CHINA'S GEOSTRATEGY

AND

INTERNATIONAL BEHAVIOUR

CHINA'S GEOSTRATEGY
AND
INTERNATIONAL BEHAVIOUR

By

AKSHAYA HANDA

(Established 1870)

United Service Institution of India

New Delhi

Vij Books India Pvt Ltd

New Delhi (India)

Published by

Vij Books India Pvt Ltd
(Publishers, Distributors & Importers)
2/19, Ansari Road
Delhi – 110 002
Phones: 91-11-43596460, 91-11-47340674
Fax: 91-11-47340674
e-mail: vijbooks@rediffmail.com

Copyright © 2014, United Service Institution of India, New Delhi

ISBN: 978-93-82652-66-3

CONTENTS

CONTENTS

FOREWORD

The role of Geography, history and politics in formulating National Strategy is undeniable. As regions strive to maximise their natural advantages while mitigating their limitations they establish precedents which become historic milestones for predicting their future actions. These acquire greater importance when we consider that geography changes little with time.

China too is similarly defined by significant geographical advantages and limitations. The fact that it is protected by natural barriers in the East, South and West; that large distances are an accepted fact in the third largest country of the world; that despite being the third largest country in terms of land mass it has just one-third the arable land per person compared to the rest of the world; that the arable land is concentrated in the east of the country populated essentially by the Hans; that its sea access is limited by a virtual wall of islands which can be used to choke it; that it always had one of the largest and presently has the largest population of the world to feed; have all had a defining influence on China. Historically thus the Chinese system of governance based on the ruler's 'Mandate of Heaven' was indicative of their endeavour for social stability and order which was characterised by tight centralised control and a strong bureaucracy. Endeavours to transfer prosperity from one area to another and an open / shut dynamic with respect to the outside world have again been evident as recurrent themes in the Chinese history. Chinese historical behaviour is also indicative of their endeavour in maintaining buffer zones along its borders and a demographic invasion of these frontiers. To many these would seem as an apt description of the present Communist regime, it is no surprise then that many believe the present regime is yet another dynasty in the evolving Chinese history.

The Chinese government today is facing the same dilemmas that had historically dogged the previous regimes. Faced with disparate development and rising inequalities amongst the population, the Chinese development model is being questioned both by scholars, critics outside and to some extent by its people. Keeping internal strife at bay requires transfer of prosperity; the latter in turn requires sustained creation of wealth, which in turn is dependent upon access to international markets and access to the sea. It is no surprise then that the Chinese have included strategic resources, trade routes and sea access as part of issues on which they would accept no compromises. Internal stability issues are raising their head in the historic buffer zones of Xinjiang and Tibet. Territorial integrity therefore forms an important component of the Chinese 'Core Interests' concept. The Chinese use both the 'carrot and stick' method to control and manage this. Hence, alongside the promise of prosperity use of the Armed/ Security Forces and demographic integration (what many term as 'invasion' which is being resisted by the locals) are increasingly visible. Calls for maintaining the party's control over the Armed Forces and voices which believe that depoliticized Armed Forces were a historical blunder which led to the collapse of the Soviet Union and Warsaw Pact – are also becoming louder. This in turn permits the Armed Forces to position themselves as the final arbitrators of regime preservation. Their exalted pre-eminence is visible in the Chinese foreign policy and are lending a degree of assertiveness to it. What is becoming an issue of concern to the international community is that the aggressiveness is being supported by other tools of the government-administrative, policy support, economic etc – in what the Chinese call the 'combination punches'.

This aggressiveness is not limited to their periphery alone. The Chinese pursuit of resources to fuel its emergence as an economic power – places it in conflict with both the international powers and often with local regimes. Many critics and even some allies have been warning of the Chinese demographic invasion in its wake. This pursuit has led to a reorientation of the Chinese Foreign Policy as Deng Xiaoping's dictum of, "hide your strength, bide your time" is being challenged and is in the process of being shelved. In turn this implies possibilities of Chinese involvement in the internal affairs of other states.

In all this, China itself is changing. China of this day is a far cry from the Communist regime established by Mao. The process initiated by Deng Xiaoping (through the 3rd Plenary Session of the 11th Central Committee of the Communist Party of China from 18 to 22 Dec 1978) has made China an economic giant which many believe is Communist only in name. Even while the Third Plenum of November 2013 seeks to strengthen the process, it has also recognized vulnerabilities in the society, which many believe have the potential of resulting in an internal collapse. In such an environment, China's ability to implement in letter and spirit, the 60 odd decisions that it had announced needs to be watched carefully. Also, the spiral effect of their implementation needs to be guarded against as they have the potential to de-stabilize the region. For example, even as China has been making efforts to export labour to ensure employment for its burgeoning population, its decision to conditionally lift the restriction on more than one child, would have implications for the next generation. Similarly, even while it seeks to restrain political dissent through restrictions on social media, its decision to dissolve the system of labour camps, one of its main tools to rein in dissent, appears to be countering the first. Does this indicate a renewed political confidence or decisions taken under social pressure? More contentious decisions like residency reforms, increased role for the markets and reforming the State Owned Enterprises are likely to challenge the entrenched interests and put pressure on the central leadership. Would a leadership under pressure domestically, become more assertive in its external relations, as some believe? Answers to these and other questions require to be sought through an understanding of their aspirations and behaviour.

This book is an important and valuable contribution as it attempts to understand the geographical and historical dimensions of the Chinese strategic problems and the solutions they have historically applied, to overcome these. What emerges, are patterns of behaviour, which are indicative of the Chinese geo-strategy, which are validated with the Chinese behaviour in the recent past. The patterns which thus emerge are important pointers and lessons in managing a relationship with China.

I am delighted to congratulate Col Akshaya Handa for his timely work of immense value to the geo-strategic community and to the USI of India, New Delhi for their support and encouragement to the author.

Mehta

Noida

12 May 2014

(RK Mehta)

Lt Gen (Retd)

ACKNOWLEDGMENTS

USI has been the pillar of my academics for last two and a half decades plus, since I first became a member. Hence it was a great honour when the institute permitted me to express my small research effort through their portal. To be thus acknowledged by the institute one has grown to revere, is a feeling beyond words and I cannot thank USI and CS3 in particular to permit me this opportunity.

This paper had been first written as my MPhil dissertation and the immense role played by my guide deserves heartfelt gratitude. Professor Rakesh Datta of the Department of Defence and National Security Studies, Panjab University, Chandigarh tolerated me despite a number of our heated arguments and guided me through the issues involved, forever goading me to take it to a logical and meaningful conclusion. He had planted the seed for this thought process and nursed it as it germinated into a plant.

No acknowledgments can be complete for me without acknowledging the roles of Lt Gen RK Mehta, PVSM, AVSM, YSM, VSM (Retd) and Maj Gen SK Razdan KC, VSM (Retd), who have guided me in my professional career and academic life in general and this effort in particular. They were the ones who channelized my reading and goaded me to write my ideas. If this effort is worthwhile the credit goes to them if otherwise, its just that I need to work harder to achieve the standards they set for me.

The role played by my parents and beautiful better half of going through and checking the innumerable drafts is immeasurable and I can only be thankful that they allowed me to be a part of their lives.

Finally my children Sanah and Bruno - who patiently allowed me to be an absent parent as I laboured - need my special thanks as I endeavour to make it up to them in the days ahead.

INTRODUCTION

On 25 Jan 1904, Halford J Mackinder of London School of Economics gave a lecture at the Royal Geographical Society 'The Geographical Pivot of History.'[1] The theme was **seeking a geographical causation in History**. In over a century plus since then many aspects of the paper have been discussed and criticised, not the least for the author's closeness with the British politicians of the day and in the words of Pascal Veiner 'a pessimistic reading of the position of Britain in the world'.[2] However, the broad thrust of the author – **of geographically designed strengths and limitations contributing heavily in the formulation of the nation's geo-strategy** – has been accepted by most. So we have a Russia which historically has tried to create buffer zones around its borders.[3] An Israel which faces main threats from the North / North East and internal dissension[4] and therefore seeks to maintain internal unity and divide its neighbours in the North and South. A Germany which – lacking strategic depth and unable to survive simultaneous attacks from France and Russia –tried to either avoid an alliance between the two or defeat one to end the threat of an alliance.[5] A Poland – which has partial protection from the South by the Carpathian and Tatra Mountains but open plains on all other flanks

---

1   Mackinder HJ 'The Geographical Pivot of History' the Geographical Journal volume 23 No 4, April 1904 pages 421-437.

2   Venier Pascal 'The Geographical Pivot of History and the Early Twentieth Century Geopolitical Culture' The Geographical Journal volume 170 No 4, December 2004 pages 330-336.

3   Based on the steppes, Russian boundaries have no major geographical features for its protection necessitating buffer states all around.

4   Protected from the South by the Sinai Desert, Arabian Desert South East of Eilat-Aqaba and East of Jordan River, Israel is vulnerable from the North and North East. In all its three manifestations Israel has been most threatened from these directions.

5   It is believed that the German pre-emptive attack against France in WW I was a response to the 1907 Triple Entente Treaty which allied Russia, France and UK. Hitler similarly had sought peace with Russia prior to opening WW II campaign against France. Post WW II German interests were tied to France through Europe and against USSR however, the eruption of the EU crisis in 2008 led to German flirtation again with Russia.

(and is thus difficult to defend with limited obstacles of some shallow rivers) – which has existed only as either a buffer state between Russia and Germany (and a buffer respected by both) or as an ally of either of the two or some outside power to guarantee its independence. [6]

It is not to say that Geography is fatalistic however, a geographical and historical context to current events does help in a better understanding of the present day behaviour and future strategy of a region. Some scholars were therefore not surprised that the Arab Spring began in a lesser known Arab nation of Tunisia. The Arab Revolt for Democracy began in what in historical terms was the most advanced society in the Arab World – the one physically closest to Europe – yet it also began in a part of that country which since antiquity had been ignored and suffered consequent underdevelopment.[7]

There was a period – immediately after the collapse of the Soviet Union – in which many believed that the Geography was no longer relevant and that modern technology would conquer and surmount it – maybe even without a war (just as it had done against the Soviet Union) or by air power (as in Bosnia). But even as Bosnia, Somalia and Rwanda proved the limitations of these notions, Afghanistan and Iraq once again reiterated how Geography stamped its authority on aspirations and behaviour of a region and therefore could not be ignored.

In conclusion of his lecture, Mackinder mentions China, and calls it the 'yellow peril to the world's freedom'[8] as it combined an 'oceanic frontage to the resources of the great continent.'[9] China as a nation has been an enigma to most Indians. While a section tends to view it from the prism of what it calls the betrayal of 1962, others see it as an irrefutable partner in progress and global geo-politics. While the truth would lie somewhere in the various shades of grey between the two extremes, it is important to understand the Chinese geo-strategy and when a particular extreme view would be relevant.

---

6   It is not a surprise that Poland was one of the first ex Warsaw Pact countries which sought NATO membership.

7   Kaplan Robert 'The Revenge of Geography' page 167 Kindle Edition.

8   Mackinder HJ 'The Geographical Pivot of History' The Geographical Journal volume 23 No 4, April 1904 page 437.

9   Ibid.

Chapter 1

GEOGRAPHY OF CHINA: LANDMASS

China[1] stretches some 5,026 kms across the East Asian landmass. It is bordered by seas and waters eastward, with the East China Sea, Korea Bay, Yellow Sea, Taiwan Strait, and South China Sea, and bordered by landmasses on its three other sides, from North Korea to Vietnam.

Internally,[2,3] China must be divided into two parts: the Chinese heartland and the non-Chinese buffer regions surrounding it. There is a line in China called the 15-inch isohyet, east of which more than 15 inches of rain fall each year and west of which the annual rainfall is less. The vast majority of Chinese live east and south of this line, in the region known as Han China — the Chinese heartland. The region is home to the ethnic Han, whom the world regards as the Chinese. It is important to understand that more than a billion people live in this area, which is about half the size of the United States. (See Fig. 1.1)[4]

The Chinese heartland is divided into two parts, northern and southern, which in turn is represented by two main dialects, Mandarin in the north and Cantonese in the south. These dialects share a writing system but are almost mutually incomprehensible when spoken. It is defined by two major rivers — the Yellow River in the north and the Yangtze in the South, along with a third lesser river in the south, the Pearl. The heartland is China's agricultural region. However — and this is the single most important fact about China — it has about one-third the arable land per person as the rest of the world. This

---

1   http://en.wikipedia.org/wiki/Geography_of_China.

2   http://www.defenceviewpoints.co.uk/articles-and-analysis/the-geopolitics-of-china.

3   http://books.google.co.in/books?id=5V1dlG5_oSAC&pg=PA26&lpg=PA26&dq=15+inch+is ohyet+line+china&source=bl&ots=tCqJwGmMXD&sig=GMuxFfHcle9rbmjzA8wZz_1SZhY& hl=en&sa=X&ei=tegEUoi0HsXJrAe86YHoDg&ved=0CDgQ6AEwAg#v=onepage&q=15%20 inch%20isohyet%20line%20china&f=false

4   In this regard see http://www.defenceviewpoints.co.uk/images/dv/15inchisohyet.jpg.

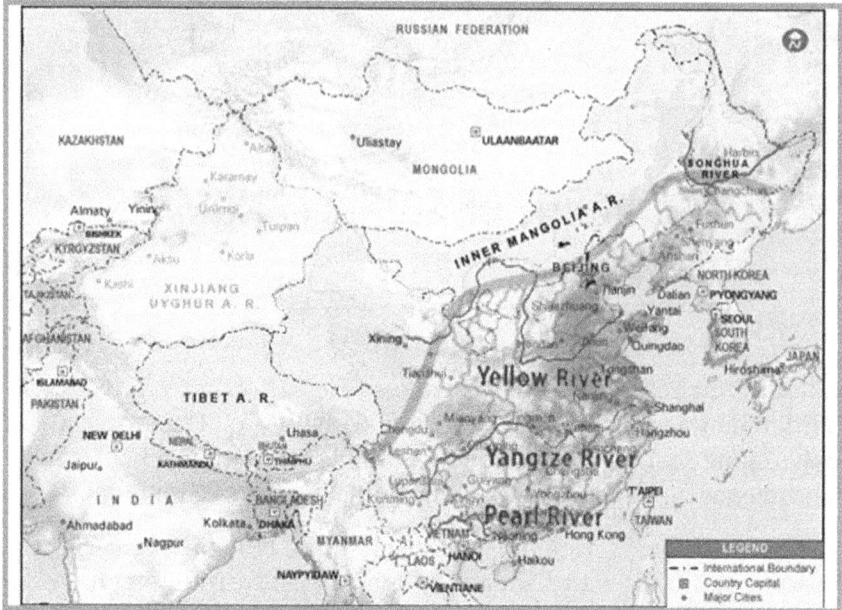

Fig. 1.1

pressure has defined modern Chinese history — both in terms of living with it and trying to move beyond it. (See Fig. 1.2)[5]

A ring of non-Han regions surround this heartland — Tibet, Xinjiang province, Inner Mongolia and Manchuria (a historical name given to the region north of North Korea that now consists of the Chinese provinces of Heilongjiang, Jilin and Liaoning).

Officially China has been divided into five homogeneous physical macro-regions: Eastern China (subdivided into the **Northeast Plain**, **North Plain**, and **Southern Hills**), **Xinjiang-Mongolia**, and the **Tibetan-highlands.** The eastern and southern half of the country, its seacoast fringed with offshore islands, is a region of fertile lowlands and foothills with most of the agricultural output and human population. The western and northern half of China is a region of sunken basins (Gobi, Taklamakan), rolling plateaus, and towering massifs, including a portion of the highest tableland on earth (Tibetan Plateau) with lower agricultural possibilities and thus, far less populated. China's sense of itself is based on the cultural differences that obtain between this surrounding belt of desert and the sown one of China proper, that is

---

5   In this regard see http://www.defenceviewpoints.co.uk/images/dv/chinadialects.jpg.

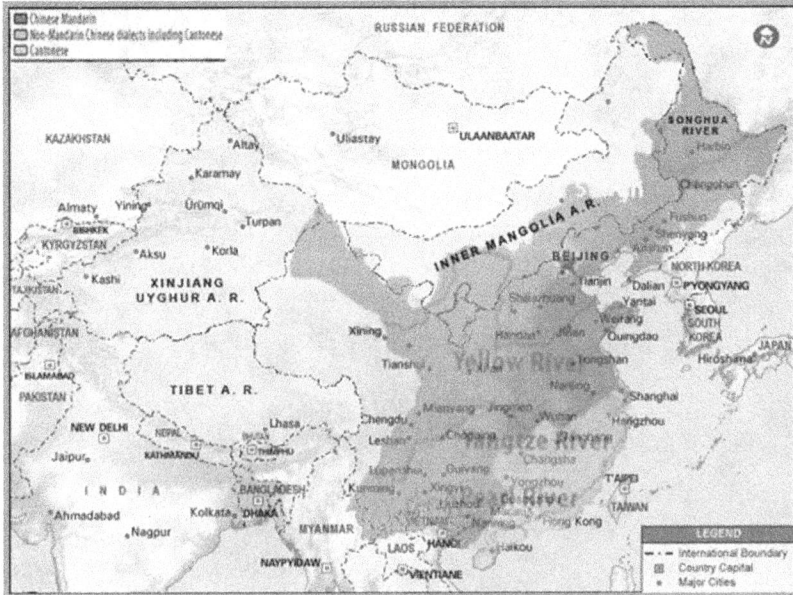

Fig. 1.2

between the pastoral and the arable. China's ethnic geography reflects this 'core-periphery structure', with the core being the arable central plain or inner China and the periphery being the pastoral frontiers or outer China.[6] This is what the building of the Great Wall was ultimately about. The Great Wall served to reinforce the ecological distinction that translated into political differences.[7] (See Fig. 1.3)[8]

Traditionally, the Chinese population centred around the Chinese Northern plain and oriented itself toward its own enormous inland market, developing as an imperial power whose centre lay in the middle and lower reaches of the Yellow River on the northern plains. More recently, the 18,000 km coastline has been used extensively for export-oriented trade, making a power shift, with the coastline provinces becoming the leading economic centres.

---

6   Kaplan Robert 'The Revenge of Geography' page 3075 Kindle Edition.

7   Grygiel Jakub J 'Great Powers and Geopolitical Change' Baltimore: John Hopkins University Press page 133.

8   https://www.google.co.in/maps?t=m&ll=30.730798199999985%2C76.7651793&spn=0.18741 332662345048%2C0.29072721689414205&output=classic&dg=opt.

Fig. 1.3

With an area of about 9.6 million km², the People's Republic of China is the third largest country in total area behind Russia and Canada, and very similar to the United States. This figure is sometimes challenged by border disputes, most notably about Taiwan, Aksai Chin, the Trans-Karakoram Tract, and South Tibet.[9]

China is diverse with snow-capped mountains, deep river valleys, broad basins, high plateaus, rolling plains, terraced hills, sandy dunes, low-latitude glaciers and other landforms present in myriad variations. In general, the land is high in the west and descends to the east coast. Mountains (33%), plateaus (26%) and hills (10%) account for nearly 70% of the country's land surface. Most of the arable land and population are based in lowland plains (12%) and basins (19%), though some of the greatest basins are filled with deserts. The country's rugged terrain presents problems for the construction of overland transportation infrastructure and requires

---

9   The CIA's The World Factbook gives 9,826,630 km2 ("CIA World Fact Book - Geography Note"), the United Nations Statistics Division gives 9,629,091 km2 ("Population by Sex, Rate of Population Increase, Surface Area and Density". Demographic Yearbook 2005. UN Statistics Division), and the Encyclopædia Britannica gives 9,522,055 km². ("United States". Encyclopædia Britannica).

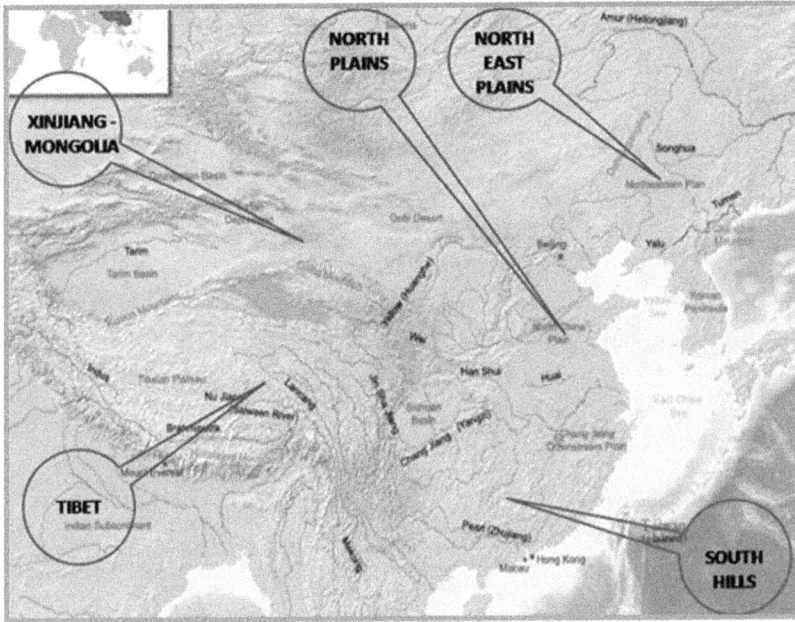

Fig. 1.4

extensive terracing to sustain agriculture, but are conducive to the development of forestry, mineral and hydropower resources and tourism. (See Fig. 1.4)[10]

Northeast Plain

Northeast of Shanhaiguan, a narrow sliver of flat coastal land opens up into the vast Manchurian Plain. The plains extend north to the crown of the "Chinese rooster," near where the Greater and Lesser Hinggan (also called Khingan Ranges) ranges converge. The Changbai Mountains to the east divide China from the Korean peninsula.

North Plain

(a) The Taihang forms the western side of the triangular North China Plain. The other two sides are the Pacific Coast to the east and the Yangtze River to the southwest. The vertices of this triangle are Beijing to the north, Shanghai to the southeast and Yichang to the southwest. This alluvial plain, fed by the Yellow and Yangtze Rivers, is one of the most heavily

---

10 http://en.wikipedia.org/wiki/File:ChinaGeography.png

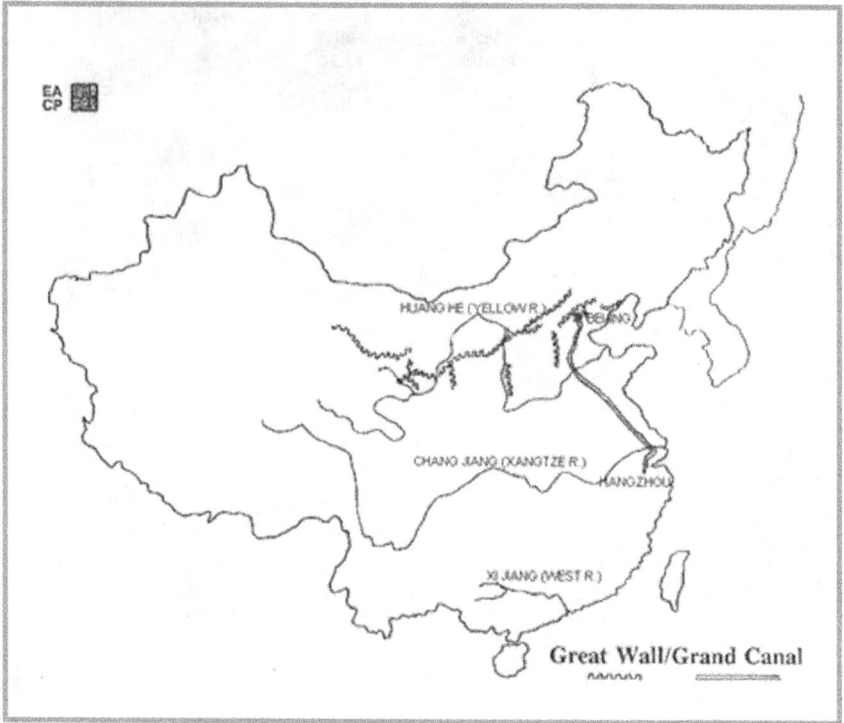

Fig. 1.5

populated regions of China. The only mountains in the plain are the Taishan in Shandong and Dabie Mountains of Anhui.

(b) Beijing, situated at the north tip of the North China Plain, is shielded by the intersection of Taihang and Jingdu Mountains. Further north are the drier grasslands of the Inner Mongolian Plateau. To the south are agricultural regions, traditionally home to sedentary populations. **The Great Wall of China** was built in the mountains across the mountains that mark the southern edge of the Inner Mongolian Plateau. The Ming-era walls run 2,000 km east-to-west from Shanhaiguan on the Bohai Coast to the Hexi Corridor in Gansu. (See Fig. 1.5)[11]

(c) Flowing from its source in the Qingzang highlands, the Yellow River courses toward the sea through the North China Plain, the historic centre of Chinese expansion and influence. Han Chinese people have farmed the rich alluvial soils since

---

11 http://afe.easia.columbia.edu/china/geog/M_Wall.htm

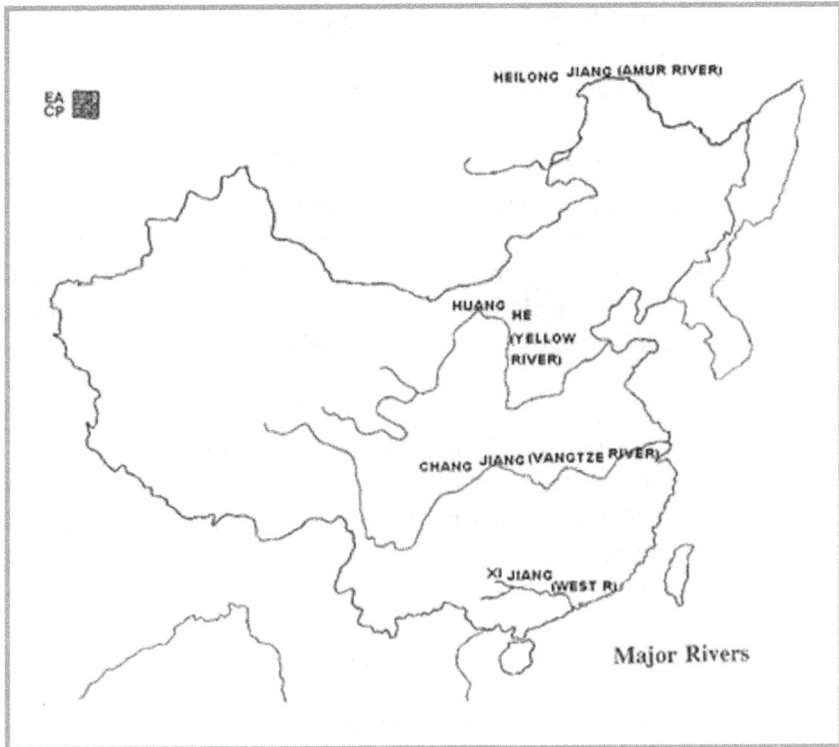

Fig. 1.6

ancient times, constructing the **Grand Canal** for north-south transport during the Imperial Era.

(d) The plain is a continuation of the Dongbei (Manchurian) Plain to the northeast but is separated from it by the Bohai Gulf, an extension of the Yellow Sea. (See Fig. 1.6)[12]

(e) There is a steep drop in the river level in the North China Plain, where the river continues across the delta, it transports a heavy load of sand and mud which is deposited on the flat plain. The flow is aided by man made embankments. As a result, the river flows on a raised ridge fifty meters above the plain. Water logging, floods, and course changes have recurred over the centuries. Traditionally, rulers were judged by their concern for or indifference to preservation of the embankments. In the modern era, China has undertaken extensive flood control and conservation measures.

---

12 http://afe.easia.columbia.edu/china/geog/M_rivr.htm

(f)   Like other densely populated areas of China, the plain is subject to floods and earthquakes. The mining and industrial centre of Tangshan, 165 km east of Beijing, was levelled by an earthquake in July 1976, it was believed to be the largest earthquake of the 20th century by death toll.

(g)   The Hai River, like the Pearl River, flows from west to east. Its upper course consists of five rivers that converge near Tianjin, then flow seventy kms before emptying into the Bohai Gulf. The Huai River, rises in Henan Province and flows through several lakes before joining the Pearl River near Yangzhou.

South Hills

(a)   East of the Tibetan Plateau, deeply folded mountains fan out toward the Sichuan Basin, which is ringed by mountains in 1000-3000 mtrs elevation. The floor of the basin has an average elevation of 500mtrs and is home to one of the most densely farmed and populated regions of China. The Sichuan Basin is capped in the north by the eastward continuation of the Kunlun range, the Qinling and Dabashan ranges. The Qinling and Dabashan ranges form a major north-south divide across China Proper, the traditional core area of China. (See Fig. 1.7)[13]

(b)   Southeast of the Tibetan Plateau and south of the Sichuan Basin is the Yunnan-Guizhou Plateau, which occupy much of southwest China. This plateau, with an average elevation of 2000 mtrs, is known for limestone landscape.

(c)   The Qin Mountains, a continuation of the Kunlun Mountains, divides the North China Plain from the Yangtze River Delta and is the major physiographic boundary between the two great parts of China Proper. It is a cultural boundary as it influences the distribution of customs and language. South of the Qinling mountain range divide are the densely populated and highly developed areas of the lower and middle plains of the Yangtze River and, on its upper reaches, the Sichuan Basin, an area encircled by a high barrier of mountain ranges.

(d)   The country's longest and most important waterway, the Yangtze River, is navigable for the majority of its length and has a vast hydroelectric potential. Rising on the Qingzang Plateau, the Yangtze River traverses 6,300 km through the heart of the

---

13 http://afe.easia.columbia.edu/china/geog/M_Mt.htm

EA
CP

ALTAI MOUNTAINS

GREATER KHINGAN RANGE

DZUNGARIAN BASIN

TIAN SHAN

DAMIR MU

TARIM BASIN

GOBI DESERT

ORDOS DESERT

TAKLA MAKAN DESERT

KUNLUN MOUNTAINS

TAIHANG MTS.

QINLING MOUNTAINS

TIBETAN PLATEAU

HIMALAYA RANGE

MT. EVEREST

NANLING MOUNTAINS

Mountains and Deserts

Fig. 1.7

country, draining an area of 1.8 million km² before emptying into the East China Sea. Roughly 300 million people live along its middle and lower reaches. (See Fig. 1.8)[14]

(e) The area is a large producer of rice and wheat. The Sichuan Basin, due to its mild, humid climate and long growing season, produces a variety of crops. It is a leading silk-producing area and an important industrial region with substantial mineral resources.

(f) The Nanling Mountains, the southernmost of the east-west mountain ranges, overlook areas in China with a tropical climate. The climate allows two crops of rice to be grown per year. Southeast of the mountains lies a coastal, hilly region of small deltas and narrow valley plains. The drainage area of the Pearl River and its associated network of rivers occupies much

---

14 http://afe.easia.columbia.edu/china/geog/M_rivr.htm

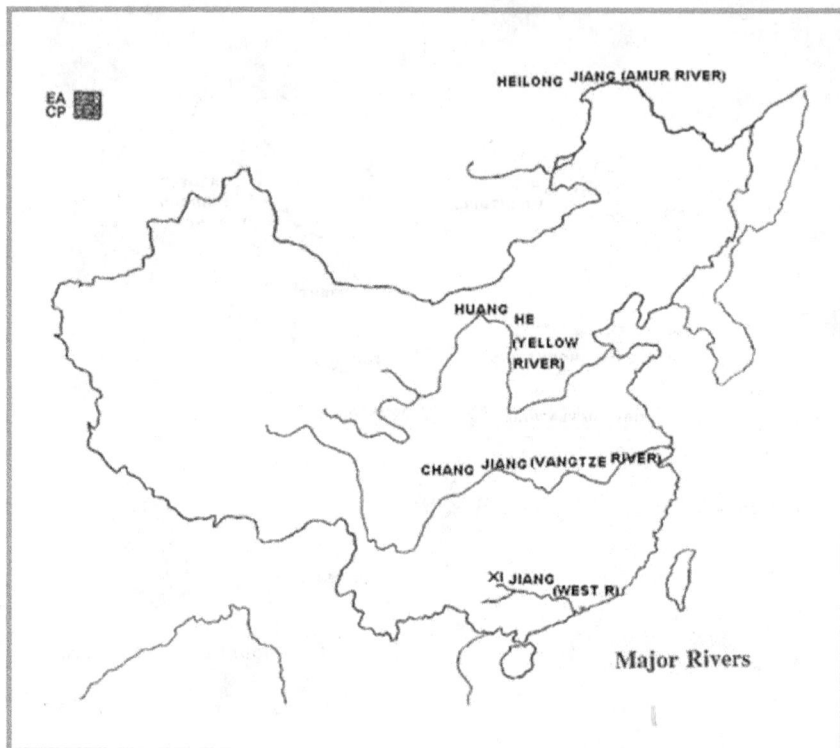

HEILONG JIANG (AMUR RIVER)

HUANG HE
(YELLOW
RIVER)

CHANG JIANG (VANGTZE RIVER)

XI JIANG
(WEST R)

Major Rivers

Fig. 1.8

of the region to the south. West of the Nanling, the Yunnan-Guizhou Plateau rises in two steps, averaging 1,200 and 1,800 mtrs in elevation, respectively, toward the precipitous mountain regions of the eastern Qingzang Plateau.

(g) South of the Yangtze, the landscape is more rugged. Like Shanxi Province to the north, each of Hunan and Jiangxi has a provincial core in a river basin that is surrounded by mountains. The Wuling range separates Guizhou from Hunan. The Luoxiao and Jinggang divides Hunan from Jiangxi, which is separated from Fujian by the Wuyi Mountains. The southeast coastal provinces, Zhejiang, Fujian and Guangdong have rugged coasts, with pockets of lowland and mountainous interior. The Nanling, an east-west mountain range, across northern Guangdong, seals off Hunan and Jiangxi from Guangdong.

Xinjiang-Mongolia

(a) Northwest of the Tibetan Plateau, between the northern slope of Kunlun and southern slope of Tian Shan, is the vast Tarim Basin of Xinjiang, which contains the Taklamakan Desert. The Tarim Basin, the largest in China, measures 1500 kms from east to west and 600 kms from north to south at its widest. Average elevation in the basin is 1000mtrs. To east, the basin descends into the Hami-Turpan Depression of eastern Xinjiang, where the dried lake bed of Lake Ayding at 154mtrs below sea level, is the lowest surface point in China and the third lowest in the world. With temperatures that have reached 49.6°C, the lake bed ranks as one the hottest places in China. North of Tian Shan is Xinjiang's second great basin, the Jungar, which contains the Gurbantünggüt Desert. The Jungar Basin is enclosed to the north by the Altay Mountains which separates Xinjiang from Russia and Mongolia.

(b) Northeast of the Tibetan Plateau, the Altun Shan-Qilian Mountains range branches off the Kunlun and creates a parallel mountain range running east-west. In between in northern Qinghai is the Qaidam Basin, with elevation of 2,600-3,000m and numerous brackish and salt lakes. North of the Qilian is Hexi Corridor of Gansu, a natural passage between Xinjiang and China proper that was part of the ancient Silk Road and traversed by modern highway and rail lines to Xinjiang. Further north, the Inner Mongolian Plateau, between 900-1500 mtrs in elevation, arcs north up the spine of China and becomes the Greater Hinggan Range of Northeast China.

(c) Between the Qinling and the Inner Mongolian Plateau is Loess Plateau, the largest of its kind in the world, covering 650000 km² in Shaanxi, parts of Gansu and Shanxi provinces, and some of Ningxia-Hui Autonomous Region. The plateau is 1000-1500 mtrs in elevation and is filled with loess, a yellowish, loose soil that travels easily in the wind. Eroded loess silt give the Yellow River its colour and name. The Loess Plateau is bound to the east by the Luliang Mountain of Shanxi, which has a narrow basin running north to south along the Fen River. Further east is the Taihang Mountains of Hebei, the dominant topographical feature of North China.

(d) **Mineral Resources.**[15,16,17] Xinjiang's landscape is composed of five major components, including the three large mountains of Altay, Tianshan, and Kunlun and the two great basins of Junggar and Tarim. It's said to be a place of "treasure on every mountain, oil in every basin".

(i) The three large mountains are all mountains of treasures and abundant in gold, jewels and precious metals. The Altay Mountain in the north means "the place producing gold". As a saying goes, there are seventy-two ditches in Altay Mountain and each ditch has gold and jewels. The Altun Mountain in the south is also named after gold. Since there is a large gold deposit and no inhabitants, illegal mining is frequently reported.

(ii) The two basins abound in oil, natural gas, sylvite, mirabilite, vermiculite and bentonite, which are of high economic value.

(iii) Other minerals include petroleum, natural gas, coal, gold, copper, nickel, lead, zinc, asbestos, salts, bentonite, limestone and vermiculite etc.

(iv) There are altogether 171 known ores in China, 138 of which are found in Xinjiang. Among them are seven energy minerals, forty-two metal minerals, seventy non-metallic minerals and three underground water resources. Among the 117 ores with proved recoverable reserves, five ores reserves rank as the top one of the country, twenty-four are among the top five and forty-three are in the top ten.

(v) Xinjiang's various basins, large or small, are rich in oil and gas resources with a reserve of more than 30 billion tons, which account for one-third of the country's total.

(vi) Xinjiang's coal resources constitute for more than 40 percent of China's total coal reserve and rank the number one in the whole country. There are only ten basins in the world with over 500 billion tons coal resources, and Xinjiang has two of them.

---

15 http://english.ts.cn/topic/content/2008-01/11/content_2389669.htm.

16 http://www.china.org.cn/english/MATERIAL/139230.htm.

17 http://www.huachun.com.cn/hc/en/news_view.asp?newsid=463

(vii) Further studies suggest huge deposits of shale gas in the Tarim and Jungar basin in the region.[18]

(viii) Sylvite is a scarce resource in China and it has long depended on imports, but Lop Nor of Xinjiang is abundant in sylvite resources and has a huge reserve. Large scale exploitation of sylvite in Lop Nor can effectively ease conflicts between supply and demand of sylvite.

(ix) There are rich resources of building materials, such as marble, granite, asbestos ore and limestone, with great variety and good quality.

Tibetan Highlands

The world's tallest mountains, the Himalayas, Karakorum, Pamirs and Tian Shan divide China from South and Central Asia. Eleven of the 17 tallest mountain peaks are located on China's western borders. They include world's tallest peak Mt. Everest (8848m) in the Himalayas on the border with Nepal and the world's second tallest peak, K2 (8611m) on the border with Pakistan. From these towering heights in the west, the land descends in steps like a terrace. North of the Himalayas and east of the Karakorum/Pamirs is the vast Tibetan Plateau, the largest and highest plateau in the world, also known as the "Roof of the World." The plateau has an average elevation of 4,000m above sea level and covers an area of 2.5 million square kms, or about one-fifth of China's land mass. In the north, the plateau is hemmed in by the Kunlun Mountains, which extends eastward from the intersection of the Pamirs, Karakorum and Tian Shan.

---

18 http://in.images.search.yahoo.com/images/view;_ylt=A2oKiZevLjtR9VcALGy9HAx.;_ylu=X3 oDMTBIMTQ4cGxyBHNIYwNzcgRzbGsDaW1n?back=http%3A%2F%2Fin.images.search.ya-hoo.com%2Fsearch%2Fimages%3F_adv_prop%3Dimage%26va%3Dshale%2Bgas%2Bdep osits%2Bchina%26fr%3Dchr-greentree_gc%26tab%3Dorganic%26ri%3D1&w=500&h=379 &imgurl=blogs.worldwatch.org%2Frevolt%2Fwp-content%2Fuploads%2F2012%2F08%2Fa eb6708d6720111024-china-shale-gas-deposits-500x379.jpg&rurl=http%3A%2F%2Fblogs. worldwatch.org%2Frevolt%2Fchina-has-high-hopes-for-shale-gas-the-thorny-road-of-honor %2F&size=77.4+KB&name=aeb6708d6720111024-%3Cb%3Echina%3C%2Fb%3E-%3Cb%3E-shale%3C%2Fb%3E-%3Cb%3Egas%3C%2Fb%3E-%3Cb%3Edeposits%3C%2Fb%3E-500x3 79&p=shale+gas+deposits+china&oid=c5c79951fdc64826a1dcf6591c929552&fr2=&fr=chr-greentree_gc&tt=aeb6708d6720111024-%253Cb%253Echina%253C%252Fb%253E-%253Cb%253Eshale%253C%252Fb%253E-%253Cb%253Egas%253C%252Fb%253E-%253Cb%253Edeposits%253C%252Fb%253E-500x379&b=0&ni=112&no=1&ts=&tab=organi c&sigr=12vq27ifv&sigb=140l2crc6&sigi=13erhl817&.crumb=5ZjJlJtunKD

(a) **The geography of Tibet:**[19] consists of the high mountains, lakes and rivers lying between Central, East and South Asia. Tibet is often called "the roof of the world," comprising table-lands averaging over 4,950 metres above the sea with peaks at 6,000 to 7,500 m, including Mount Everest. It is bounded on the north and east by the Central China Plain, on the west by the Kashmir Region of India and on the south by Nepal, India and Bhutan. Most of Tibet sits atop a geological structure known as the Tibetan Plateau which includes the Himalaya and many of the highest mountain peaks in the world. High mountain peaks include Changtse, Lhotse, Makalu, Gauri Sankar, Gurla Mandhata Cho Oyu, Jomolhari, Gyachung Kang, Gyala Peri, Mount Kailash, Kawagebo, Khumbutse, Melungtse, Mount Nyainqentanglha Namcha Barwa, Mount Nyainqentanglha, Shishapangma and Yangra . Mountain passes include Cherko la, and North Col. Smaller mountains include Mount Gephel and Gurla Mandhata.

(b) **Regions:** Physically, Tibet may be divided into two parts, the "lake region" in the west and north-west, and the "river region", which spreads out on three sides of the former on the east, south, and west. The region names are useful in contrasting their hydrological structures, and also in contrasting their different cultural uses which is nomadic in the "lake region" and agricultural in the "river region".

(i) **River Region:** On the south the "river region" is bounded by the Himalayas, on the north by a broad mountain system. The system at no point narrows to a single range; generally there are three or four across its breadth. As a whole the system forms the watershed between rivers flowing to the Indian Ocean – the Indus, Brahmaputra and Salween and its tributaries – and the streams flowing into the undrained salt lakes to the north. The "river region" is characterized by fertile mountain valleys and includes the Yarlung Tsangpo River (the upper courses of the Brahmaputra) and its major tributary, the Nyang River, the Salween, the Yangtze, the Mekong, and the Yellow River. The Yarlung Tsangpo Canyon, formed by a horseshoe bend in the river where it flows around Namcha Barwa, is the deepest, and possibly longest canyon in the world. Among the mountains there are many narrow valleys. The valleys of Lhasa, Shigatse, Gyantse and the Brahmaputra are free from permafrost, covered with good soil and groves of trees, well irrigated, and richly cultivated. The South Tibet Valley is formed by the Yarlung Zangbo River during its middle reaches, where it travels from west to east. The valley is approximately 1200 kms long and 300 kms wide. The valley descends from 4500 metres above sea level to 2800 metres. The mountains on either side of the valley are usually around 5000 metres high. Lakes here include Lake Paiku and Lake Puma Yumco.

(ii) **Lake Region:** The "lake region" extends from the Pangong Tso Lake in Ladakh, Lake Rakshastal, Yamdrok Lake and Lake Manasarovar near the source of the Indus River, to the sources of the Salween, the Mekong and the Yangtze. Other lakes include Dagze Co, Nam Co, and Pagsum Co. The lake region is an arid and wind-swept desert. This region is called the Chang Tang (Byang sang) or 'Northern Plateau' by the people of Tibet. It is some 1100 km broad, and covers an area about equal to that of France. Due to the extremely high mountain barriers it has a very arid alpine climate with annual precipitation around 100 mm and possesses no river outlet. The mountain ranges are spread out, rounded, disconnected, separated by flat valleys relatively of little depth. The country is dotted over with large and small lakes, generally salt or alkaline, and intersected by streams. Due to the presence of discontinuous permafrost over the Chang Tang, the soil is boggy and covered with tussocks of grass, thus resembling the Siberian tundra. Salt and fresh-water lakes are intermingled. The lakes are generally without outlet, or have only a small effluent. The deposits consist of soda, potash, borax and common salt. The lake region is noted for a vast number of hot springs, which are widely distributed between the Himalaya and 34° N., but are most numerous to the west of Tengri Nor (north-west of Lhasa). So intense is the cold in this part of Tibet that these springs are sometimes represented by columns of ice, the nearly boiling water having frozen in the act of ejection.

(c) **The Mineral Resources of Tibet:**[20] 'Like the Taklamakan Desert of Xinjiang, the sprawling, mountainous Tibetan

---

20 http://www.lhassa.org/en/geography-of-tibet/mineral-resources-of-tibet.php

plateau, rich in copper and iron ore, accounts for much of territory of China, thus clarifying with horror with which Beijing views Tibetan autonomy, let alone independence. Without Tibet there is a much reduced China and a virtually expanded Indian Subcontinent.[21] The mineral resources of Tibet are exceptional, which include the largest uranium reserve of the world and 94 types of other different minerals. These Include:

(i) **Chromite** which is frequently employed in organic chemistry to produce oxidations, and in industry for the tanning of the skins.

(ii) **Corundum**, is used primarily for manufacture of aluminium.

(iii) **Crystal.**

(iv) **Copper**.

(v) **Volcanic ash** which consists of salt, potassium, calcium and magnesium as well as manganese and iron oxides.

(vi) **Magnesite**, used in mechanical engineering.

(vii) **Sulphur.**

(viii) **Mica** which is used in the quarter wave plates, being useful in polarimetry with the study of the luminous vibrations.

Rivers and Drainage

(a) China has 50,000 rivers, each with a catchment area greater than 100 square kms. The rivers in China have a total length of 420,000 kms. 1500 of Chinese rivers have a catchment area exceeding 1000 square kms. The majority of rivers flow west to east into the Pacific Ocean. The Yangtze (Chang Jiang) rises in Tibet, flows through Central China and enters the Yellow Sea near Shanghai. The Yangtze is 6300 kms long and has a catchment area of 1.8 million square kms. It is the third longest river in the world, after the Amazon and the Nile. The second longest river in China is the Huang He (Yellow River). It rises in Tibet and travels circuitously for 5464 kms through North China, it empties into the Bo Hai Gulf on the north coast of the Shandong Province. It has a catchment area of 752,000 square kms. The Heilongjiang (Heilong or Black Dragon River) flows for 3,101 kms in Northeast China and an

---

21 Kaplan Robert 'The Revenge of Geography' page 3280 Kindle Edition.

additional 1,249 kms in Russia, where it is known as the Amur. The longest river in South China is the Zhujiang (Pearl River), which is 2,214 kms long. Along with its three tributaries, the Xi (West), Dong (East), and Bei (North) rivers, it forms the Pearl River Delta near Guangzhou, Zhuhai, Macau, and Hong Kong. Other major rivers are the Liaohe in the north east, Haihe in the north, Qiantang in the east, and Lancang in the southwest.

(b)   Inland drainage involving upland basins in the north and northeast accounts for 40 percent of the country's total drainage area. Many rivers and streams flow into lakes or diminish in the desert. Some are used for irrigation.

(c)   'The yellow river derives its waters from the snows of Tibet, and for part of its course flows near the Mongolian steppe.[22] Tibet with the headwaters of the Yellow, Yangzi, Mekong, Salween, Brahmaputra, Indus and Sutlej rivers, may constitute the world's most enormous store house of fresh water, even as China by 2030 is expected to fall short of its water demands by 25 percent.[23] This store house provides water to almost all the countries in the neighbourhood. 'By expanding its borders, China has become the source of transboundary river flows to the largest number of countries in the world – from Russia to India, and from Kazakhstan to the Indo-China Peninsula.'[24] This is already leading to disputes which are only likely to intensify in the future. 'China is now involved in water disputes with almost all its riparian neighbours ranging from big Russia and India to weak clients like North Korea and Myanmar.'[25,26]

---

22 Lattimore Owen, 'Inner Asian Frontiers: Chinese and Russian Margins of Expansion', The Journal of Economic History, Cambridge, England May 1947.

23 Sinha Uttam Kumar, 'Tibet's Watershed Challenge', Washington Post 14 June 2010.

24 Chellaney Brahma 'Asia's Water Crisis and the New Security Risks' USI Journal Jan-Mar 2012 page 55.

25 Ibid page 56.

26 China has 7% of the world's fresh water supply for 20% of the population. This scarcity becomes all the more acute due to the pollution of the water. 'If the air in large cities is turning poisonous, the quality of water too, is declining fast over the entire country. An official of the China Geological Survey recently reported that the groundwater of 90% of Chinese cities is polluted, with two-thirds of those cities having "severely polluted" water. Spills from China's coal and chemical industries have periodically shut down the use of China's rivers and streams as they killed fish and poisoned humans. A Chinese study showed that in 40 years there were 3,600 spillage accidents related to the chemical industry, about 900 of which were on a large scale. The seriousness of the threat to water supply was brought home dramatically this week when thousands

(d) China's territorial waters are principally marginal seas of the western Pacific Ocean. These waters lie on the indented coastline of the mainland and approximately 5,000 islands. The Yellow Sea, East China Sea, and South China Sea are marginal seas of the Pacific Ocean. More than half the coastline, predominantly in the south, is rocky; most of the remainder is sandy. The Bay of Hangzhou roughly divides the two kinds of shoreline.

---

of dead pigs (cause unknown), dumped upstream by farmers, floated down the Huangpu river that supplies drinking water to Shanghai'. See http://timesofindia.indiatimes.com/home/opinion/edit-page/Chinas-Achilles-heel-is-pollution/articleshow/18993032.cms

Chapter 2

GEOGRAPHY OF CHINA: SEA ACCESS

Significant achievements have been made by China in ocean-going transportation and container transportation capacity. "By the end of 1997, merchant ships had increased to 320,000 with a total dead-weight tonnage of close to 50 million, of which more than 23 million were of the fleets in foreign trade transportation[1]." At present, China has 15 harbours each with an annual handling capacity of more than 10 million tons. The harbours with annual handling capacity above 10,000 tons number 200. Since 2008 Chinese ports have handled the maximum container traffic in the world.[2] In recent years, China's coastal shipbuilding industry has shown a trend of rapid development.

Resultantly, China is acutely aware of the importance of the sea routes. "As a member of the IMO China has signed bilateral maritime transportation agreements with 51 countries, making positive efforts to promote international cooperation and exchanges in maritime transportation. At the 16th to 20th sessions of the IMO, China was successively elected as an A-level council member state. China has also acceded to 30-some conventions formulated by the IMO."[3]

China supports the principle of the freedom of the seas. However it's ability in defending SLOCs is limited – a virtual wall of islands along with the Korean Peninsula bar its access to the Pacific. North to South these include – the Korean Peninsula, Japan, Senkaku/Diaoyu, Taiwan,[4] Paracel Islands, Philippines, Spratly Islands and Malaysia.

---

1   http://www.apcss.org/Publications/Ocasional%20Papers/OPSloc.htm

2   http://unctad.org/en/Docs/rmt2011ch4_en.pdf

3   http://www.apcss.org/Publications/Ocasional%20Papers/OPSloc.htm

4   In General Douglas MacArthur's words, Taiwan is 'an unsinkable aircraft carrier that dominates

Further ahead, the Malacca Straits exists as another major dilemma for the Chinese sea-borne trade as they provide the sole economically viable access to the Indian Ocean Region. 'In terms of geography, China is as blessed by its seaboard and its proximity to water as it is by its continental interior. China dominates the East Asian coastline on the Pacific in the temperate and tropical zones, and on its southern border is close enough to the Indian Ocean to contemplate being linked to it in years ahead by roads and energy pipelines. But whereas China is in a generally favourable position along its land borders, it faces a more hostile environment at sea. The Chinese Navy sees little but trouble and frustration in what it calls the First Island Chain, which, going from north to south comprises Japan, the Ryuku Islands, the so called half Island of the Korean Peninsula, Taiwan, the Philippines, Indonesia and Australia.'[5]

Yellow Sea

'Jutting out from Manchuria, of which it is a natural geographical appendage, the Korean peninsula commands all maritime traffic in North East China and more particularly, traps in its armpit the Bohai Sea, home to China's largest offshore oil reserve.'[6] (See Fig. 2.1)[7]

The Yellow Sea[8] is the name given to the northern part of the East China Sea, which is a marginal sea of the Pacific Ocean. It is located between mainland China and the Korean Peninsula. Its name comes from the sand particles from Gobi Desert sand storms that turn the surface of the water golden yellow. The innermost bay of the Yellow Sea is called the Bohai Sea (previously Pechihli Bay or Chihli Bay). Into it flow both the Yellow River (through Shandong province and its capital Jinan) and Hai He (through Beijing and Tianjin). Deposits of sand and silt from those rivers contribute to the sea colour.

Major Islands of the Sea. Major islands of the sea include Anmado, Baengnyeong do, Daebudo, Deokjeokdo, Gageodo, Ganghwa do, Hauido, Heuksando, Hongdo, Jejudo, Jindo, Muuido,

---

the centre point of China's convex seaboard, from which an outside power like the United States can radiate power along China's coastal periphery. Holmes and Yoshihara, 'Command of the Sea with Chinese Characteristics'.

5 Kaplan Robert 'The Revenge of Geography' page 3420 Kindle Edition.

6 Ibid' page 3364 Kindle Edition.

7 http://en.wikipedia.org/wiki/File:Bar-tailed_Godwit9may.gif

8 http://en.wikipedia.org/wiki/Yellow_Sea

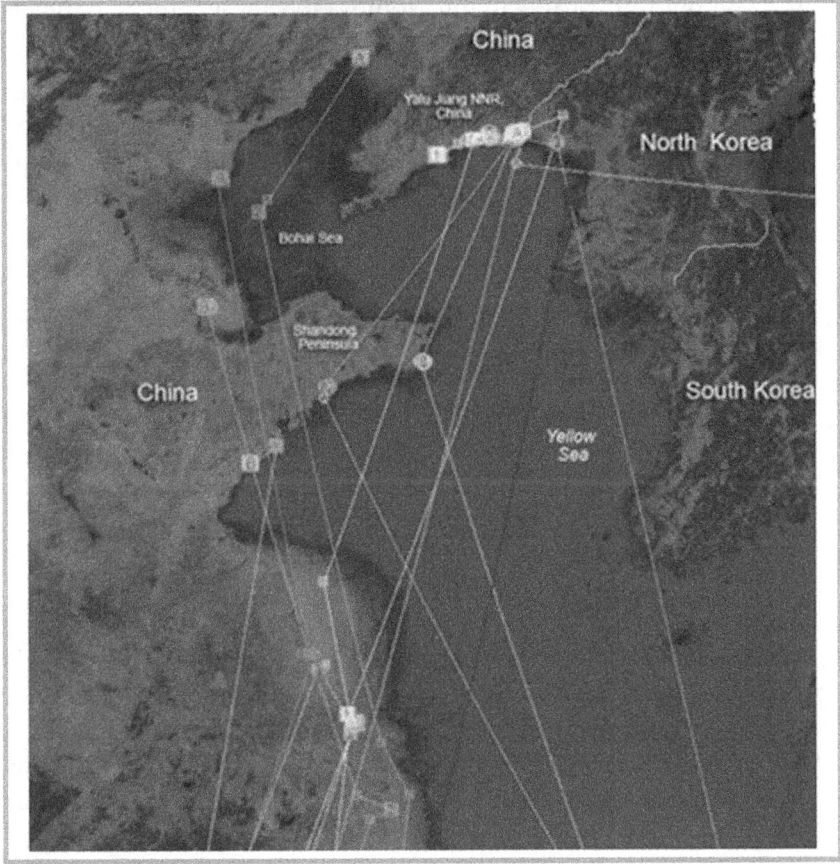

Fig. 2.1

Sido, Silmido, Sindo, Wando, Yeong jongdo and Yeonpyeong do. All of these are in South Korea.

Economy

(a) The coast of the Yellow Sea is very densely populated, at approximately 250 people/km². The sea waters had been used for fishing by the Chinese, Korean and Japanese ships for centuries. Especially rich in fish are the bottom layers. The intensity of fishing has been gradually increasing for China and Korea and decreasing for Japan. For example, the production volumes for China rose from 619,000 tonnes in 1985 to 1,984,400 tonnes in 1996. All species are over fished, however, and while the total catchments are rising, the fish population is continuously declining for most species leading to conflicts of interests.

(b) **Oil exploration has been successful in the Chinese and North Korean portions of the sea**, with the proven and estimated reserves of about 9 and 20 billion tonnes, respectively. However, the study and exploration of the sea is somewhat hindered by insufficient sharing of information between the involved countries.

(c) Navigation is another traditional activity in the Yellow Sea. The main Chinese ports are **Dalian, Tianjin, Qingdao** and **Qinhuangdao**. The major South Korean ports on the Yellow Sea are Incheon, Gunsan and Mokpo, and that for North Korea is Nampho, the outport of Pyongyang. The Bohai Train Ferry provides a shortcut between the Liaodong Peninsula and Shandong.

East China Sea

The East China Sea[9] is a marginal sea east of China. It is a part of the Pacific Ocean and covers an area of 1,249,000 square kms. It is bounded on the east by Kyūshū and the Ryukyu Islands of Japan, on the south by the island of Taiwan, and on the west by mainland China and the Asian continent. It is connected with the South China Sea by the Taiwan Strait and with the Sea of Japan by the Korea Strait; it opens in the north to the Yellow Sea.

States with borders on the sea (clockwise from north) include: South Korea, Japan, Republic of China (Taiwan) and the People's Republic of China. (See Fig. 2.2) [10]

Islands and Reefs (See Fig. 2.3)[11]

(a) Senkaku Islands (Japanese) or Diaoyu Islands (Chinese).

(b) Tong Island.

(c) Cluster of submerged reefs in the northern East China Sea. These including Socotra Rock, also called Suyan Rock or Ieodo, Hupijiao Rock and Yajiao Rock.

---

9   http://en.wikipedia.org/wiki/East_China_Sea

10 http://en.wikipedia.org/wiki/File:East_China_Sea_Map.jpg

11 http://www.bbc.co.uk/news/world-asia-20730880

Fig. 2.2

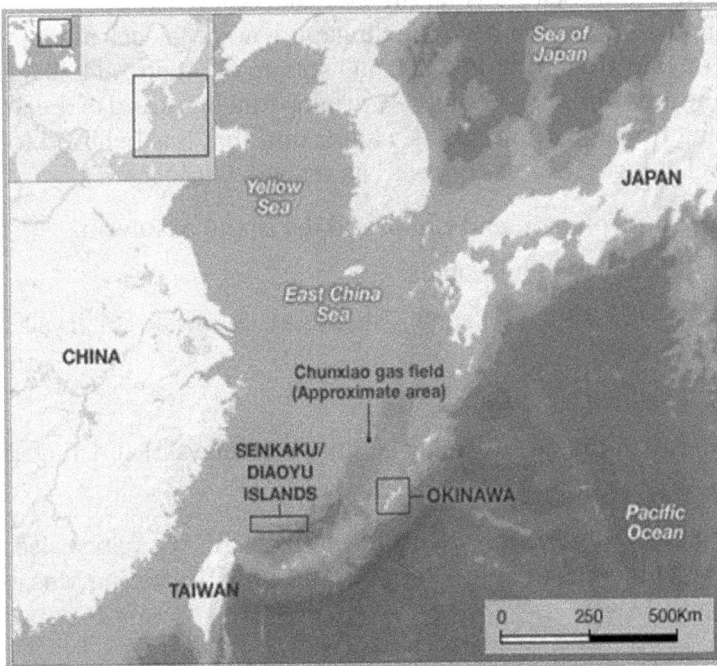

Fig. 2.3

Economic Importance[12]

(a) The East China Sea is of great economic interest to all three countries because of its proven or suspected hydrocarbon resources, its fishery resources and its sea-floor deposits of metals. The various estimates of proven and potential hydrocarbon resources vary considerably. Although these reserves are not particularly high by international standards, they are important in view of the crucial role of hydrocarbon imports in both Japan and China and the desire of both countries to reduce their high dependence on energy from the Middle East. Currently, the most important hydrocarbon resource in the East China Sea is gas. Although gas accounts for only about 3 per cent of China's total energy consumption, its consumption is rising quickly, driven by a policy of reducing the high level of environmentally damaging coal consumption. In 2007, despite its own growing gas production, China has started to import gas in the form of LNG.

(b) Its islands are rich fishing grounds and lie on the key shipping lanes especially those coming from North China.

South China Sea

The South China Sea[13] is a marginal sea that is part of the Pacific Ocean, encompassing an area from the Singapore and Malacca Straits to the Strait of Taiwan of around 3,500,000 square kilometres (1,400,000 sq mi). The area's importance largely results from one-third of the world's shipping transiting through its waters, and that it is believed to hold huge oil and gas reserves beneath its seabed. It is located

(a) South of mainland China and the island of Taiwan.

(b) West of the Philippines.

(c) North West of Sabah (Malaysia), Sarawak (Malaysia) and Brunei.

(d) North of Indonesia.

(e) North east of the Malay Peninsula (Malaysia) and Singapore.

(f) East of Vietnam.

States and territories with borders on the sea (clockwise from north) include: the People's Republic of China (including Macau and

---

12 http://www.japanfocus.org/-Reinhard-Drifte/3156

13 http://en.wikipedia.org/wiki/South_China_Sea

Hong Kong), the Republic of China (Taiwan), Philippines, Malaysia, Brunei, Indonesia, Singapore, Thailand, Cambodia, and Vietnam.

Islands and Seamounts

(a) The minute South China Sea Islands, collectively an archipelago, number in the hundreds. The sea and its mostly uninhabited islands are subject to competing claims of sovereignty by several countries. These claims are also reflected in the variety of names used for the islands and the sea.

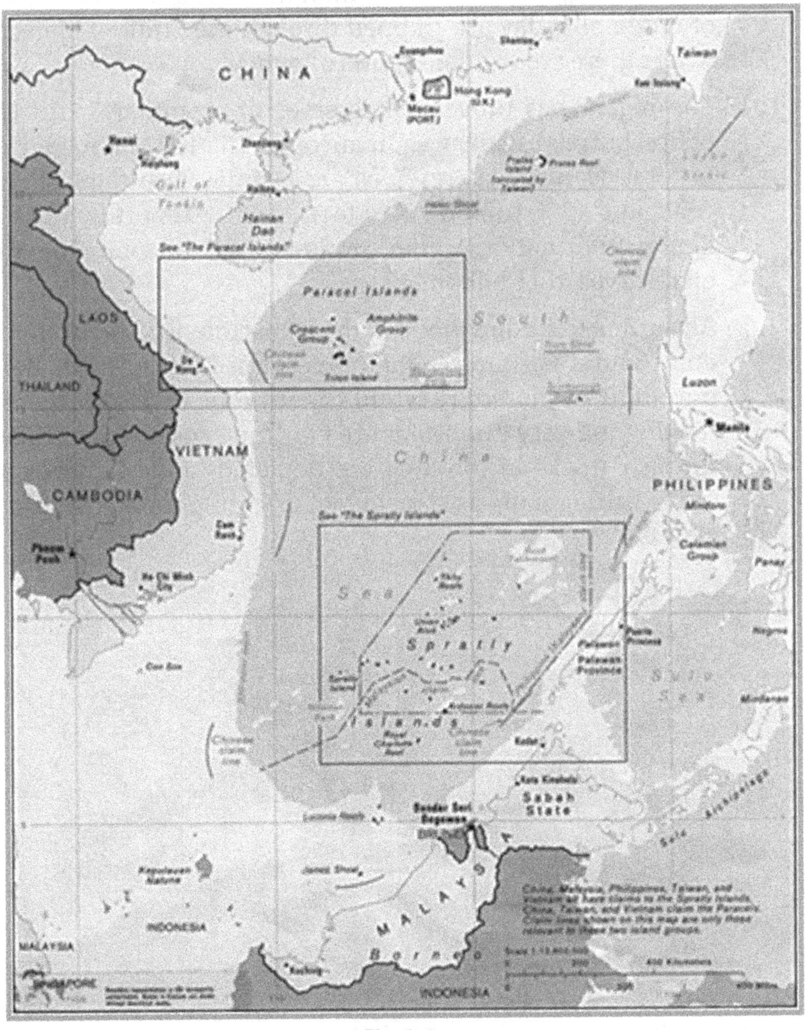

Fig. 2.4

(b) The South China Sea contains over 250 small islands, atolls, cays, shoals, reefs, and sandbars, most of which have no indigenous people, many of which are naturally under water at high tide, and some of which are permanently submerged. (See Fig. 2.4)[14]

Economic Importance

(a) It is an extremely significant body of water in a geopolitical sense. It is the second most used sea lane in the world, while in terms of world annual merchant fleet tonnage, over 50% passes through the Strait of Malacca, the Sunda Strait, and the Lombok Strait. Over 1.6 million m^3 (10 million barrels) of crude oil a day are shipped through the Strait of Malacca, where there are regular reports of piracy.

(b) The region has proven oil reserves of around 1.2 km^3 (7.7 billion barrels), with an estimate of 4.5 km^3 (28 billion barrels) in total. Natural gas reserves are estimated to total around 7,500 km^3 (266 trillion cubic feet). A 2013 report by the U.S. Energy Information Administration raised the total estimated oil reserves to 11 billion barrels.

(c) According to studies made by the Department of Environment and Natural Resources, Philippines, this body of water holds one third of the entire world's marine biodiversity, thereby making it a very important area for the ecosystem. However the fish stocks in the area are depleted, and countries are using fishing bans as a means of asserting their sovereignty claims.

14 http://en.wikipedia.org/wiki/File:Schina_sea_88.png

Chapter 3

CHINESE HISTORY

General

The Chinese record their history[1] as a succession of ruling dynasties till the formation of the Republic of China and then the People's Republic of China. Chinese civilization originated in various regional centres along both the Yellow River and the Yangtze River valleys in the Neolithic era, but the Yellow River is said to be the cradle of Chinese civilization. With thousands of years of continuous history, China is one of the world's oldest civilizations. The written history of China can be found as early as the Shang Dynasty (1700–1046 BC), although ancient historical texts such as the *Records of the Grand Historian* (ca. 100 BC) and *Bamboo Annals* assert the existence of a Xia Dynasty before the Shang. Much of Chinese culture, literature and philosophy further developed during the Zhou Dynasty (1045–256 BC).The Zhou Dynasty began to bow to external and internal pressures in the 8th century BC, and the kingdom eventually broke apart into smaller states, beginning in the Spring and Autumn Period and reaching full expression in the Warring States period. In between eras of multiple kingdoms, Chinese dynasties have ruled parts or all of China. This practice began with the Qin Dynasty: in 221 BC, Qin Shi Huang united the various warring kingdoms and created the first Chinese empire. Successive dynasties in Chinese history developed bureaucratic systems that enabled the Emperor of China to directly control vast territories.

Palaeolithic

What is now China was inhabited by *Homo erectus* more than a million years ago. Perhaps the most famous specimen of *Homo erectus* found in China is the so-called Peking Man discovered in 1923-27.

---

1 http://en.wikipedia.org/wiki/History_of_China

Neolithic

The Neolithic age in China can be traced back to between 12,000 and 10,000 BC. Early evidence for proto-Chinese millet agriculture is radiocarbon-dated to about 7000 BC. Farming gave rise to the Jiahu culture (7000 to 5800 BC). Excavation of a Peiligang culture site in Xinzheng county, Henan, found a community that flourished in 5,500-4,900 BC, with evidence of agriculture, constructed buildings, pottery, and burial of the dead. In late Neolithic times, the Yellow River valley began to establish itself as a centre of Yangshao culture (5000 BC to 3000 BC), and the first villages were founded. Later, Yangshao culture was superseded by the Longshan culture, which was also cantered on the Yellow River from about 3000 BC to 2000 BC.

Xia Dynasty

The Xia Dynasty of China (from 2100 to 1600 BC) is the first dynasty to be described in ancient historical records such as Sima Qian's *Records of the Grand Historian* and *Bamboo Annals*. Although there is disagreement as to whether the dynasty actually existed, there is some archaeological evidence pointing to its possible existence. Sima Qian, writing in the late 2nd century BC, dated the founding of the Xia Dynasty to around 2200 BC, but this date has not been corroborated. Most archaeologists now connect the Xia to excavations at Erlitou in central Henan province, where a bronze smelter from around 2000 BC was unearthed. According to mythology, the dynasty ended around 1600 BC as a consequence of the Battle of Mingtiao.

Shang Dynasty

(a) Archaeological findings providing evidence for the existence of the Shang Dynasty, between 1600–1046 BC, are divided into two sets. The Shang Dynasty featured 31 kings, from Tang of Shang to King Zhou of Shang. In this period, the Chinese worshipped many different gods — weather gods and sky gods — and also a supreme god, named Shangdi, who ruled over the other gods. Those who lived during the Shang Dynasty also believed that their ancestors — their parents and grandparents — became like gods when they died, and that their ancestors wanted to be worshipped, too, like gods. Each family worshipped its own ancestors.

(b) The *Records of the Grand Historian* states that the Shang

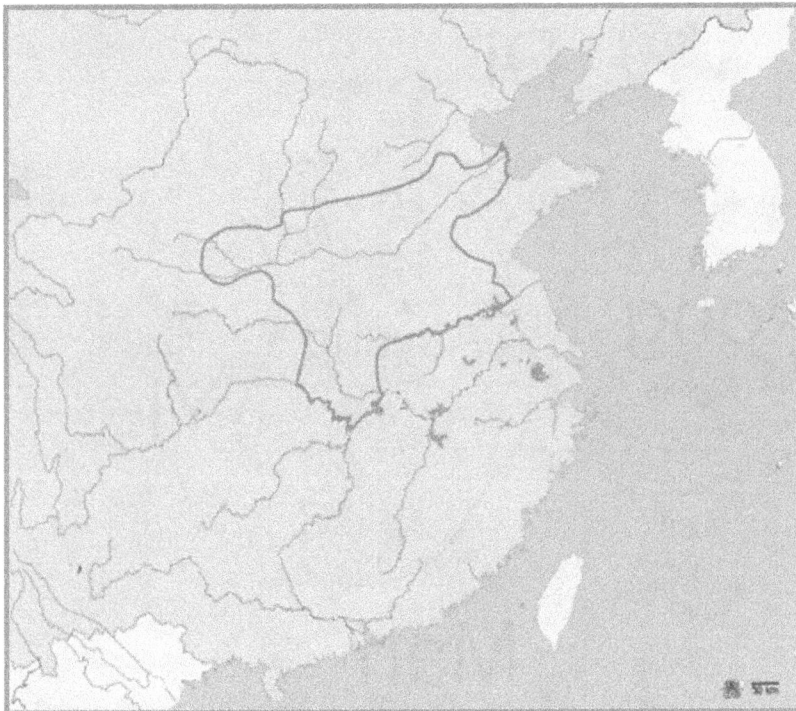

Fig. 3.1

Dynasty moved its capital six times (See Fig. 3.1 and 3.2)[2,3]. The final (and most important) move to Yin in 1350 BC led to the dynasty's golden age. The term Yin Dynasty has been synonymous with the Shang dynasty in history, although it has lately been used to specifically refer to the latter half of the Shang Dynasty.

(c) Chinese historians living in later periods were accustomed to the notion of one dynasty succeeding another, but the actual political situation in early China is known to have been much more complicated. Hence, as some scholars of China suggest, the Xia and the Shang can possibly refer to political entities that existed concurrently, just as the early Zhou is known to have existed at the same time as the Shang.

2   http://en.wikipedia.org/wiki/File:Shang_dynasty.svg
3   http://depts.washington.edu/chinaciv/1xarshang.htm

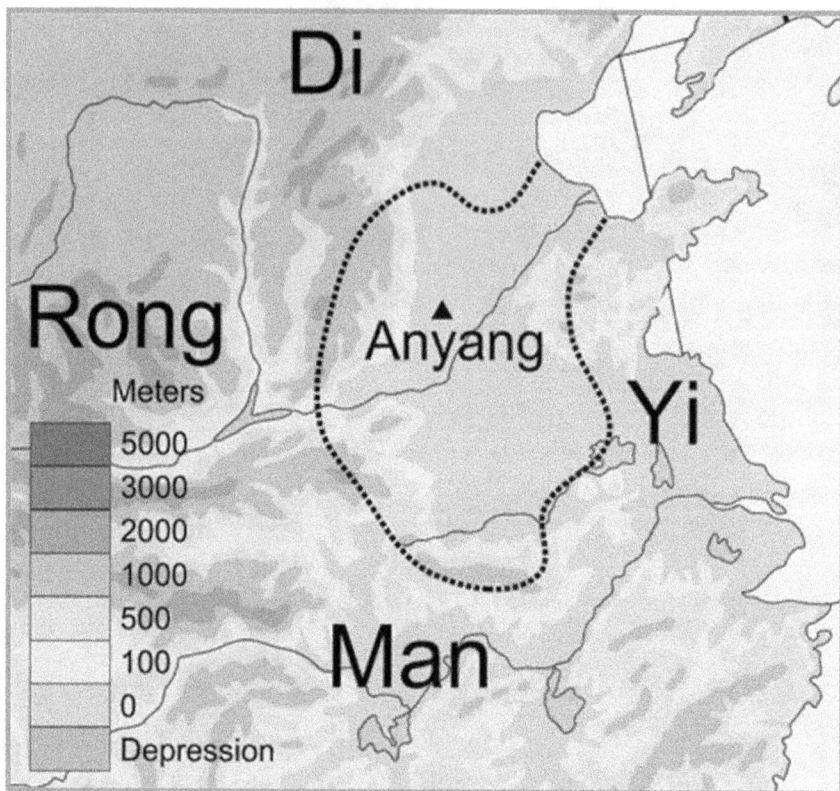

Fig. 3.2

Zhou Dynasty

(a) The Zhou Dynasty (See Fig. 3.3)[4] was the longest-lasting dynasty in Chinese history, from 1066 BC to approximately 256 BC. By the end of the 2nd millennium BC, the Zhou Dynasty began to emerge in the Yellow River valley, overrunning the territory of the Shang. The Zhou appeared to have begun their rule under a semi-feudal system. The Zhou lived west of the Shang, and the Zhou leader had been appointed "Western Protector" by the Shang. The ruler of the Zhou, King Wu, with the assistance of his brother, the Duke of Zhou, as regent, managed to defeat the Shang at the Battle of Muye.

(b) The king of Zhou at this time invoked the concept of the Mandate of Heaven to legitimize his rule, a concept that

---

4 http://en.wikipedia.org/wiki/File:Zhou_dynasty_1000_BC.png

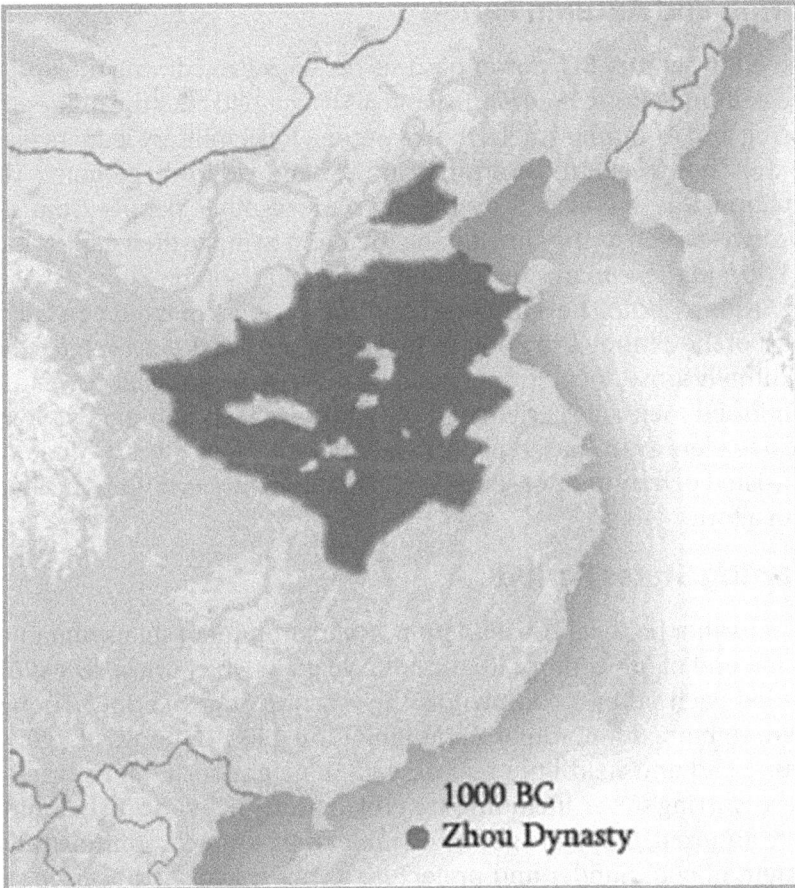

1000 BC
● Zhou Dynasty

Fig. 3.3

would be influential for almost every succeeding dynasty. Like Shangdi, Heaven ruled over all the other gods, and it decided who would rule China. It was believed that a ruler had lost the Mandate of Heaven when natural disasters occurred in great number, and when, more realistically, the sovereign had apparently lost his concern for the people. In response, the royal house would be overthrown, and a new house would rule, having been granted the Mandate of Heaven.

Spring and Autumn Period

In the 8th century BC, power became decentralized during the Spring and Autumn period (See Fig. 3.4 and 3.5)[5,6], named after the influential Spring and Autumn Annals. In this period, local military leaders used by the Zhou began to assert their power and vie for hegemony. The situation was aggravated by the invasion of other people from the northwest, such as the Qin, forcing the Zhou to move their capital east to Luoyang. This marks the second major phase of the Zhou dynasty: the Eastern Zhou. The Spring and Autumn Period is marked by a falling apart of the central Zhou power. In each of the hundreds of states that eventually arose, local strongmen held most of the political power and continued their subservience to the Zhou kings in name only. Some local leaders even started using royal titles for themselves. China now consisted of hundreds of states, some of them only as large as a village with a fort.

Warring States Period

After further political consolidation, seven prominent states remained by the end of 5th century BC, and the years in which these few states battled each other are known as the Warring States Period. Though there remained a nominal Zhou king until 256 BC, he was largely a figurehead and held little real power. As neighbouring territories of these warring states, including areas of modern Sichuan and Liaoning, were annexed, they were governed under the new local administrative system of commander and prefecture . This system had been in use since the Spring and Autumn Period, and parts can still be seen in the modern system of Sheng & Xian (province and county).The final expansion in this period began during the reign of Ying Zheng, the king of Qin. His unification of the other six powers, and further annexations in the modern regions of Zhejiang, Fujian, Guangdong and Guangxiin 214 BC, enabled him to proclaim himself the First Emperor (Qin Shi Huang). (See Fig. 3.6)[7]

Qin Dynasty

   (a)   Historians often refer to the period from Qin Dynasty to the end of Qing Dynasty as Imperial China. Though the unified

---

5   http://en.wikipedia.org/wiki/File:Chinese_plain_5c._BC-en.svg

6   http://depts.washington.edu/chinaciv/1xarzhou.htm

7   http://en.wikipedia.org/wiki/File:Streitende-Reiche2.jpg

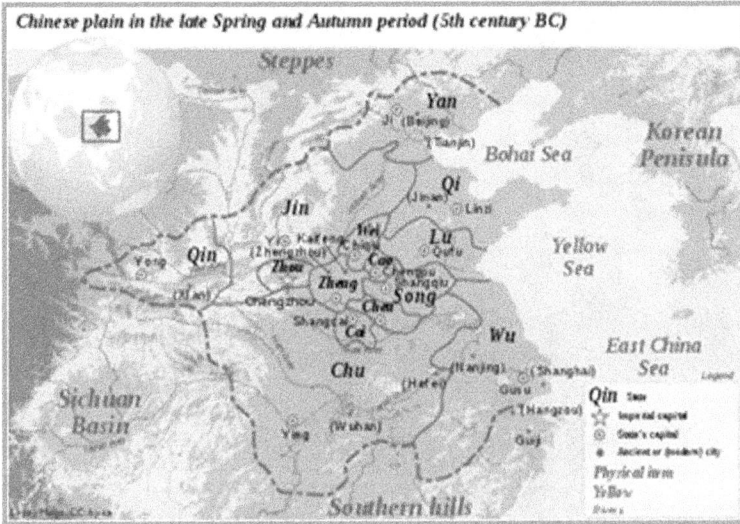

Chinese plain in the late Spring and Autumn period (5th century BC)

Fig. 3.4

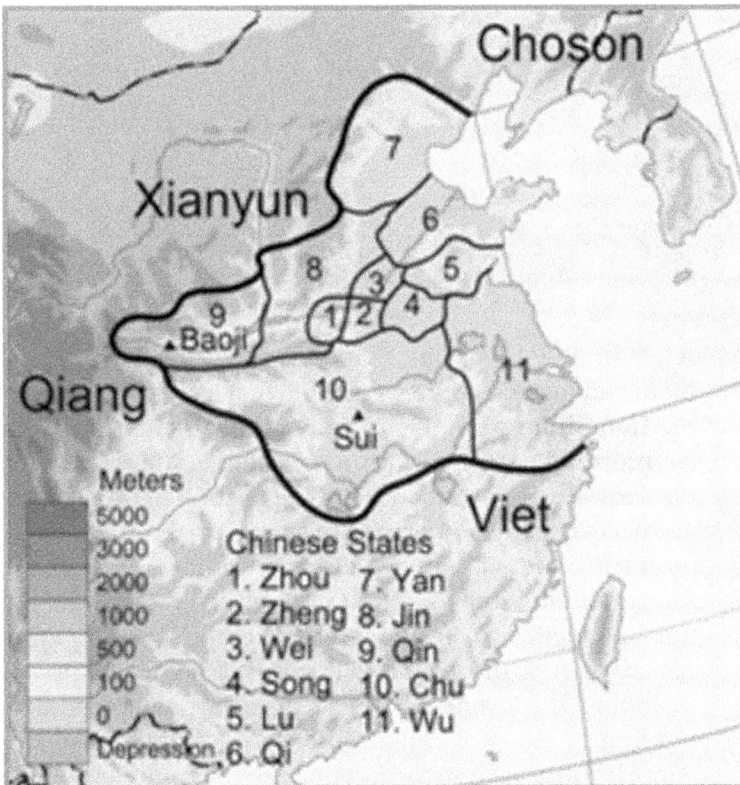

Fig. 3.5

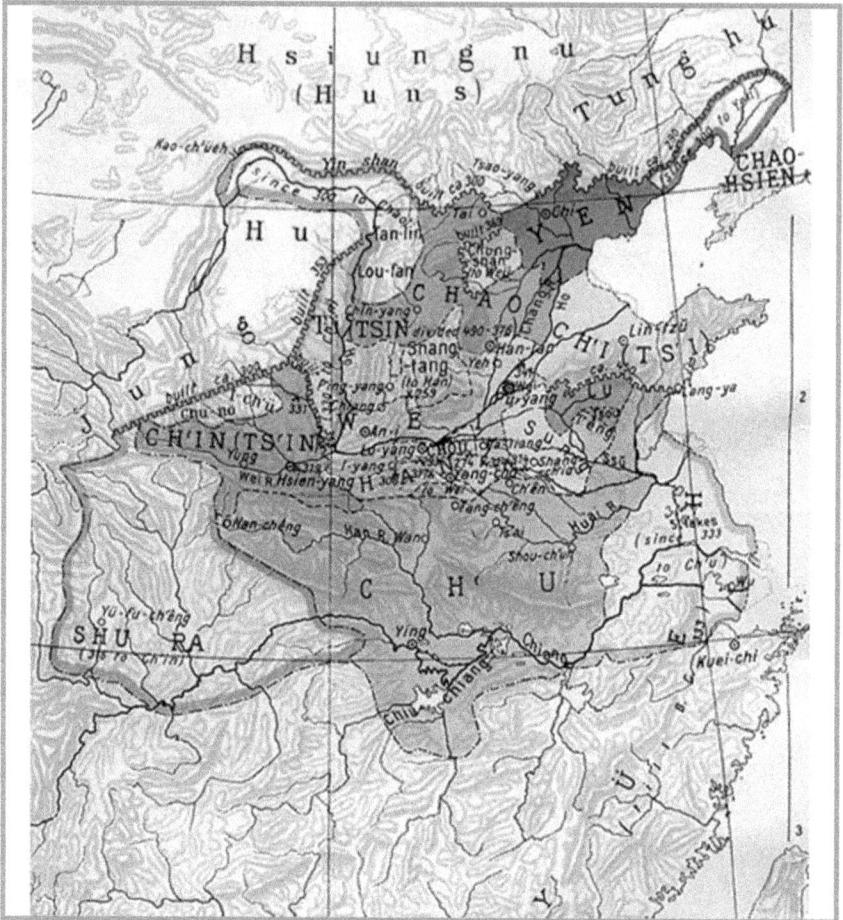

Fig. 3.6

reign of the First Qin Emperor lasted only 12 years, he managed to subdue great parts of what constitutes the core of the Han Chinese homeland and to unite them under a tightly centralized Legalist government seated at Xianyang (close to modern Xi'an). The doctrine of Legalism that guided the Qin emphasized strict adherence to a legal code and the absolute power of the emperor. This philosophy, while effective for expanding the empire in a military fashion, proved unworkable for governing it in peacetime. The Qin Emperor presided over the brutal silencing of political opposition, including the event known as the burning of books and burying of scholars. This would be the impetus behind the later Han synthesis incorporating the more moderate schools

Fig. 3.7

of political governance. (See Fig. 3.7)[8]

(b) The Qin Dynasty is well known for beginning the Great Wall of China, which was later augmented and enhanced during the Ming Dynasty. The other major contributions of the Qin include the concept of a centralized government, the unification of the legal code, development of the written language, measurement, and currency of China after the tribulations of the Spring and Autumn and Warring States Periods. Even something as basic as the length of axles for carts was made uniform to ensure a viable trading system throughout the empire.

8   http://en.wikipedia.org/wiki/File:Qin_empire_210_BCE.png

Western Han Dynasty

(a) The Han Dynasty was founded by Liu Bang, who emerged victorious in the civil war that followed the collapse of the unified but short-lived Qin Dynasty. A golden age in Chinese history, the Han Dynasty's long period of stability and prosperity consolidated the foundation of China as a unified state under a central imperial bureaucracy, which was to last intermittently for most of the next two millennium. During the Han Dynasty, territory of China was extended to most of China proper and to areas far west. Confucianism was officially elevated to orthodox status and was to shape the subsequent Chinese Civilization. Art, Culture and Science all advanced to unprecedented heights. With the profound and lasting impacts of this period of Chinese history, the dynasty name "Han" had been taken as the name of the Chinese people, now the dominant ethnic group in modern China, and had been commonly used to refer to Chinese language and written characters. (See Fig. 3.8 and 3.9)[9,10]

(b) After the initial Laissez-faire policies of Emperors Wen and Jing, the ambitious Emperor Wu brought the empire to its zenith. To consolidate his power, Confucianism, which emphasizes stability and order in a well-structured society, was given exclusive patronage to be the guiding philosophical thoughts and moral principles of the empire. Imperial Universities were established to support its study and further development, while other thoughts were discouraged.

(c) Major military campaigns were launched to weaken the nomadic Xiongnu Empire, limiting their influence north of the Great Wall. Along with the diplomatic efforts led by Zhang Qian, the sphere of influence of the Han Empire extended to the states in the Tarim Basin, opened up the Silk Road that connected China to west, stimulating prosperous bilateral trades and cultural exchange. To the south, various small kingdoms far beyond the Yangtze River Valley were formally incorporated into the empire.

(d) After Emperor Wu, the empire slipped into gradual stagnation and decline. Economically, the state treasury was strained by

9 http://en.wikipedia.org/wiki/File:Han_map.jpg

10 http://depts.washington.edu/chinaciv/1xarhan1.htm

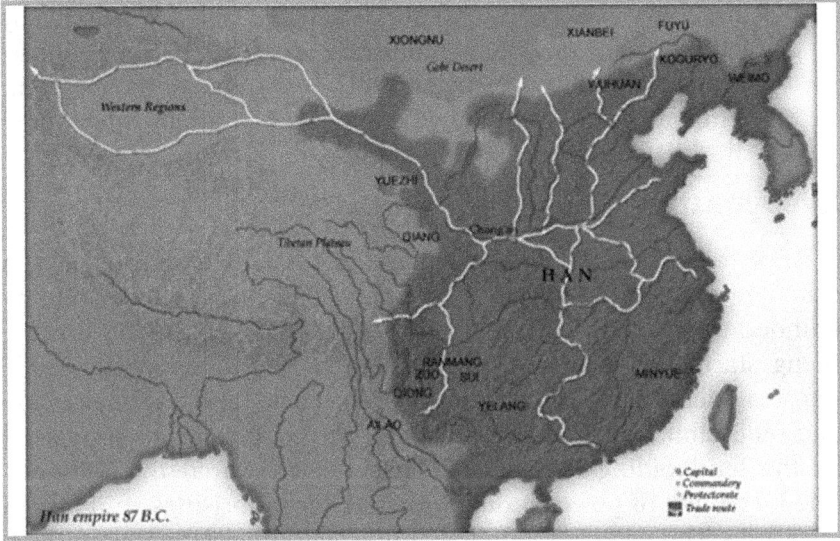

Fig. 3.8

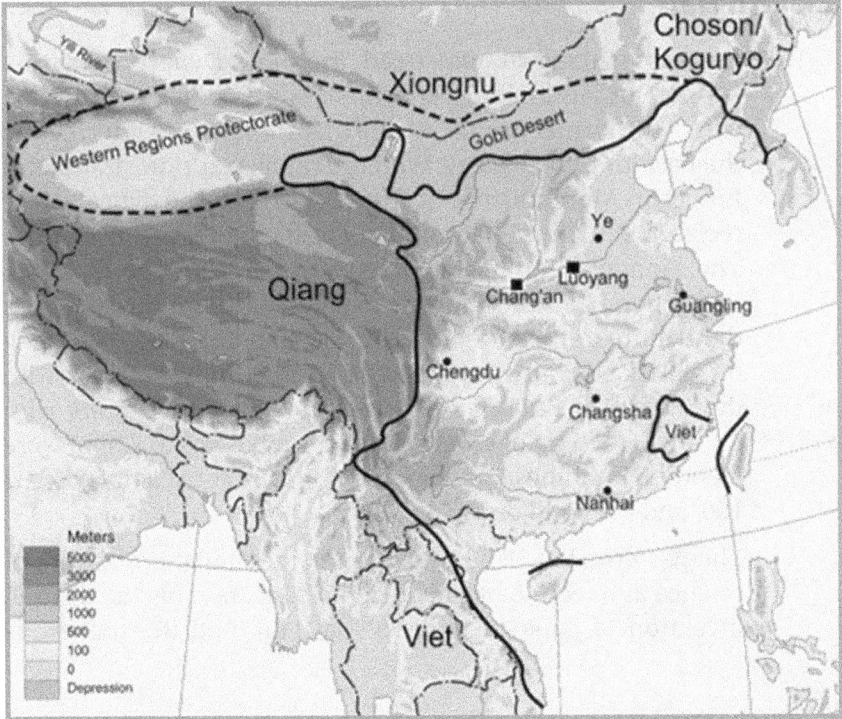

Fig. 3.9

excessive campaigns and projects, while land acquisitions by elite families gradually drained the tax base. Various consort clans exerted increasing control over strings of incompetent emperors and eventually the dynasty was briefly interrupted by the usurpation of Wang Mang.

Xin Dynasty

In AD 9, the usurper Wang Mang claimed that the Mandate of Heaven called for the end of the Han dynasty and the rise of his own, and he founded the short-lived Xin ("New") Dynasty (See Fig. 3.10)[11]. Wang Mang started an extensive program of land and other economic reforms, including the outlawing of slavery and land nationalization and redistribution. These programs, however, were never supported by the landholding families, because they favoured the peasants. The instability of power brought about chaos, uprisings, and loss of territories. This was compounded by mass flooding of the Yellow River; silt build-up caused it to split into two channels and displaced large numbers of farmers. Wang Mang was eventually killed in Weiyang Palace by an enraged peasant mob in AD 23.

Eastern Han

(a) Emperor Guangwu reinstated the Han Dynasty with the support of landholding and merchant families at Luoyang, *east* of the former capital Xi'an. Thus, this new era is termed as the Eastern Han Dynasty. With the capable administrations of Emperors Ming and Zhang, former glories of the dynasty were reclaimed, with brilliant military and cultural achievements. The Xiongnu Empire was decisively defeated. The diplomat and general Ban Chao further expanded the conquests across the Pamirs to the shores of the Caspian Sea thus reopening the Silk Road, and bringing trade, foreign cultures, along with the arrival of Buddhism. With extensive connections with the west, the first of several Roman embassies to China were recorded in Chinese sources, coming from the sea route in AD 166, and a second one in AD 284.

(b) The Eastern Han Dynasty was one of the most prolific era of science and technology in ancient China, notably the historic invention of paper making by Cai Lun, and the numerous

---

11 http://en.wikipedia.org/wiki/File:%E6%96%B0%E8%8E%BD%E6%97%B6%E6%9C%9F%E7%9 6%86%E5%9F%9F%E5%9B%BE%EF%BC%88%E7%B9%81%EF%BC%89.png

鮮卑

挹婁

匈　奴

北沃沮

夫余

下

烏桓

月氏

羌　氐

夫甘都盧

哀牢

新莽時疆域
（9年～23年）

Fig. 3.10

contributions by the polymath Zhang Heng.

(c) By the 2nd century, the empire declined amidst land acquisitions, invasions, and feuding between consort clans and eunuchs. The Yellow Turban Rebellion broke out in AD 184, ushering in an era of warlords. In the ensuing turmoil, three states tried to gain predominance in the period of the Three Kingdoms. This time period has been greatly romanticized in works such as *Romance of the Three Kingdoms*.

Wei, Shu and Wu Period

After Cao Cao reunified the north in 208, his son proclaimed the Wei dynasty in 220. Soon, Wei's rivals Shu and Wu proclaimed their independence, leading China into the Three Kingdoms Period (See Fig. 3.11)[12]. This period was characterized by a gradual decentralization of the state that had existed during the Qin and Han dynasties, and an increase in the power of great families. Although the Three Kingdoms were reunified by the Jin Dynasty in 280, this structure was essentially the same until the Wu Hu uprising.

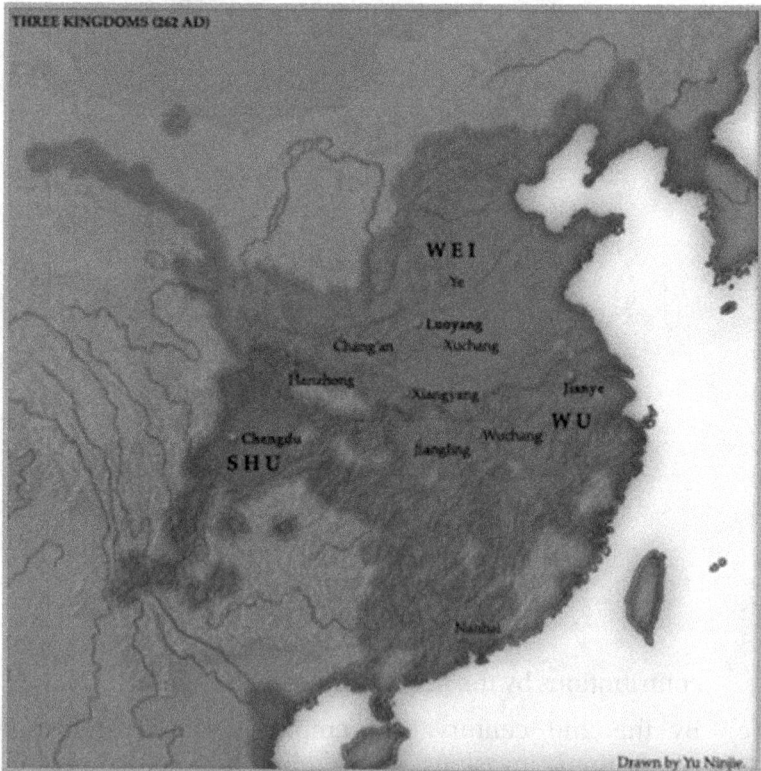

Fig. 3.11

---

12 http://en.wikipedia.org/wiki/File:China_5.jpg

Wu Hu Period

Taking advantage of **civil war in the Jin Dynasty**, the contemporary non-Han Chinese (Wu Hu) ethnic groups controlled much of the country in the early 4th century and provoked large-scale Han Chinese migrations to south of the Yangtze River. In AD 303 the Di people rebelled and later captured Chengdu, establishing the state of Cheng Han. Under Liu Yuan, the Xiongnu rebelled near today's Linfen County and established the state of Han Zhao. Liu Yuan's successor Liu Cong captured and executed the last two Western Jin emperors. Sixteen kingdoms were a plethora of short-lived non-Chinese dynasties that came to rule the whole or parts of northern China in the 4th and 5th centuries. Many ethnic groups were involved, including ancestors of the Turks, Mongols, and Tibetans. Most of these nomadic peoples had, to some extent, been "sinicized" long before their ascent to power. In fact, some of them, notably the Qiang and the Xiongnu, had already been allowed to live in the frontier regions within the Great Wall since late Han times.

Southern and Northern Dynasties

(a) Signalled by the collapse of East Jin Dynasty in AD 420, China entered the era of the Southern and Northern Dynasties (See Fig. 3.12)[13]. The Han people managed to survive the military attacks from the nomadic tribes of the north, such as the Xianbei, and their civilization continued to thrive.

(b) In southern China, fierce debates about whether Buddhism should be allowed to exist were held frequently by the royal court and nobles. Finally, near the end of the Southern and Northern Dynasties era, both Buddhist and Taoist followers compromised and became more tolerant of each other.

(c) In 589, Sui annexed the last Southern Dynasty, Chen, through military force, and put an end to the era of Southern and Northern Dynasties.

Sui Dynasty

The Sui Dynasty (See Fig. 3.13 and 3.14)[14,15], which managed to reunite the country in 589 after nearly four centuries of political fragmentation,

---

13 http://en.wikipedia.org/wiki/File:Northern_and_Southern_Dynasties_560_CE.png

14 http://en.wikipedia.org/wiki/File:Cheui_Dynasty_581_CE.png

15 http://depts.washington.edu/chinaciv/1xarsui1.htm

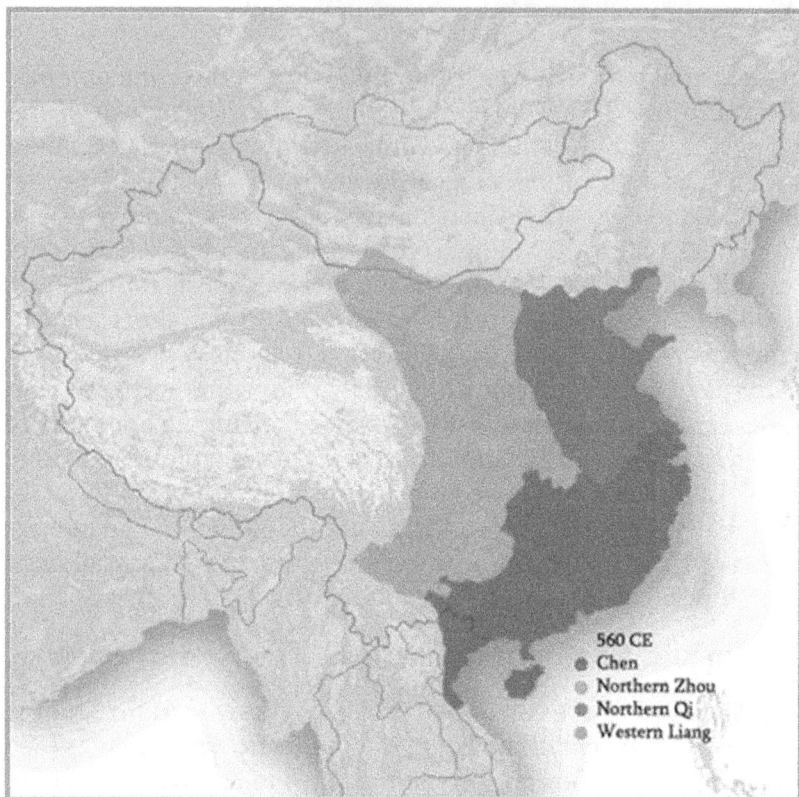

Fig. 3.12

played a role more important than its length of existence would suggest. The Sui brought China together again and set up many institutions that were to be adopted by their successors, the Tang. These included the government system of Three Departments and Six Ministries, standard coinage, improved defence and expansion of the Great Wall, and official support for Buddhism. Like the Qin, however, the Sui **overused their resources and collapsed.**

Tang Dynasty

(a) Tang Dynasty (See Fig. 3.15 and 3.16)[16,17] was founded by

---

16 http://en.wikipedia.org/wiki/File:Tang_Dynasty_circa_700_CE.png
17 http://depts.washington.edu/chinaciv/1xartang.htm

Fig. 3.13

Emperor Gaozu on 18 June 618. It was a golden age of Chinese civilization with significant developments in art, literature, particularly poetry, and technology. Buddhism became the predominant religion for common people.

(b) Started by the second emperor, Taizong, military campaigns were launched to dissolve threats from nomadic tribes, extend the border, and submit neighbouring states into a tributary system. Military victories in the Tarim Basin kept the Silk Road open, connecting the capital Chang'an to Central Asia and areas far to the west. In the south, lucrative maritime trade routes began from port cities such as Guangzhou. There was extensive trade with distant foreign countries, and many foreign merchants settled in China, boosting a vibrant cosmopolitan culture. The Tang culture and social systems

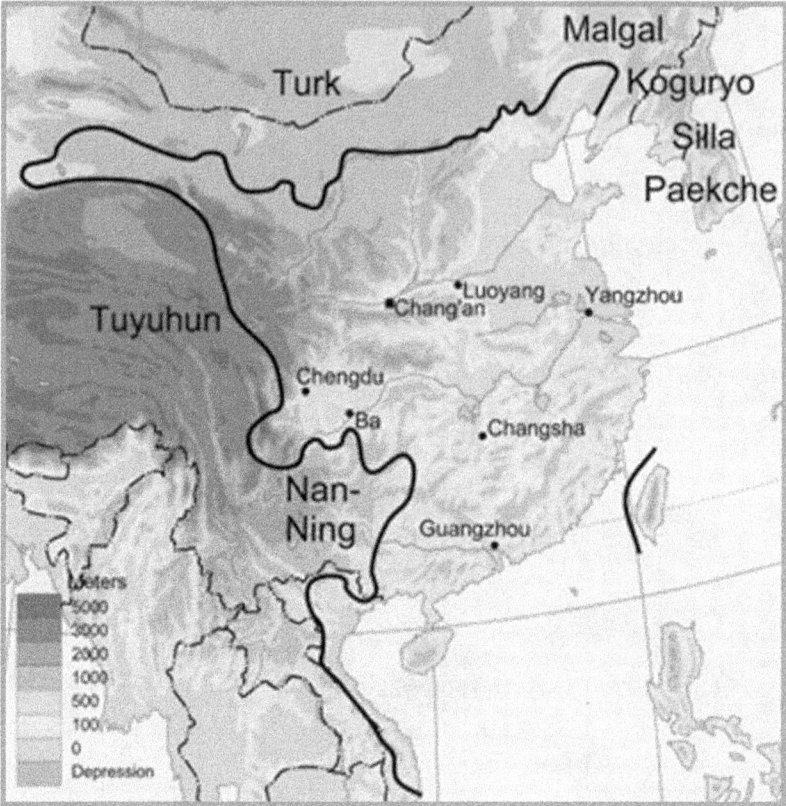

Fig. 3.14

were admired and adapted by neighbouring countries like Japan. Internally, the **Grand Canal**[18] linked the political heartland in Chang'an to the economic and agricultural centres in the eastern and southern parts of the empire.

(c) Underlying the prosperity of the early Tang Dynasty was a strong centralized bureaucracy with efficient policies. The government was organized as "Three Departments and Six Ministries" to separately draft, review, and implement

---

18 As noted by Kaplan Robert in 'The Revenge of Geography' page 3065 Kindle Edition. Built between AD 605 and 611, linking the Yellow and the Yangtze rivers and China's famine-prone north with its economically productive south, with its rice surpluses – had, according to British historian John Keay, "a similar effect to the building of the first transcontinental railroads in North America". The author calls it the key to Chinese unity as it reduced the North's conquest of the South. Thereby it helped consolidate the core geography of agrarian China.

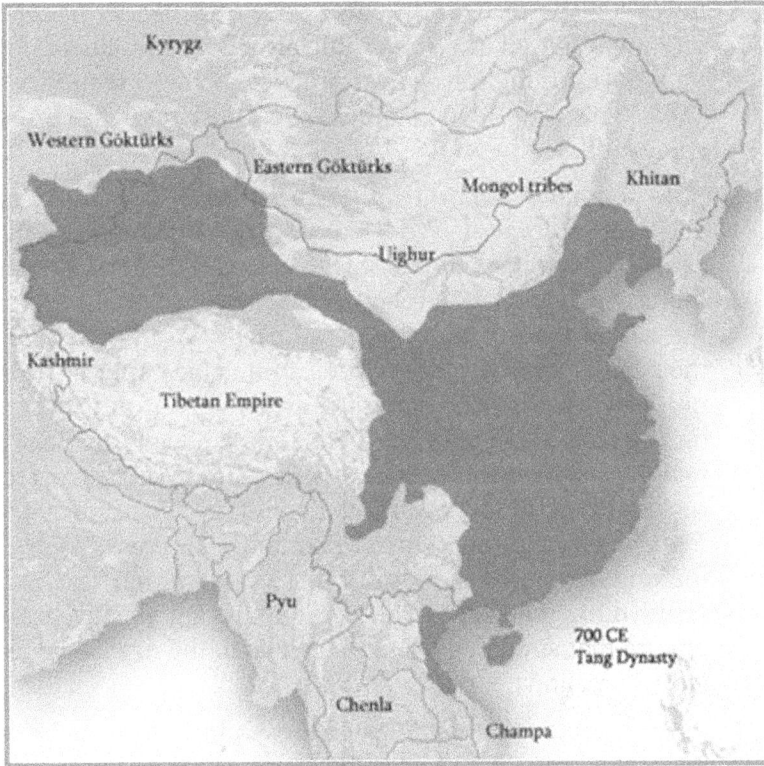

Fig. 3.15

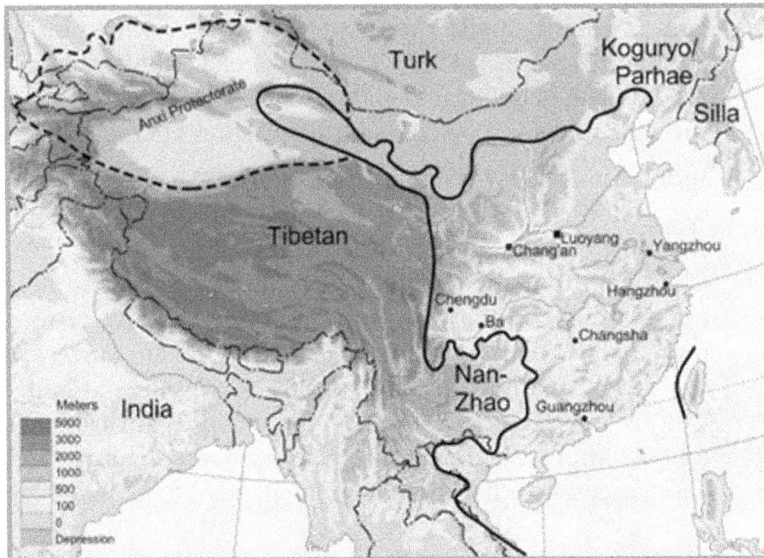

Fig. 3.16

policies. These departments were run by royal family members as well as scholar officials who were selected from imperial examinations. These practices, which matured in the Tang Dynasty, were to be inherited by the later dynasties with some modifications.

(d) The Tang land policy – the "Equal-field system" – claimed all lands as imperially owned, and were granted evenly to people according to the size of the households. The associated military policy – the "Fubing system" – conscripted all men in the nation for a fixed duty period each year in exchange for their land rights. These policies stimulated rapid growth of productivity, while boosting the army without much burden on the state treasury. However, lands gradually fell into the hands of private land owners, and standing armies were to replace conscription towards the middle period of the dynasty. The dynasty continued to flourish under Empress Wu Zetian, the only empress regent in Chinese history, and reached its zenith during the reign of Emperor Xuanzong, who oversaw an empire that stretched from the Pacific to the Aral Sea with at least 50 million people.

(e) At the zenith of prosperity of the empire, the An Lushan Rebellion was a watershed event that devastated the population and drastically weakened the central imperial government. Regional military governors, known as Jiedushi, gained increasingly autonomous status while formerly submissive states raided the empire. Nevertheless, after the An Lushan Rebellion, the Tang civil society recovered and thrived amidst the weakened imperial bureaucracy.

(f) From about 860, the Tang Dynasty declined due to a series of rebellions within China itself and in the former subject Kingdom of Nanzhao to the south. One warlord, Huang Chao, captured Guangzhou in 879, killing most of the 200,000 inhabitants, including most of the large colony of foreign merchant families there. In late AD 880, Luoyang surrendered to Huang Chao, and on 5 January 881 he conquered Chang'an. The emperor Xizong fled to Chengdu, and Huang established a new temporary regime which was eventually destroyed by Tang forces. Another time of political chaos followed.

Five Dynasties and Ten Kingdoms

The period of political disunity between the Tang and the Song, known as the Five Dynasties and Ten Kingdoms period (See Fig. 3.17 and 3.18)[19,20], lasted little more than half a century, from AD 907 to 960. During this brief era, when China was in all respects a multi-state system, five regimes rapidly succeeded one another in control of the old Imperial heartland in northern China. During this same time, sections of southern and western China were occupied by ten, more stable, regimes so the period is also referred to as the Ten Kingdoms.

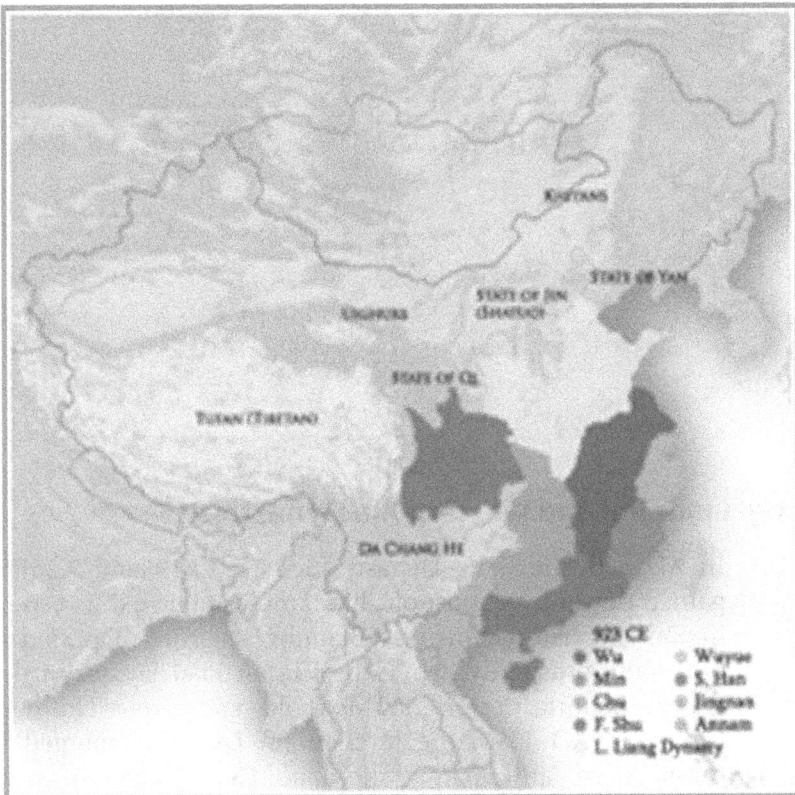

Fig. 3.17

---

19 http://en.wikipedia.org/wiki/File:Five_Dynasties_Ten_Kingdoms_923_CE.png

20 http://depts.washington.edu/chinaciv/1xarfive.htm

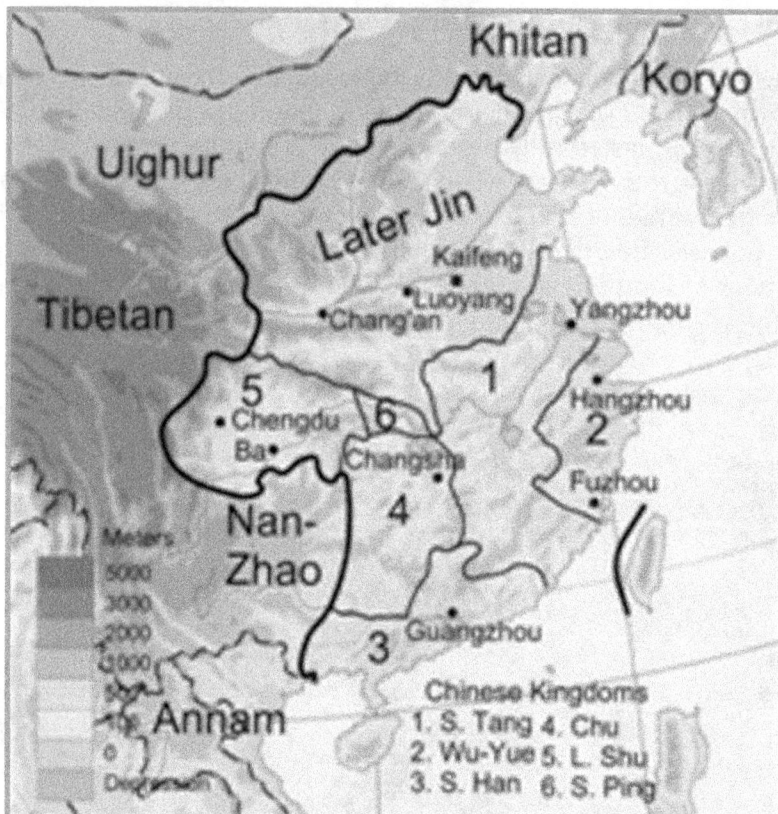

Fig. 3.18

Song, Liao, Jin, and Western Xia Dynasties

(a) In AD 960, the Song Dynasty (See Fig. 3.19 and 3.20)[21,22] gained power over most of China and established its capital in Kaifeng (later known as Bianjing), starting a period of economic prosperity, while the Khitan Liao Dynasty ruled over Manchuria, present-day Mongolia, and parts of Northern China. In AD 1115, the Jurchen Jin Dynasty emerged to prominence, annihilating the Liao Dynasty in 10 years. Meanwhile, in what are now the north western Chinese provinces of Gansu, Shaanxi, and Ningxia, there emerged a Western Xia Dynasty from AD 1032 to AD 1227, established by Tangut tribes. The Jin Dynasty took power over Northern China and Kaifeng from the Song Dynasty, which moved its

21 http://depts.washington.edu/chinaciv/1xarsong.htm
22 http://www.paulnoll.com/China/Dynasty/dynasty-Song.html

Fig. 3.19

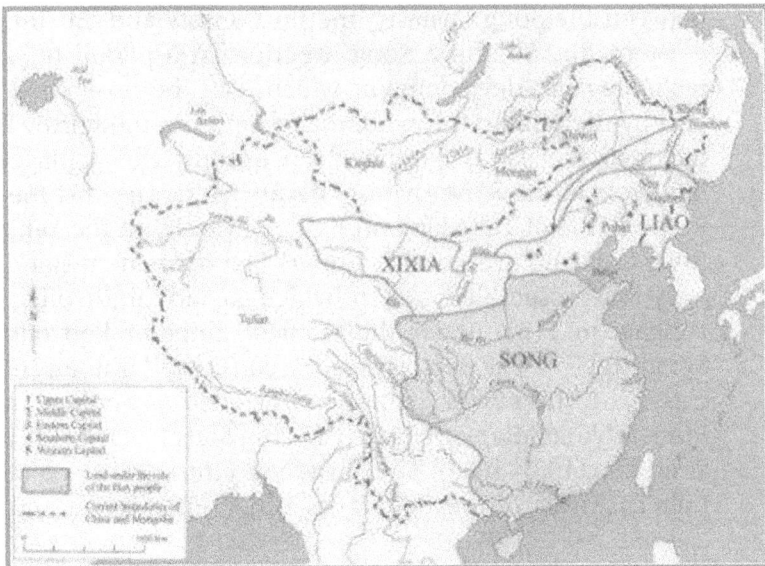

Fig. 3.20

Fig. 3.21

capital to Hangzhou.

(b)   The Southern Song Dynasty (See Fig. 3.21)[23] also suffered the humiliation of having to acknowledge the Jin Dynasty as formal overlords. In the ensuing years, China was divided between the Song Dynasty, the Jin Dynasty and the Tangut Western Xia. Southern Song experienced a period of great technological development which can be explained in part by the military pressure that it felt from the north. This included the use of gunpowder weapons, which played a large role in the Song Dynasty naval victories against the Jin in the Battle of Tangdao and Battle of Caishi on the Yangtze River in 1161. Furthermore, China's first permanent standing navy was assembled and provided an admiral's office at Dinghai in 1132, under the reign of Emperor Renzong of Song. (c)   The Song Dynasty is considered by many to be classical China's high point in science and technology, with **innovative scholar-officials** such as Su Song (1020–1101) and Shen Kuo (1031–1095). There was court intrigue between the political rivals of the Reformers and Conservatives, led by

23 http://www.paulnoll.com/China/Dynasty/dynasty-Song.html

the chancellors Wang Anshi and Sima Guang, respectively. By the mid-to-late 13th century, the Chinese had adopted the dogma of Neo-Confucian philosophy formulated by Zhu Xi. Enormous literary works were compiled during the Song Dynasty, such as the historical work of the *Zizhi Tongjian* (Comprehensive Mirror to Aid in Government). Culture and the arts flourished, with grandiose artworks such as *Along the River During the Qingming Festival* and *Eighteen Songs of a Nomad Flute*, along with great Buddhist painters like the prolific Lin Tinggui.

Yuan (Great Khanate) Dynasty

(a) The Jurchen-founded Jin Dynasty was defeated by the **Mongols**, who then proceeded to defeat the Southern Song in a long and bloody war, the first war in which firearms played an important role. During the era after the war, later called the **Pax Mongolica**, adventurous Westerners such as Polo travelled all the way to China and brought the first reports of its wonders to Europe. In the Yuan Dynasty, the Mongols were divided between those who wanted to remain based in the steppes and those who wished to adopt the customs of the Chinese.

(b) The Mongols call this the period of the rule of the four Khanates. (See Fig. 3.22)[24]

(c) Kublai Khan, grandson of Genghis Khan, wanting to adopt the customs of China, established the Yuan Dynasty (See Fig. 3.23)[25]. This was the first dynasty to rule the whole of China from Beijing as the capital. Beijing had been ceded to Liao in AD 938 with the Sixteen Prefectures of Yan Yun.

(d) Before that, it had been the capital of the Jin, who did not rule all of China. Before the Mongol invasion, Chinese dynasties reportedly had approximately 120 million inhabitants; after the conquest was completed in 1279, the 1300 census reported roughly 60 million people. While it is tempting to attribute this major decline solely to Mongol ferocity, scholars today have mixed sentiments regarding this subject. Scholars such as Frederick W. Mote argue that the wide drop in numbers

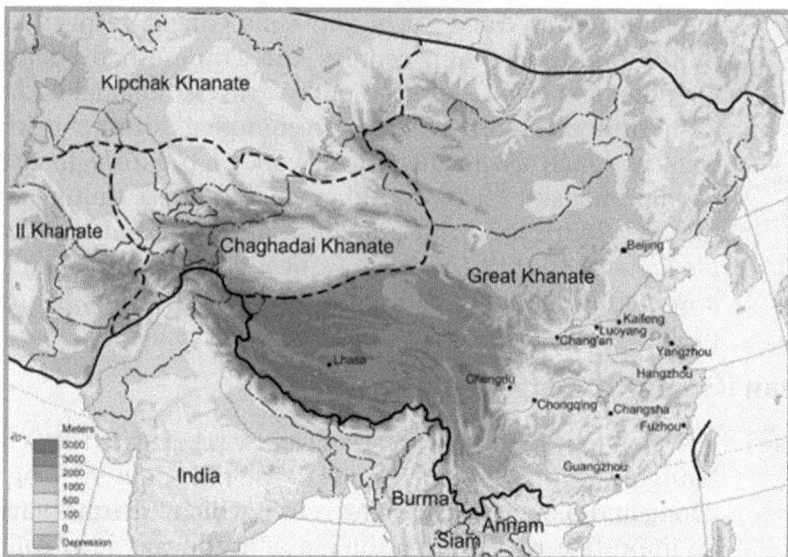

Fig. 3.22

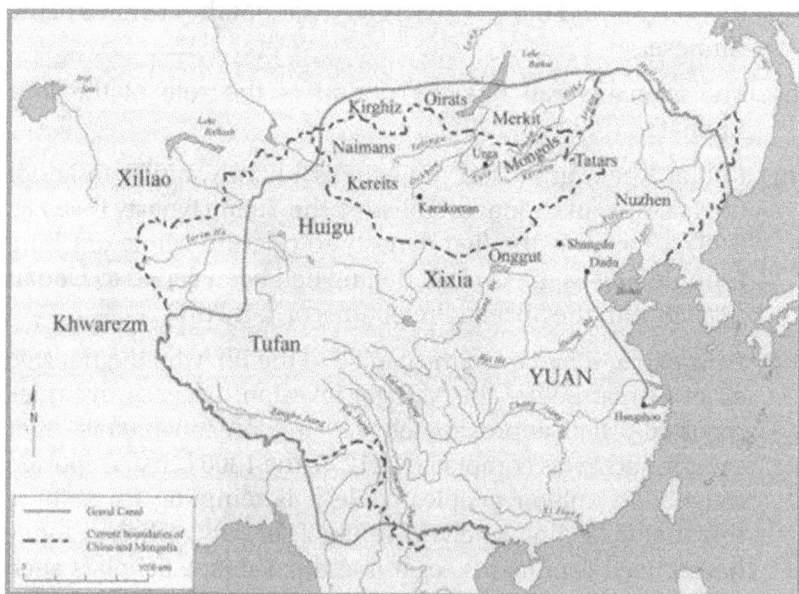

Fig. 3.23

reflects an administrative failure to record rather than an actual decrease; others such as Timothy Brook argue that the Mongols created a system of enserfment among a huge portion of the Chinese populace, causing many to disappear from the census altogether; other historians like William McNeill and David Morgan argue that the Bubonic Plague was the main factor behind the demographic decline during this period.   (e)
In the 14th century, China suffered additional depredations from epidemics of plague. The Black Death is estimated to have killed 25 million people or 30% of the population of China.

Ming Dynasty

(a) Throughout the Yuan Dynasty, which lasted less than a century, there was relatively strong sentiment among the populace against the Mongol rule. The frequent natural disasters since the 1340s finally led to peasant revolts. The Yuan Dynasty was eventually overthrown by the Ming Dynasty in 1368. (See Fig. 3.24)[26]

(b) Urbanization increased as the population grew and as the division of labour grew more complex. Large urban centres, such as Nanjing and Beijing, also contributed to the growth of private industry. In particular, small-scale industries grew up, often specializing in paper, silk, cotton, and porcelain goods. For the most part, however, relatively small urban centres with markets proliferated around the country. Town markets mainly traded food, with some necessary manufactures such as pins or oil.

(c) Despite the xenophobia and intellectual introspection characteristic of the increasingly popular new school of neo-Confucianism, China under the early Ming Dynasty was not isolated. Foreign trade and other contacts with the outside world, particularly Japan, increased considerably. Chinese merchants explored all of the Indian Ocean, reaching East Africa with the voyages of Zheng He.

(d) Zhu Yuanzhang or Hong-wu, the founder of the dynasty, laid the foundations for a state interested less in commerce and more in extracting revenues from the agricultural sector.

---

26 http://depts.washington.edu/chinaciv/1xarming.htm

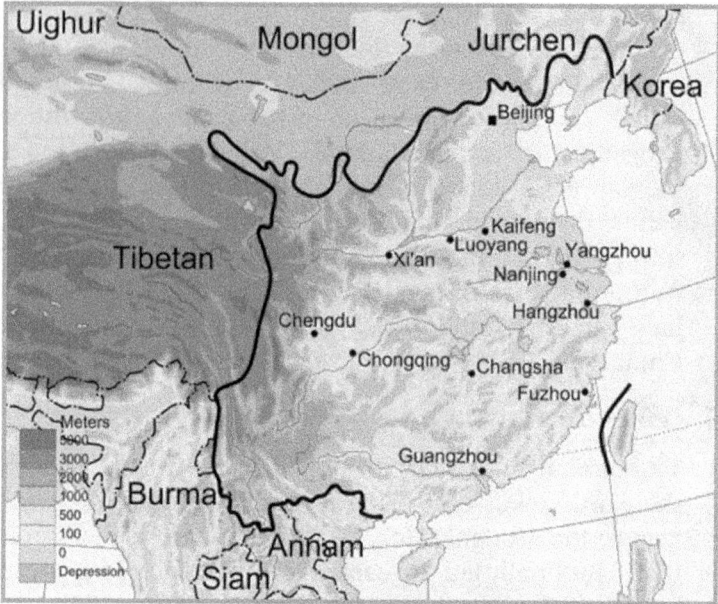

Fig. 3.24

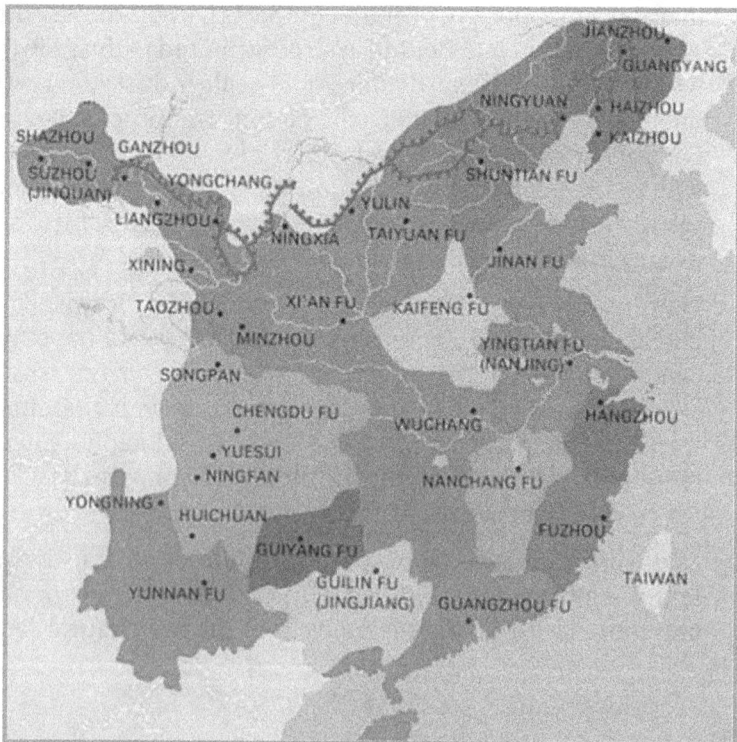

Fig. 3.25

Perhaps because of the Emperor's background as a peasant, the Ming economic system emphasized agriculture, unlike that of the Song and the Mongolian Dynasties, which relied on traders and merchants for revenue. Neo-feudal landholdings of the Song and Mongol periods were expropriated by the Ming rulers. Land estates were confiscated by the government, fragmented, and rented out. Private slavery was forbidden. Consequently, after the death of Emperor Yong-le, independent peasant landholders predominated in Chinese agriculture. These laws might have paved the way to removing the worst of the poverty during the previous regimes. (See Fig. 3.25)[27]

(e) The dynasty had a strong and complex central government that unified and controlled the empire. The emperor's role became more autocratic, although Zhu Yuanzhang necessarily continued to use what he called the "Grand Secretaries" to assist with the immense paperwork of the bureaucracy, including memorials (petitions and recommendations to the throne), imperial edicts in reply, reports of various kinds, and tax records. It was this same bureaucracy that later prevented the Ming government from being able to adapt to changes in society, and eventually led to its decline.

(f) Emperor Yong-le strenuously tried to extend China's influence beyond its borders by demanding other rulers send ambassadors to China to present tribute. A large navy was built, including four-mast ships displacing 1,500 tons. A standing army of 1 million troops (some estimate as many as 1.9 million) was created. The Chinese armies conquered Vietnam for around 20 years, while the Chinese fleet sailed the China seas and the Indian Ocean, cruising as far as the east coast of Africa. Several maritime Asian nations sent envoys with tribute for the Chinese emperor. Domestically, the Grand Canal was expanded and proved to be a stimulus to domestic trade. Over 100,000 tons of iron per year were produced. Many books were printed using movable type. The imperial palace in Beijing's Forbidden City reached its current splendour. It was also during these centuries that the potential of south China came to be fully exploited. New crops were widely cultivated and industries such as those producing porcelain

---

27 http://www.paulnoll.com/China/Dynasty/dynasty-Ming.html

and textiles flourished.

(g)   In 1449 Esen Tayisi led an Oirat Mongol invasion of northern China which culminated in the capture of the Zhengtong Emperor at Tumu. In 1542 the Mongol leader Altan Khan began to harass China along the northern border. In 1550 he even reached the suburbs of Beijing. The empire also had to deal with Japanese pirates attacking the south-eastern coastline; General Qi Jiguang was instrumental in defeating these pirates. The deadliest earthquake of all times, the Shaanxi earthquake of 1556 that killed approximately 830,000 people, occurred during the Jiajing Emperor's reign.

(h)   During the Ming dynasty the last construction on the Great Wall was undertaken to protect China from foreign invasions. While the Great Wall had been built in earlier times, most of what is seen today was either built or repaired by the Ming. The brick and granite work was enlarged, the watch towers were redesigned, and cannons were placed along its length.

Qing Dynasty

(a)   The Qing Dynasty (1644–1911) (See Fig. 3.26 and 3.27)[28,29] was the last imperial dynasty in China. Founded by the Manchus, it was the second non-Han Chinese dynasty. The Manchus were formerly known as *Jurchen*, residing in the north-eastern part of the Ming territory outside the Great Wall. They emerged as the major threat to the late Ming Dynasty after Nurhaci united all Jurchen tribes and established an independent state. However, the Ming Dynasty would be overthrown by Li Zicheng's peasant's rebellion, with Beijing captured in 1644 and the last Ming Emperor Chongzhen committed suicide. The Manchu allied with the Ming Dynasty general Wu Sanguito seize Beijing, which was made the capital of the Qing dynasty, and then proceeded to subdue the remaining Ming's resistance in the south. The decades of Manchu conquest caused enormous loss of lives and the economic scale of China shrank drastically. Nevertheless, the Manchus adopted the Confucian norms of traditional Chinese government in their rule and were considered a Chinese dynasty.

---

28 http://www.paulnoll.com/China/Dynasty/dynasty-Qing.html
29 http://depts.washington.edu/chinaciv/1xarqing.htm

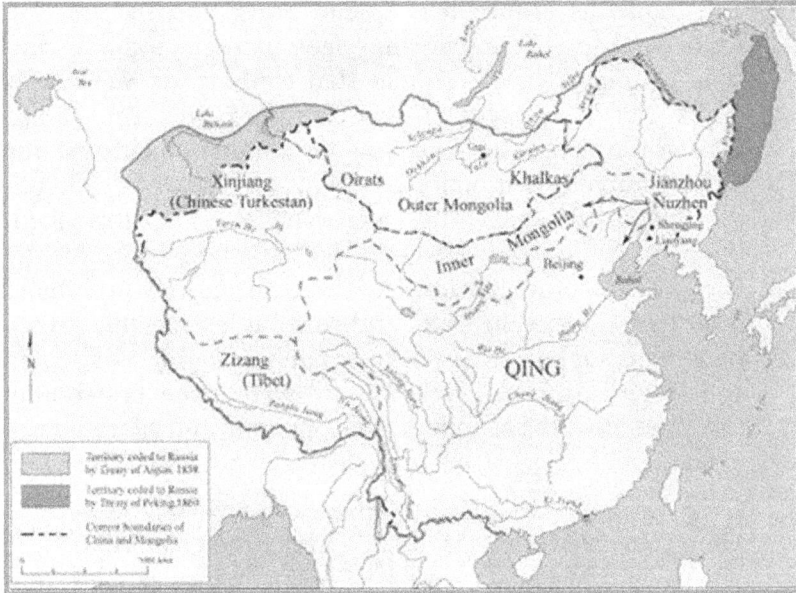

Fig. 3.26

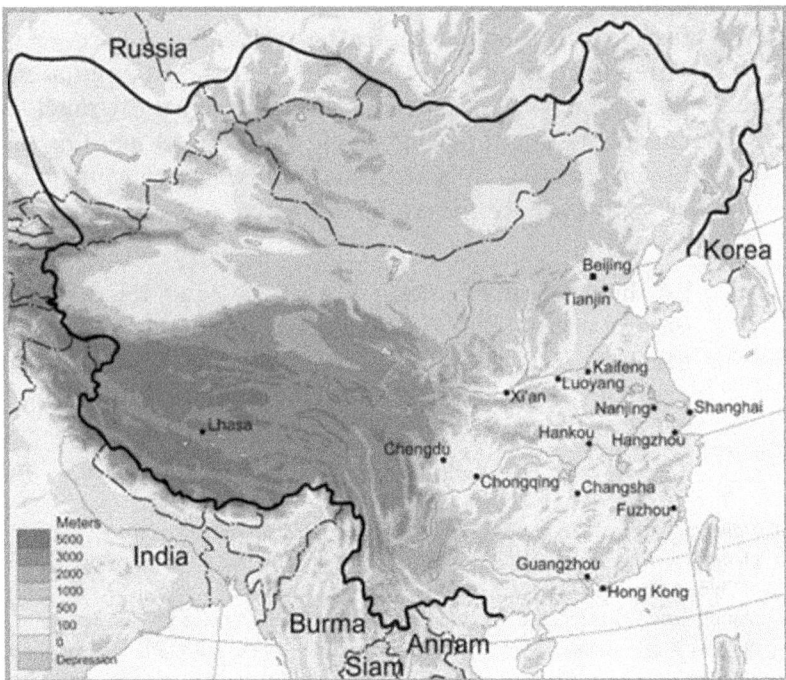

Fig. 3.27

(b)   The Manchus **enforced a 'queue order'**, forcing the Han Chinese to adopt the Manchu queue hairstyle and Manchu-style clothing. The traditional Han clothing, or *Hanfu*, was also replaced by Manchu-style clothing *Qipao*. The Kangxi Emperor ordered the creation of Kangxi Dictionary, the most complete dictionary of Chinese characters ever put together at the time. The Qing dynasty set up the "Eight Banners" system that provided the basic framework for the Qing military organization. The banner-men were prohibited from participating in trade and manual labour unless they petitioned to be removed from banner status. They were considered a form of nobility and were given preferential treatment in terms of annual pensions, land and allotments of cloth.

(c)   Over the next half-century, all areas previously under the Ming Dynasty were consolidated under the Qing. Xinjiang,[30] Tibet,[31] and Mongolia were also formally incorporated into Chinese territory. Between 1673 and 1681, the Emperor Kangxi suppressed an uprising of three generals in Southern China who had been denied hereditary rule to large fiefdoms granted by the previous emperor; he also put down a Ming restorationist invasion from Taiwan, called the Revolt of the Three Feudatories. In 1683, the Qing staged an amphibious assault on southern Taiwan, bringing down the rebel Grand Duchy of Tungning, which was founded by the Ming loyalist Koxinga in 1662 after the fall of the Southern Ming, and had served as a base for continued Ming resistance in Southern China.

(d)   By the end of Qianlong Emperor's long reign, the Qing Empire was at its zenith. China ruled more than one-third of the world's population, and had the largest economy in the world. By area of extent, it was one of the largest empires ever in history.

---

30 Xinjiang only became a part of China in the middle of the eighteenth century, when the Qing emperor Qianlong conquered huge areas of western territory, consequently doubling the size of China and fixing a firm western border with Russia. See Robert Kaplan 'The Revenge of Geography' page 3243 Kindle Edition and Spence, 'The Search for Modern China', page 97.

31 Chinese official history tells us that Tibet came under Chinese rule during the reign of Kabulai Khan. The counter-argument is that Kabulai Khan was the grandson of Changez Khan and was a Mongol secondly Kabulai Khan defeated the Tibetans and established their ruler as his prefecture - a sort of tributary system implying that Tibet was never ruled by Beijing till 1949.

(e) In the 19th century, the empire was internally stagnated and externally threatened by imperialism. The defeat by the British Empire in the First Opium War (1840) led to the Treaty of Nanking (1842), under which Hong Kong was ceded and opium import was legitimized. Subsequent military defeats and unequal treaties with other imperial powers would continue even after the fall of the Qing Dynasty.

(f) Internally, the Taiping Rebellion (1851–1864), a quasi-Christian religious movement led by the "Heavenly King" Hong Xiuquan, would raid roughly a third of Chinese territory for over a decade until they were finally crushed in the Third Battle of Nanking in 1864. Arguably one of the largest wars in the 19th century in terms of troops involvement, there was massive loss of lives, with a death toll of about 20 millions. A string of rebellions would follow, which included Punti–Hakka Clan Wars, Nien Rebellion, Muslim Rebellion, and Panthay Rebellion. Although all rebellions were eventually put down at enormous cost and casualties, the central imperial authority was seriously weakened.

(g) In response to calamities within the empire and threats from imperialism, the Self-Strengthening Movement was an institutional reform in the second half of the nineteenth century. The aim was to modernize the empire, with prime emphasis on strengthening the military. However, the reform was undermined by corrupt officials, cynicism, and quarrels within the imperial family. As a result, the "Beiyang Fleet" were soundly defeated in the First Sino-Japanese War (1894-1895).Guangxu Emperor and the reformists then launched a more comprehensive reform effort, the Hundred Days' Reform (1898), but it was shortly overturned by the conservatives under Empress Dowager Cixi in a military coup.

(h) At the turn of the 20th century, a conservative anti-imperialist movement, the Boxer Rebellion, violently revolted against foreign suppression over vast areas in Northern China. The Empress Dowager, probably seeking to ensure her continual grip on power, sided with the Boxers as they advanced on Beijing. In response, a relief expedition of the Eight-Nation Alliance invaded China to rescue the besieged foreign missions. Consisting of British, Japanese, Russian, Italian, German, French, US and Austrian troops, the alliance defeated the Boxers and demanded further concessions from

Fig. 3.28

the Qing government.

(i) The early 1900s saw **increasing civil disorder**, despite reform talk by Cixi and the Qing government. Slavery in China was abolished in 1910. The Xinhai Revolution in 1911 overthrew the Qing's imperial rule.

Republic of China

(a) Frustrated by the Qing court's **resistance to reform** and by China's weakness, young officials, military officers, and students began to advocate the overthrow of the Qing Dynasty and the creation of a republic. They were inspired by the revolutionary ideas of Sun Yat-sen.

(b) A revolutionary military uprising, the Wuchang Uprising, began on 10 October 1911, in Wuhan. The provisional government of the Republic of China was formed in Nanjing on 12 March 1912 (See Fig. 3.28)[32]. Sun Yat-sen was declared President, but Sun was forced to turn power over to Yuan Shikai, who commanded the New Army and was Prime Minister under the Qing government, as part of the agreement to let the last Qing monarch abdicate (a decision Sun would later regret). Over the next few years, Yuan proceeded to abolish the national and provincial assemblies, and declared himself emperor in late 1915. Yuan's imperial ambitions were fiercely opposed by his subordinates; faced with the prospect of rebellion, he abdicated in March 1916, and died in June of that year.

(c) Yuan's death in 1916 left a power vacuum in China; the republican government was all but shattered. This ushered in the warlord Era, during which much of the country was ruled by shifting coalitions of competing provincial military leaders.

(d) In 1919, the May Fourth Movement began as a response to the terms imposed on China by the Treaty of Versailles ending World War I, but quickly became a protest movement about the domestic situation in China. The discrediting of liberal Western philosophy amongst Chinese intellectuals was followed by the adoption of more radical lines of thought. This in turn planted the seeds for the irreconcilable conflict between the left and right in China that would dominate Chinese history for the rest of the century.

(e) In the 1920s, Sun Yat-sen established a revolutionary base in south China, and set out to unite the fragmented nation. With assistance from the Soviet Union(themselves fresh from a socialist uprising), he entered into an alliance with the fledgling Communist Party of China. After Sun's death from cancer in 1925, one of his protégés, Chiang Kai-shek, seized control of the *Kuomintang* (Nationalist Party or KMT) and succeeded in bringing most of south and central China under its rule in a military campaign known as the Northern Expedition (1926-1927). Having defeated the warlords in south and central China by military force, Chiang was able to secure the nominal allegiance of the warlords in the North. In 1927, Chiang turned on the CPC and relentlessly chased the CPC armies and its leaders from their bases in southern and

---

32 http://www.paulnoll.com/China/Dynasty/dynasty-ROC.html

eastern China. In 1934, driven from their mountain bases, the CPC forces embarked on the Long March across China's most desolate terrain to the northwest, where they established a guerrilla base at Yan'an in Shaanxi Province. During the Long March, the communists reorganized under a new leader, Mao Zedong (Mao Tse-tung).

(f) The bitter struggle between the KMT and the CPC continued, openly or clandestinely, through the 14-year long Japanese occupation of various parts of the country (1931–1945). The two Chinese parties nominally formed a united front to oppose the Japanese in 1937, during the Sino-Japanese War (1937-1945), which became a part of World War II.

(g) Following the defeat of Japan in 1945, the war between the KMT and the CPC resumed, after failed attempts at reconciliation and a negotiated settlement. By 1949, the CPC had established control over most of the country. When Chiang was defeated by CPC forces in mainland China in 1949, he retreated to Taiwan with his government and his most disciplined troops, along with most of the KMT leadership and a large number of their supporters; Chiang Kai-shek had taken effective control of Taiwan at the end of WWII as part of the overall Japanese surrender, when Japanese troops in Taiwan surrendered to Republic of China troops.

Chapter 4

ECONOMY

The People's Republic of China (PRC) is the **world's second largest economy**[1] by **nominal GDP** and by **purchasing power parity** after the United States. It is the world's fastest-growing major economy, with growth rates averaging 10% over the past 30 years. China is also the largest exporter and second largest importer of goods in the world. On a per capita income basis, China ranked 90th by nominal GDP and 91st by GDP (PPP) in 2011, according to the International Monetary Fund (IMF). The provinces in the coastal regions of China tend to be more industrialized, while regions in the hinterland are less developed. Most economic growth of China is created from Special Economic Zones of the People's Republic of China. However, still an estimated 100 million Chinese live below the poverty line[2] in 2012,and this has been estimated despite China setting a poverty line nearly 20% below the world standard.[3]

History

(a)   By 1949, continuous foreign invasions, frequent revolutions and restorations, and civil wars had left the country with a fragile economy with little infrastructure. As Communist ascendancy seemed inevitable, almost all hard and foreign currency in China country were transported to Taiwan in 1948, making the war-time inflation even worse.

---

1   http://en.wikipedia.org/wiki/Economy_of_the_People%27s_Republic_of_China

2   http://articles.economictimes.indiatimes.com/2012-06-21/news/32352617_1_sustainable-development-wen-jiabao-countries.

3   http://www.economist.com/blogs/analects/2013/02/chinas-poor.

(b) Since the formation of the PRC, an enormous effort was made towards creating economic growth and entire new industries were created. Tight control of budget and money supply reduced inflation by the end of 1950. Though most of it was done at the expense of suppressing the private sector of small to big businesses. In the beginning of the Communist party's rule, the leaders of the party had agreed that for a nation such as China, which does not have any heavy industry and minimal secondary production, capitalism is to be utilized to help the building of the "New China" and finally merged into communism.

(c) The new government nationalized the country's banking system and brought all currency and credit under centralized control. It regulated prices by establishing trade associations and boosted government revenues by collecting agricultural taxes.

(d) Meanwhile, in fulfilment of their revolutionary promise, China's communist leaders completed land reform within two years of coming to power, eliminating landlords and redistributing their land and other possessions to peasant households.

(e) Mao tried in 1958 to push China's economy to new heights. Under his highly touted "Great Leap Forward", agricultural collectives were reorganized into enormous communes where men and women were assigned in military fashion to specific tasks. Peasants were told to stop relying on the family, and instead adopted a system of communal kitchens, mess halls, and nurseries. Wages were calculated along the communist principle of "From each according to his ability, to each according to his need", and sideline production was banned as incipient capitalism. All Chinese citizens were urged to boost the country's steel production by establishing "backyard steel furnaces" to help overtake the West. The Great Leap Forward quickly revealed itself as a giant step backwards. Over-ambitious targets were set, falsified production figures were duly reported, and Chinese officials lived in an unreal world of miraculous production increases. By 1960, agricultural production in the countryside had slowed dangerously and large areas of China were gripped by a devastating famine.

(f) For the next several years, China experienced a period of relative stability. Agricultural and industrial production returned to normal levels, and labour productivity began to rise. Then, in 1966, Mao proclaimed a Cultural Revolution to "put China back on track". Under orders to "Destroy the Four Olds" (old thoughts, culture, customs and habits), universities and schools closed their doors, and students, who became Mao's "Red Guards", were sent throughout the country to make revolution, beating and torturing anyone whose rank or political thinking offended them. By 1969 the country had descended into anarchy, and factions of the Red Guards had begun to fight among themselves.

(g) Reforms began with Li Xiannian and Deng Xiaoping, Chinese leaders in the 80s. Unlike Mao, Deng and Li were pragmatic leaders, known less for their ideological commitment than for their slogan: "Who cares if a cat is black or white, as long as it catches the mice." Once they consolidated their power, they began to put their pragmatic policies to work, determined to bring China back from the devastation that the Cultural Revolution had wrought.

(h) Since 1978, China began to make major reforms to its economy. The Chinese leadership adopted a pragmatic perspective on many political and socioeconomic problems, and quickly began to introduce aspects of a capitalist economic system. Political and social stability, economic productivity, and public and consumer welfare were considered paramount and indivisible. In these years, the government emphasized raising personal income and consumption and introducing new management systems to help increase productivity. The government also had focused on foreign trade as a major vehicle for economic growth. In the 1980s, China tried to combine central planning with market-oriented reforms to increase productivity, living standards, and technological quality without exacerbating inflation, unemployment, and budget deficits. Reforms began in the agricultural, industrial, fiscal, financial, banking, price setting, and labour systems. 'During the 1980s Chinese leaders often revealed the strategy behind their country's economic opening to the West. In statement after statement, the Chinese Communists affirmed that they were taking a page out of Lenin's playbook. In the early 1920s Lenin initiated the Soviet Union's New Economic Policy (NEP), opening Russia to capitalist investment. As one might expect, the Soviet economy prospered during the

NEP period and Russia was able to lay the foundations of its military industry. Due to its proven track record, something akin to Lenin's NEP has been adopted by China.'[4]

(i) A decision was made in 1978 to permit foreign direct investment in several small "special economic zones" along the coast. The country lacked the legal infrastructure and knowledge of international practices to make this prospect attractive for many foreign businesses, however, in the early 1980s steps were taken to expand the number of areas that could accept foreign investment with a minimum of red tape, and related efforts were made to develop the legal and other infrastructures necessary to make this work well. This additional effort resulted in making 14 coastal cities and three coastal regions "open areas" for foreign investment. All of these places provide favoured tax treatment and other advantages for foreign investment. Laws on contracts, patents, and other matters of concern to foreign businesses were also passed in an effort to attract international capital to spur China's development. The largely bureaucratic nature of China's economy, however, posed a number of inherent problems for foreign firms that wanted to operate in the Chinese environment, and China gradually had to add more incentives to attract foreign capital.

(j) Deng allowed farmers to produce on their own and sanctioned the sale of surplus production and other cash crops in newly freed markets. State procurement prices were raised, and prices for many agricultural goods were left to the dictates of the market. Beginning with the poor mountain areas of Anhui and then spreading across the country, Deng and his officials broke up the communes established by Mao and replaced them with a complicated system of leases that eventually brought effective land tenure back to the household level, even though ownership of land remained collective. The Household Responsibility System allowed peasants to lease land for a fixed period from the collective, provided they delivered to the collective a minimum quota of produce, usually basic grain. They could then sell any surplus they produced, either to the state at government procurement prices or on the newly free market. They were also permitted to retain any profits they might earn. Within a decade, grain production had grown by

4   http://www.financialsensearchive.com/stormwatch/geo/pastanalysis/2007/0309.html

roughly 30%, and production of cotton, sugarcane, tobacco, and fruit had doubled.

(k) As the reforms fuelled production increased surprising even the reformers, the scale of change grew bolder, and by the mid-1980s, the party leadership had begun the more complicated and politically delicate task of transforming the country's system of central planning and state-owned enterprise. Prior to 1978, enterprises were almost all owned by the state in one form or another. At the top of each sector were the State-owned Enterprises (SOEs), answerable to the national government. Below these were other enterprises reporting to provincial, municipal, or county authorities. Private enterprises, meaning family-run shops, were not allowed until after 1978, and even then they were limited to seven employees.

(l) China's SOEs were typical of large industrial firms in a centrally planned economy. They functioned not only as industrial units but also as social agencies, providing housing, day care, education, and health care for the workers and their families. The largest enterprises included hundreds of thousands of employees, only a small proportion of whom were directly engaged in production.

(m) The upside of this system was that Chinese workers could expect both lifetime employment and an extensive, firm-based welfare system-the so-called "iron rice bowl". All welfare entitlements in this system were accounted for as costs of production and were deducted from revenues before the calculation of the profits that were to be remitted to the state. There was no national social security system because none was needed.

(n) Following the Chinese Communist Party's Third Plenum, held in October 2003, Chinese legislators unveiled several proposed amendments to the state constitution. One of the most significant was a proposal to provide protection for private property rights. Legislators also indicated there would be a new emphasis on certain aspects of overall government economic policy, including efforts to reduce unemployment (then in the 8–10% range in urban areas), to rebalance income distribution between urban and rural regions, and to maintain economic growth while protecting the environment and improving social equity. The National People's Congress approved the amendments when it met in March 2004.

(o) The Fifth Plenum in October 2005 approved the 11th Five-Year Economic Program (2006–2010) aimed at building a "socialist harmonious society" through more balanced wealth distribution and improved education, medical care, and social security. On March 2006, the National People's Congress approved the11th Five-Year Program. The plan called for a relatively conservative 45% increase in GDP and a 20% reduction in energy intensity (energy consumption per unit of GDP) by 2010.

(p) China's economy grew at an average rate of 10% per year during the period 1990–2004, the highest growth rate in the world. China's GDP grew 10.0% in 2003, 10.1%, in 2004, and even faster 10.4% in 2005 despite attempts by the government to cool the economy. China's total trade in 2010 surpassed $2.97 trillion, making China the world's second-largest trading nation after the U.S. Such high growth is necessary if China is to generate the 15 million jobs needed annually—roughly the size of Ecuador or Cambodia—to employ new entrants into the national job market.

(q) China launched its Economic Stimulus Plan to specifically deal with the Global financial crisis of 2008–2009. It has primarily focused on increasing affordable housing, easing credit restrictions for mortgage and SMEs, lower taxes such as those on real estate sales and commodities, pumping more public investment into infrastructure development, such as the rail network, roads and ports. By the end of 2009 it appeared that the Chinese economy was showing signs of recovery. At the 2009 Economic Work Conference in December '**managing inflation expectations**' was added to the list of economic objectives, suggesting a strong economic upturn and a desire to take steps to manage it.

(r) In 2011, the IMF warned that government controlled banks could be building up imbalances that could hamper growth and leave the system "severely impacted". In 2011, the IMF predicted that China's GDP (purchasing power parity adjusted) would overtake that of the United States in 2016. The state favours state-owned enterprises despite lower productivity; this crowds out competition.

(s) In 2012, Amnesty International reported that forced evictions that resulted from a construction boom caused by excessive stimulus spending were a serious threat to China's social and political stability. Due to the corruption and political uncertainties of the one-party state and the limited economic freedom in an economy dominated by large state owned enterprises, many skilled professionals are either leaving the country or preparing safety nets for themselves abroad. Corruption continued to grow worse in the PRC as it dropped from 75th to 80th place in Transparency International's index of state corruption.

Government's Role

(a) Since 1949 the government, under socialist political and economic system, has been responsible for planning and managing the national economy. In the early 1950s, the foreign trade system was monopolized by the state. Nearly all the domestic enterprises were state-owned and the government had set the prices for key commodities, controlled the level and general distribution of investment funds, determined output targets for major enterprises and branches, allocated energy resources, set wage levels and employment targets, operated the wholesale and retail networks, and steered the financial policy and banking system. In the countryside from the mid-1950s, the government established cropping patterns, set the level of prices, and fixed output targets for all major crops.

(b) Since 1978 when economic reforms were instituted, the government's role in the economy has lessened by a great degree. Industrial output by state enterprises slowly declined, although a few strategic industries, such as the aerospace industry have today remained predominantly state-owned. While the role of the government in managing the economy has been reduced and the role of both private enterprise and market forces increased, the government maintains a major role in the urban economy. With its policies on such issues as agricultural procurement the government also retains a major influence on rural sector performance. The State Constitution of 1982 specified that the state is to guide the country's economic development by making broad decisions on economic priorities and policies, and that the State Council, which exercises executive control, was to direct its subordinate bodies in preparing and implementing the national economic plan and the state budget. A major portion of the government system (bureaucracy) is devoted to managing the economy in a top-down chain of command with all but a few of the more than 100 ministries, commissions, administrations, bureaus, academies, and corporations under the State Council being concerned with economic matters.

(c) The whole policy-making process involves extensive consultation and negotiation. Economic policies and decisions adopted by the National People's Congress and the State Council are to be passed on to the economic organizations under the State Council, which incorporates them into the plans for the various sectors of the economy. Economic plans and policies are implemented by a variety of direct and indirect control mechanisms. Direct control is exercised by designating specific physical output quotas and supply allocations for some goods and services. Indirect instruments—also called "economic levers"—operate by affecting market incentives. These included levying taxes, setting prices for products and supplies, allocating investment funds, monitoring and controlling financial transactions by the banking system, and controlling the allocation of key resources, such as skilled labour, electric power, transportation, steel, and chemicals (including fertilizers). The main advantage of including a project in an annual plan is that the raw materials, labour, financial resources, and markets are guaranteed by directives that have the weight of the law behind them. In reality, however, a great deal of economic activity goes on outside the scope of the detailed plan, and the tendency has been for the plan to become narrower rather than broader in scope. A major objective of the reform program was to reduce the use of direct controls and to increase the role of indirect economic levers. Major state-owned enterprises still receive detailed plans specifying physical quantities of key inputs and products from their ministries. These corporations, however, have been increasingly affected by prices and allocations that were determined through market interaction and only indirectly influenced by the central plan.

(d) Consumer spending has been subject to a limited degree of direct government influence but is primarily determined by the basic market forces of income levels and commodity prices. Before the reform period, key goods were rationed when they were in short supply, but by the mid-1980s availability had increased to the point that rationing was discontinued for everything except grain, which could also be purchased in the free markets. Collectively owned units and the agricultural sector were regulated primarily by indirect instruments. Each collective unit was "responsible for its own profit and loss", and the prices of its inputs and products provided the major production incentives.

(e) Vast changes were made in relaxing the state control of the agricultural sector from the late 1970s. The structural mechanisms for implementing state objectives—the people's communes and their subordinate teams and brigades— have been either entirely eliminated or greatly diminished. Farm incentives have been boosted both by price increases for state-purchased agricultural products, and permission to sell excess production on a free market. There was more room in the choice of what crops to grow, and peasants are allowed to contract for land that they will work, rather than simply working most of the land collectively. The system of procurement quotas (fixed in the form of contracts) has been being phased out, although the state can still buy farm products and control surpluses in order to affect market conditions.

(f) Foreign trade is supervised by the Ministry of Commerce, customs, and the Bank of China, the foreign exchange arm of the Chinese banking system, which controls access to the foreign currency required for imports. Ever since restrictions on foreign trade were reduced, there have been broad opportunities for individual enterprises to engage in exchanges with foreign firms without much intervention from official agencies.

(g) **State-Owned Enterprises.** As of 2012 large state-owned enterprises (SOEs) were the backbone of China's economy producing over 50% of its goods and services and employing over half of the workers in China. 65 of the Chinese companies in the 2012 Fortune Global 500 list, were state-owned, including State Grid Corporation of China, which operates the country's power grid, and China National Petroleum Corporation and Sinopec, oil companies. Profits of the largest state-owned enterprises were much greater than the largest firms in the private sector which were largely small and medium sized businesses. Reform efforts, spurred by problems with corruption at some firms, were focused on splitting state-owned firms or creating competing state-owned firms rather than privatization which is politically unacceptable to the ruling party. Firms attempting to maintain their position such as the State Grid point out the advantages of monopoly, using examples of disorganization such as the 2012 India blackouts. As of 2011, 35% of business activity and 43% of profits in the People's Republic of China resulted from companies in which the state owned a majority interest. Liberal critics, such as The New York Times, allege that China's state-owned companies are a vehicle for corruption by the families of ruling party leaders who have sometimes amassed fortunes while managing them.

Regional Economies

China's unequal transportation system—combined with important differences in the availability of natural and human resources and in industrial infrastructure—has produced **significant variations in the regional economies of China**. Economic development has generally been more rapid in coastal provinces than in the interior, and there are large disparities in per capita income between regions. The three wealthiest regions are along the southeast coast, centered on the Pearl River Delta; along the east coast, centered on the Lower Yangtze River; and near the Bohai Gulf, in the Beijing–Tianjin–Liaoning region. It is the rapid development of these areas that is expected to have the most significant effect on the Asian regional economy as a whole, and Chinese government policy is designed to remove the obstacles to accelerated growth in these wealthier regions.

Energy Resources

(a) Since 1980, China's energy production has grown dramatically, as has the proportion allocated to domestic consumption. Some 80 percent of all power generated is from fossil fuel at thermal plants, with about 17 percent at hydroelectric installations; only about two percent is from nuclear energy, mainly from plants located in Guangdong and Zhejiang. Though China has rich overall energy potential, most have yet to be developed. In addition, the geographical distribution of energy puts **most of these resources relatively far from their major industrial users**. Basically the **northeast is rich in coal** and **oil**, the **central part of north China has abundant coal**, and the **southwest has immense hydroelectric potential**. But the **industrialized regions around Guangzhou** and the **Lower**

Yangtze region around Shanghai have too little energy, while there is **relatively little heavy industry** located near major energy resource areas other than in the southern part of the northeast.

(b) China, due in large part to environmental concerns, has wanted to shift China's current energy mix from a heavy reliance on coal, which accounts for 70–75% of China's energy, toward greater reliance on oil, natural gas, renewable energy, and nuclear power. China has closed thousands of coal mines over the past five to ten years to cut overproduction. According to Chinese statistics, this has reduced coal production by over 25%.

(c) Since 1993, China has been a net importer of oil, a large portion of which comes from the Middle East. Imported oil accounts for 20% of the processed crude in China. Net imports are expected to rise to 3.5 million barrels (560,000 m³) per day by 2010. China is interested in diversifying the sources of its oil imports and has invested in oil fields around the world. China is developing oil imports from Central Asia and has invested in Kazakhstani oil fields. Beijing also plans to increase China's natural gas production, which currently accounts for only 3% of China's total energy consumption and incorporated a natural gas strategy in its 10th Five-Year Plan (2001–2005), with the goal of expanding gas use from a 2% share of total energy production to 4%.

(d) Moving away from coal towards cleaner energy sources including oil, natural gas, renewable energy, and nuclear power is an important component of China's development program. Beijing also intends to continue to improve energy efficiency and promote the use of clean coal technology and hydroelectric resources. In addition, the share of electricity generated by nuclear power is projected to grow from 1% in 2000 to 5% in 2030. China's renewable energy law, which went into effect in 2006, calls for 10% of its energy to come from renewable energy sources by 2020.

(e) The advent of shale gas is also likely to change the energy outlook as China is estimated by some to have the world's largest deposits of Shale Gas. 'China possesses the largest deposits of shale gas of any country in the world (886 trillion cubic feet compared with the United States' 750 trillion, the world's second-largest deposits)."[5,6]

Hydroelectric Resources

China has an abundant potential for hydroelectric power production due to its considerable river network and mountainous terrain. Most of the total hydroelectric capacity is situated in the southwest of the country, where coal supplies are poor but demand for energy is rising swiftly. The potential in the northeast is fairly small, but it was there that the first hydroelectric stations were built—by the Japanese during its occupation of Manchuria. Due to considerable seasonal fluctuations in rainfall, the flow of rivers tends to drop during the winter, forcing many power stations to operate at less than normal capacity, while in the summer, on the other hand, floods often interfere with generation.

Coal

(a) Although coal deposits are widely scattered (some coal is found in every province), most of the total is located in the northern part of the country. The province of Shanxi, in fact, is thought to contain about half of the total; other important coal-bearing provinces include Heilongjiang, Liaoning, Jilin, Hebei, and Shandong. Apart from these northern provinces, significant quantities of coal are present in Sichuan, and there are some deposits of importance in Guangdong, Guangxi, Yunnan, and Guizhou.

(b) To ensure a more even distribution of coal supplies and to reduce the strain on the less than adequate transportation network, the authorities pressed for the development of a large number of small, locally run mines throughout the country. This campaign was energetically pursued after the 1960s, with the result that thousands of small pits have been established, and they produce more than half the country's coal. This output, however, is typically expensive and is used for local consumption. It has also led to a less than stringent

---

5   http://www.foreignaffairs.com/articles/138597/aviezer-tucker/the-new-power-map?page=show

6   The process of tapping these showcases the problems of Chinese economy as most of the contracts have been landed by companies who have no experience in oil well drilling leave alone the technology for shale fracturing see http://www.reuters.com/article/2013/03/10/us-china-shale-idUSBRE9290GR20130310

implementation of safety measures in these unregulated mines, which cause several thousands of deaths each year.

(c) Coal makes up the bulk of China's energy consumption (70% in 2005), and China is the largest producer and consumer of coal in the world. As China's economy continues to grow, China's coal demand is projected to rise significantly. Although coal's share of China's overall energy consumption will decrease, coal consumption will continue to rise in absolute terms. China's continued and increasing reliance on coal as a power source has contributed significantly to putting China on the path to becoming the world's largest emitter of acid rain-causing sulphur dioxide and greenhouse gases, including carbon dioxide.

Oil and Natural Gas

(a) China's onshore oil resources are mostly located in the Northeast and in Xinjiang, Gansu, Qinghai, Sichuan, Shandong, and Henan provinces. Oil shale is found in a number of places, especially at Fushun in Liaoning, where the deposits overlie the coal reserves, as well as in Guangdong. Light oil of high quality has been found in the Pearl River estuary of the South China Sea, the Qaidam Basin in Qinghai, and the Tarim Basin in Xinjiang. The country consumes most of its oil output but does export some crude oil and oil products. China has explored and developed oil deposits in the South and East China Seas, the Yellow Sea, the Gulf of Tonkin, and the Bohai Sea.

LIKELY SHALE DEPOSITS OF CHINA[7]

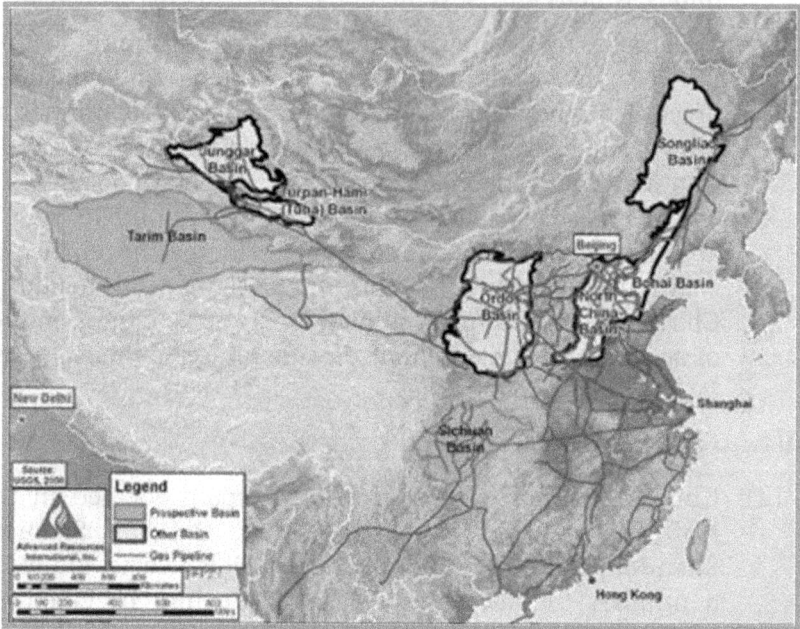

(b) The total extent of China's natural gas reserves is unknown, as relatively little exploration for natural gas has been done. Sichuan accounts for almost half of the known natural gas reserves and production. Most of the rest of China's natural gas is associated gas produced in the Northeast's major oil fields, especially Daqing oilfield. Other gas deposits have been found in the Qaidam Basin, Hebei, Jiangsu, Shanghai, and Zhejiang, and offshore to the southwest of Hainan Island.

---

7 http://in.images.search.yahoo.com/images/view;_ylt=A2oKiZevLjtR9VcALGy9HAx.;_ylu=X3
   oDMTBIMTQ4cGxyBHNlYwNzcgRzbGsDaW1n?back=http%3A%2F%2Fin.images.search.ya-
   hoo.com%2Fsearch%2Fimages%3F_adv_prop%3Dimage%26va%3Dshale%2Bgas%2Bdep
   osits%2Bchina%26fr%3Dchr-greentree_gc%26tab%3Dorganic%26ri%3D1&w=500&h=379
   &imgurl=blogs.worldwatch.org%2Frevolt%2Fwp-content%2Fuploads%2F2012%2F08%2Fa
   eb6708d6720111024-china-shale-gas-deposits-500x379.jpg&rurl=http%3A%2F%2Fblogs.
   worldwatch.org%2Frevolt%2Fchina-has-high-hopes-for-shale-gas-the-thorny-road-of-honor
   %2F&size=77.4+KB&name=aeb6708d6720111024-%3Cb%3Echina%3C%2Fb%3E-%3Cb%3E-
   shale%3C%2Fb%3E-%3Cb%3Egas%3C%2Fb%3E-%3Cb%3Edeposits%3C%2Fb%3E-500x3
   79&p=shale+gas+deposits+china&oid=c5c79951fdc64826a1dcf6591c929552&fr2=&fr=
   chr-greentree_gc&tt=aeb6708d6720111024-%253Cb%253Echina%253C%252Fb%253E-
   %253Cb%253Eshale%253C%252Fb%253E-%253Cb%253Egas%253C%252Fb%253E-
   %253Cb%253Edeposits%253C%252Fb%253E-500x379&b=0&ni=112&no=1&ts=&t
   ab=organic&sigr=12vq27ifv&sigb=140l2crc6&sigi=13erhl817&.crumb=5ZjJIJtunKD

(c) The Natural Gas production is likely to get a major boost with the advent and acquisition of Shale Gas tapping technologies as China is estimated to have some of the largest deposits of the same. 'Although China is just beginning to tap its gas deposits, by the time any Sino-Russian pipeline project could be completed, it might be churning out enough unconventional gas to be energy self-sufficient. According to Chinese government estimates, the country has enough natural gas to provide for its domestic needs for up to two centuries.'[8]

Minerals

Outdated mining and ore-processing technologies are being replaced with modern techniques, but China's rapid industrialization requires imports of minerals from abroad. In particular, iron ore imports from Australia and the United States have soared as steel production rapidly outstripped domestic iron ore production. Also **China has become increasingly active in several African countries to mine the reserves it requires for economic growth, particularly in countries such as the Democratic Republic of the Congo** and **Gabon.**

Metals and Non-metals

(a) Iron ore reserves are found in most provinces, including Hainan. Gansu, Guizhou, southern Sichuan, and Guangdong provinces have rich deposits. The largest mined reserves are located north of the Yangtze River and supply neighbouring iron and steel enterprises. With the exception of nickel, chromium, and cobalt, China is well supplied with ferroalloys and manganese. Reserves of tungsten are also known to be fairly large. Copper resources are moderate, and high-quality ore is present only in a few deposits. Discoveries have been reported from Ningxia. Lead and zinc are available, and bauxite resources are thought to be plentiful. China's antimony reserves are the largest in the world. Tin resources are plentiful, and there are fairly rich deposits of gold. China is the world's fifth largest producer of gold and in the early 21st century became an important producer and exporter of rare metals needed in high-technology industries. The rare earth

---

8 http://www.foreignaffairs.com/articles/138597/aviezer-tucker/the-new-power-map?page=show

reserves at the Bayan Obi mine in Inner Mongolia are thought to be the largest in any single location in the world.

(b) China also produces a fairly wide range of non-metallic minerals. One of the most important of these is salt, which is derived from coastal evaporation sites in Jiangsu, Hebei, Shandong, and Liaoning, as well as from extensive salt fields in Sichuan, Ningxia, and the Qaidam Basin. There are important deposits of phosphate rock in a number of areas. Pyrites occur in several places; Liaoning, Hebei, Shandong, and Shanxi have the most important deposits. China also has large resources of fluorite (fluorspar), gypsum, asbestos, and cement.

External Trade

(a) International trade makes up a sizeable portion of China's overall economy. China's industrial base by design produces more than its domestic economy can consume, so China must export goods to the rest of the world while importing raw materials. Thus external trade is essential to maintain growth – which as we have seen earlier is critical to maintaining social stability.

(b) A meaningful segment of China's trade with the Third World was financed through grants, credits, and other forms of assistance. The principal efforts were made in Asia, especially to Indonesia, Burma (now Myanmar), Pakistan, and Ceylon (now Sri Lanka), but large loans were also granted in Africa (Ghana, Algeria, Tanzania) and in the Middle East (Egypt). However, after Mao Zedong's death in 1976, these efforts were scaled back. After which, trade with developing countries became negligible, though during that time, Hong Kong and Taiwan both began to emerge as major trading partners.

(c) Since economic reforms began in the late 1970s, China sought to decentralize its foreign trade system to integrate itself into the international trading system. On November 1991, China joined the Asia-Pacific Economic Cooperation (APEC) group, which promotes free trade and cooperation in the economic, trade, investment, and technology spheres. China served as APEC chair in 2001, and Shanghai hosted the annual APEC leaders meeting in October of that year.

(d) After reaching a bilateral WTO agreement with the EU and other trading partners in summer 2000, China worked on a multilateral WTO accession package. China concluded multilateral negotiations on its accession to the WTO in September 2001. The completion of its accession protocol and Working Party Report paved the way for its entry into the WTO on December 11, 2001, after 16 years of negotiations, the longest in the history of the General Agreement on Tariffs and Trade. However, U.S. exporters continue to have concerns about fair market access due to China's restrictive trade policies and U.S. export restrictions.

(e) 'The economic downturn in Europe and the United States — China's two main customers — has exposed Chinese exports to increased competition and decreased appetite. Meanwhile, China has been unable to appropriately increase domestic demand and guarantee access to global sea-lanes independent of what the U.S. Navy is willing to allow. Those same economic stresses also challenge China domestically. The wealthier coast depends on trade that is now faltering, and the impoverished interior requires subsidies that are difficult to provide when economic growth is slowing substantially.'[9]

Chinese Investment Abroad

Outward foreign direct investment is a new feature of Chinese globalization, where local Chinese firms seek to make investments in both developing and developed countries. It was reported in 2011 that there was increasing investment by capital rich Chinese firms in promising firms in the United States. Such investments offer access to expertise in marketing and distribution potentially useful in exploiting the developing Chinese domestic market.

Mergers and Acquisitions

From 1993 to 2010, Chinese companies have been involved as either an acquirer or acquired company in 25,284 mergers and acquisitions with a total known value of US$969 billion. The number and value of deals hit a new record in 2010. 3640 deals happened in 2010 which is an increase of 17% compared to 2009. The value of deals in 2010 was US$196 billion which is an increase of 25% compared to the year before.

---

9   http://www.stratfor.com/weekly/state-world-assessing-chinas-strategy

Balance of Payments

China's economic reform and interests warrants that it pays great importance to **SLOC security.** Its import and export volume was US$ 135.63 billion in 1991, US$ 325.06 billion but by 2011 its trade with US alone was US$ 503.2 billion,[10] and total trade more than US $3 trillion,[11] and 90% of its foreign trade is by sea-transportation. An analysis of China's Exports and Imports in 2010 and 2011 taken from the WTO site is attached at appendix.[12] The same shows the following: -

(a) The major imports include manufactures, machinery and transport, office and telecom equipment and integrated circuits. These products catered for 61.57% of total imports in 2010 and 60.65% of the total in 2011.

(b) Fuel imports as a percentage of total imports was only 1.05% in 2010 and 1.15% in 2011.

While fuel imports as a percentage of total imports was not much however in real terms there exists a big imbalance between supply and demand of oil for China, which it has to import. In 2010 alone it imported nearly 200 million metric tons of crude.[13] In 2012 it rose to 271.02 million metric tons.[14] *'China, already imports 58 percent of the oil and 22 percent of the gas it uses each year'.*[15] **'By 2030, China will depend on imported oil for approximately 75 percent of its total demand'.**[16] The ensuing 'Chinese energy debate focuses both on supply security and on the need to keep energy prices as low as possible.'[17] (See Fig. 4.2)[18]

---

10 https://www.uschina.org/statistics/tradetable.html

11 http://news.xinhuanet.com/english2010/china/2011-11/03/c_131228263.htm

12 http://www.wto.org/english/res_e/statis_e/its2012_e/its12_appendix_e.htm

13 http://en.wikipedia.org/wiki/Petroleum_industry_in_China

14 http://online.wsj.com/article/SB10001424127887324081704578232650955659718.html

15 http://www.foreignaffairs.com/articles/138093/michael-t-klare/island-grabbing-in-asia

16 Commander Gurumurthy B 'A case study on Strategic and Geopolitical Impact of PLA-Pak Military Strategic Partnership and Security Implications for India', USI Journal Jan-Mar 2012 page 9.

17 Zweig David and Jianhai Bi, 'China's Global Hunt for Energy' Foreign Affairs 84, Volume No 5 (Sep-Oct 2005), page 25.

18   http://www.google.co.in/imgres?hl=en&sa=X&rlz=1C1CHMO_enIN521IN521&biw=1366&b ih=600&tbm=isch&tbnid=sRHdiy6W-ay6oM:&imgrefurl=http://www.eia.gov/countries/cab. cfm%3Ffips%3DCH&docid=BV3I30ryiIEO8M&imgurl=http://www.eia.gov/countries/analysis-briefs/China/images/crude_oil_imports_source.png&w=554&h=467&ei=AeAlUbjOE8qlrAfWu

China's crude oil imports by source, 2011
thousand barrels per day

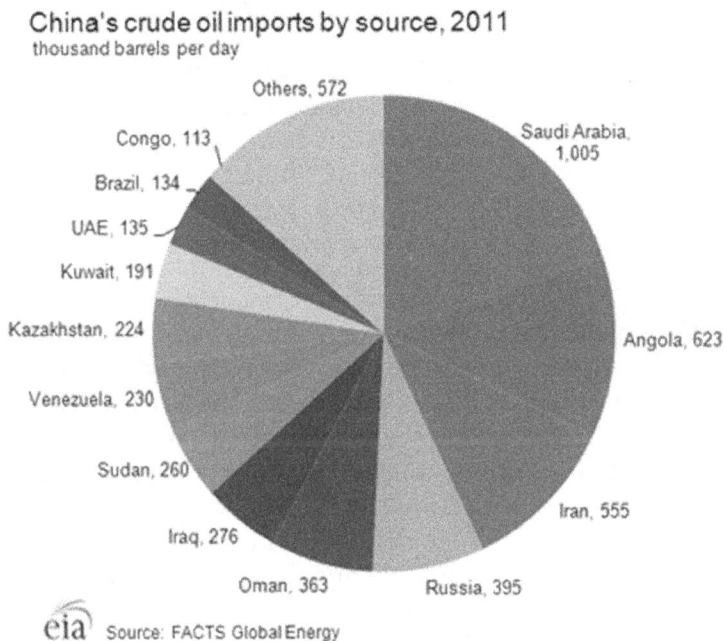

Others, 572
Congo, 113
Brazil, 134
UAE, 135
Kuwait, 191
Kazakhstan, 224
Venezuela, 230
Sudan, 260
Iraq, 276
Oman, 363
Russia, 395
Saudi Arabia, 1,005
Angola, 623
Iran, 555

eia Source: FACTS Global Energy

Fig. 4.2

Dealing with Natural Resource Deficiency

To deal with these – '**China does not come armed with a missionary approach to world affairs. It has no ideology or system of governance it seeks to spread.** Moral progress in international affairs is an American goal and not a Chinese one. And yet China is not a status quo power: for it is propelled abroad by a need to secure energy, metals and strategic minerals in order to support the rising living standard of roughly a fifth of humanity. Indeed China is able to feed 23 percent of world's population from 7 percent of the arable land – "by crowding some 2000 human beings onto each square mile of cultivated earth in the valleys and flood plains," as Fairbank points out. It now is under popular pressure to achieve something similar – that is, provide a middle-class life style for much of its urban population.'[19] 'In all of this, China is not risk-averse.'[20] 'The plain fact is that when it comes to assertive pursuit of National Interest, China has cared little about the potential impact on its image in other states. Its policies are designed to advance perceived national interests, not to seek approbation or appreciation from other states.'[21] This behaviour is raising worried eye-brows in China's neighbourhood. 'China may still be in the early phases of its continental expansion, so its grasp of the periphery is nascent. The key story line of the next few decades may be the manner in which China accomplishes this.'[22]

(a) **Afghanistan and Pakistan.** 'Eyeing some of the world's last untapped deposits of copper, iron, gold, uranium and precious gems, China is already mining for copper in war-torn Afghanistan, just south of Kabul. China has a vision of Afghanistan (and of Pakistan) as a secure conduit for roads and energy pipelines that will bring natural resources from Indian Ocean ports, linking up with Beijing's budding Central Asian dominion-of-sorts.'[23] Thus as the United States moves to defeat al Qaeda and irreconcilable elements of Taliban, it is China's geopolitical position that will be enhanced. Military deployments are ephemeral: roads, rail links and pipelines can be virtually forever.'[24,25]

(b) **Burma (now Myanmar).** Burma (now Myanmar) is a 'feeble state abundant in the very metals, hydrocarbons, and other natural resources that China desperately requires. The distance is less than five hundred miles from Burma (now Myanmar)'s Indian Ocean seaboard – where China and India are competing for development rights – to China's Yunnan Province. We are talking of a future of pipelines, in this case gas from offshore

---

19 Kaplan Robert 'The Revenge of Geography' page 3170 Kindle Edition.

20 Ibid page 3270 Kindle Edition.

21 Dr Chellany Brahma, 'Asia's Water Crisis and the New Security Risks', USI Journal Jan-Mar 2012 page 55.

22 Kaplan Robert 'The Revenge of Geography' page 3355 Kindle Edition.

23 Ibid page 3270 Kindle Edition.

24 Ibid page 3280 Kindle Edition.

25 To secure its interests China has established a security liaison with Afghanistan see http://www. c3sindia.org/afghanistan/3090.

fields in the Bay of Bengal that will extend China's reach beyond its legal border.[26,27]

(c) **Thailand.** Thailand can less and less play the role of a regional anchor and inherent balancer against China, owing to deep structural problems in Thai politics: the royal family, with an ailing king, is increasingly less of a stabilizing force; the Thai military is roiled by factionalism; and the citizenry is ideologically split between an urbane middle class and an up-and-coming rural class. China, flush with cash, is developing military relationships with Thailand.[28]

(d) **Malaysia.** 'Because all ethnic Malays are Muslims, Islam is radicalized in Malaysia, and the result is inter-communal divides between Malay, Chinese and Indian communities. Creeping Islamisation has led to seventy thousand Chinese leaving Malaysia in the past two decades, even as the country falls further under the shadow of China economically, with most of Malaysia's imports coming from there. Chinese themselves may be unpopular in Malaysia, but China "the state" is too big to resist.'[29]

(e) **Singapore.** 'The quite fear of China is most clearly revealed by the actions of Singapore, a city-state strategically located near the narrowest part of the Strait of Malacca. In Singapore, ethnic Chinese dominate the ethnic Malays by a margin of 77 percent to 14 percent. Nevertheless, Singapore fears becoming a vassal state of China, and has consequently developed a long-standing military training **relationship with Taiwan.** Recently retired Minister Mentor Lee Kuan Yew has publicly urged United States to stay militarily and diplomatically engaged in the region.'[30]

(f) **Vietnam.** 'A historic foe of China with a large Army and strategically located Naval bases that might serve as a potential

---

26 Kaplan Robert 'The Revenge of Geography' page 3317 Kindle Edition.

27 Also see http://www.c3sindia.org/eastasia/3222 and http://www.southasiaanalysis.org/node/1072.

28 Robert Kaplan 'The Revenge of Geography' page 3327 Kindle Edition.

29 Ibid page 3337 Kindle Edition.

30 Ibid page 3345 Kindle Edition.

hedge against China – with all its fears regarding its much larger northern neighbour, has no choice but to get along with it.'[31]

---

31 Ibid page 3355 Kindle Edition.

Chapter 5

RECURRENT THEMES IN CHINESE GEOGRAPHY AND HISTORY

East China

(a) The eastern and southern half of the country, its seacoast fringed with offshore islands, is a region of fertile lowlands and foothills with most of the agricultural output and human population. These agricultural lands are, in turn, divided between the comparatively dry wheat-millet area of northern China, with its short growing season, and the wet, double-cropping rice culture of China's productive South.[1] South hills is only area which allows multiple crops a year.

(b) The western and northern half of China is a region of sunken basins (Gobi, Taklamakan), rolling plateaus, and towering massifs, including a portion of the highest tableland on earth (Tibetan Plateau) with lower agricultural possibilities and thus, far less populated.

(c) Traditionally, the Chinese population is centred around the Chinese Northern plain and oriented itself toward its own enormous inland market, developing as an imperial power whose centre lay in the middle and lower reaches of the Yellow River on the northern plains.

(d) The Qin Mountains, a continuation of the Kunlun Mountains, divides the North China Plain from the Yangtze River Delta and is the major physiographic boundary between the two great parts of China Proper. It is a cultural boundary as it influences the distribution of customs and language.

(e) Transfer of prosperity from economically productive areas, to the famine and disaster prone ones has been the key to Chinese unity.

---

1   Kaplan Robert 'The Revenge of Geography' page 3065 Kindle Edition.

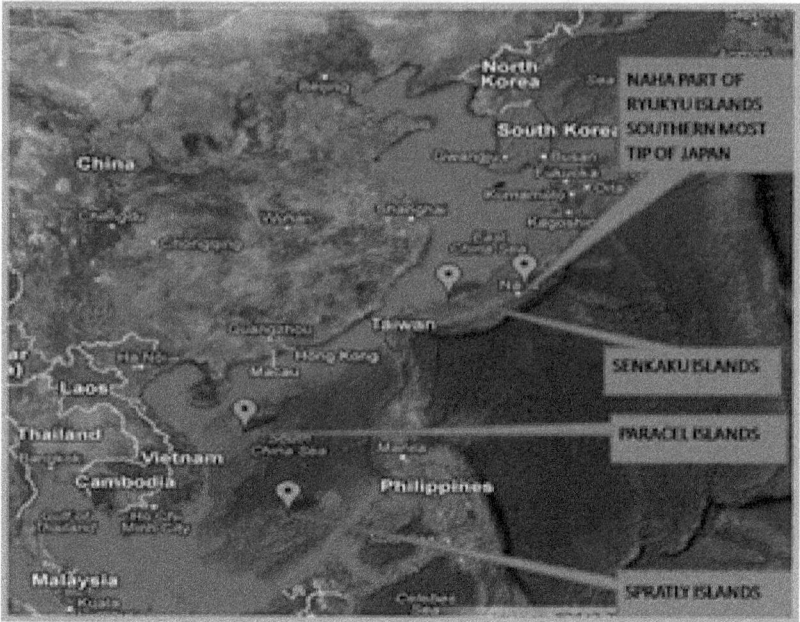

Fig. 5.1

Sea Access

A virtual wall of islands limits China's access to the oceans (See Fig. 5.1)[2]. Along with the Korean Peninsula, North to South these include – the Korean Peninsula, Japan, Senkaku / Diaoyu, Taiwan, Paracel Islands, Philippines, Spratly Islands and Malaysia. Further ahead, the Malacca Straits exists as another major dilemma for the Chinese sea-borne trade as they provide the sole economically viable access to the Indian Ocean Region.

System of Governance

(a) **Validity of Rulers.**

(i) Since the time of the Zhou Dynasty the Chinese rulers invoked the concept of the Mandate of Heaven to legitimize their rule. Like Shangdi, Heaven ruled over all the other gods, and it decided who would rule China. It was believed that a ruler had lost the Mandate of Heaven when natural disasters occurred in great number, and when, more realistically, the sovereign had apparently lost

2 https://www.google.co.in/maps?t=m&ll=30.730798199999985%2C76.7651793&spn=0.18741 332662345048%2C0.29072721689414205&output=classic&dg=opt

his concern for the people. In response, the royal house would be overthrown, and a new house would rule, having been granted the Mandate of Heaven.

(ii) Traditionally, rulers were judged by their concern for or indifference towards the people. Hence, large infrastructure projects were undertaken to protect the population from natural disasters. These include the Great Wall (constructed to protect against the raids from the North), the Great Canal (thereby transport water from the South to the North China) and preservation of the embankments of the yellow river. Notably, the Xin and the Yuan Dynasty were over thrown in the face of natural disasters. In the modern era, China has undertaken extensive flood control and conservation measures.

(iii) 'One of the Confucian myths of the state was Government by Virtue.'[3]

(b) **History of Strong Bureaucracy.**

(i) Successive dynasties in Chinese history developed bureaucratic systems that enabled the Emperor of China to directly control vast territories.

(ii) The Sui Dynasty, in the sixth century is credited with having set up many institutions that were to be adopted by their successors, these included the government system of Three Departments and Six Ministries which essentially was the foundation of their bureaucracy – which lasted through the various rulers and dynasty changes.

(iii) The Ming dynasty had a strong and complex central government that unified and controlled the empire. The emperor's continued to use what he called the "Grand Secretaries" to assist with the immense paperwork of the bureaucracy, including memorials (petitions and recommendations to the throne), imperial edicts in reply, reports of various kinds, and tax records.

(iv) The effectiveness of the system is visible from the fact that record of complex bureaucratic operations like population census is available since 1300 AD.

---

3   Kaplan Robert 'The Revenge of Geography' page 3118 Kindle Edition.

(c) **Tight Centralised Control.**

(i) The Qin dynasty experimented first with a tightly centralized Legalist government seated at Xianyang. The doctrine of Legalism that guided the Qin emphasized strict adherence to a legal code and the absolute power of the emperor. Their other major contributions include the concept of a centralized government, the unification of the legal code, development of the written language, measurement, and currency. Even something as basic as the length of axles for carts had to be made uniform to ensure a viable trading system throughout the empire.

(ii) The Qin Emperor presided over the brutal silencing of political opposition, including the event known as the burning of books and burying of scholars. This would be the impetus behind the governance pattern of later dynasties especially in the Han, Sui, Tang, Song, Laio, Jin, Ming and Qing dynasties.

(iii) The Tang dynasty even experimented with Centralised land Control. Their land policy – the "Equal-field system" – claimed all lands as imperially owned, and were granted evenly to people according to the size of the households. The Ming dynasty again tried the system when land estates were confiscated by the government, fragmented, and rented out.

(iv) On the other extreme during the Qing dynasty the control was even extended to hair styles and clothing of individuals.

(d) **Stability and Order.** Since the time of the Western Han Dynasty, Confucianism, which emphasizes stability and order in a well-structured society, was given exclusive patronage to be the guiding philosophical thoughts and moral principles of the empire. 'The goal of its rulers has been preserving unity and preventing chaos. Its people have been more concerned with order, satisfying material needs of the present life and tranquil safety, rather than worrying about afterlife and Nirvana.'[4]

(i) The Chinese record their own history as a succession of ruling dynasties that begins with the legendary Xia

---

dynasty (2100-1600 BC), and ended in 1911-12 with the formation of the Republic of China–which was soon followed by the establishment of the People's Republic of China in 1949. Although Chinese history is regarded as a succession of dynasties, during certain parts of Chinese history the land area we call China today was under the control of a number of different kingdoms. After the fall of the great Han dynasty around 220 AD, China fell apart into many smaller kingdoms, and was only reunited over three hundred years later by the short, but powerful Sui dynasty (580-618 AD). During the Song dynasty (960-1279 AD), invading tribes set up the Jin and Liao kingdoms in northeast China, and a large kingdom of Tibetan-related peoples called Xixia existed in western China. Therefore, when thinking about Chinese history, it is important to imagine it as a complex picture of unity and disunity over a very long time span.

(ii) In a general sense, there was a pattern of dynastic rise and fall, often reflected in historical accounts, poetry, and other literature of China. **According to the pattern, a dynasty is:-**

- ▶ Founded by force during a period of disorder.
- ▶ Vigorous rulers create a stable, prosperous state that secures or extends the borders.
- ▶ After a period of success and stability (which often entails population growth), leadership declines, wealth concentrates into fewer hands, and the population outstrips resources.
- ▶ The dynasty collapses due to internal uprisings— sometimes coupled with foreign invasions.
- ▶ After a period of weakness and disunion, the cycle starts again with dynamic leadership (sometimes foreign, as in the case of the Mongols and Manchus), often in a climate of lowered population and redistributed wealth.

(iii) **Concerns of Government Stability.**

- ▶ Social harmony was a key component of the ideas of Confucian statecraft. If rulers and subjects alike acted in proper accord with their positions, all would be well with the realm. It was up to the ruler to set the example by behaving properly so as to preserve the supernatural permission —or right to rule—known as the Mandate of Heaven. If a ruler was out of sync with the heavens, then chaos in society was sure to follow. What was feared most in this ideal system was instability and chaos. Instability was the result of any number of factors, including famine, invasion, unfair conscription of labourers and troops, over-taxation, and incompetent, corrupt, or malicious rulers. When conditions become unstable, popular uprisings can result that may prove difficult or impossible to quell.

▶ According to legend, the empire of China's first emperor, Qin Shi Huangdi, was brought down by a popular rebellion ignited by a group of workers on the Great Wall. Delayed because of a rainstorm, they were sentenced to death – but chose rebellion instead. In the first half of the 20th century, popular uprisings lead by Sun Yat-sen's Nationalist Party brought down the Manchu government. Not long after, other popular forces, led by the Communists, took advantage of chaos within China caused by a weak central government, local warlords, and foreign invasion, to bring their movement to power over most of the territory in 1949. During the rule of Chairman Mao Zedong, particularly from 1966 to 1976, young minds and emotions were whipped into widespread chaos that endangered the vitality of the state.

(e) Hence China's current system, of governance is not much different from its inheritance. 'China's nominal Communist rulers constitute the latest of some twenty five Chinese dynasties going back four thousand years.'[5]

Aggression from Northern Aliens and Other Non-Han States

(a) The threat to China **came mainly over the millennia from the Eurasian steppe-land**, so that the interplay between the indigenous Chinese and the Manchurians, Mongols and Turkic peoples of the high desert has formed one of the central themes of Chinese history. That is why the capital cities of early Chinese dynasties were often built on the Wei River, upstream from meeting with the Yellow, where there

5   Kaplan Robert 'The Revenge of Geography' page 3148 Kindle Edition.

was enough rainfall for sedentary agriculture, yet safe from the nomadic tribes of the Inner Mongolian plateau just to the north.[6]

(b)   Relations, often antagonistic, between nomadic Turkic and Mongol peoples of the northern steppes and forests and the settled agriculturalists of the North China Plain go back far into antiquity. Among the northern invaders were the Xiongnu and Xianbei, who were followed in later centuries by the Qidan (Khaitan), Jurched, Mongol, Turk, and Manchu (Manju) peoples. During periods of division, small states appeared and disappeared in northern China on the borders with the steppes. This was especially so between the Han and Tang dynasties. During this time many such states had Creole-cultures that combined steppe and sedentary cultures. Among these peoples were a group known as the Toba, whose descendants were among the founders of the great Tang dynasty.

(c)   Besides the northern steppes and north-eastern forests, alien states existed at times in other border areas. Among these were the Tibetan empire in the west, the Nanzhao in the southwest, the Tangut (Xixia) empire of the northwest, and the Uigur kingdom farther to the north in Xinjiang. Many smaller kingdoms existed as well, including the little-known Parhae kingdom located in parts of present-day northeast China and North Korea.

(d)   Nomads on the northern steppe depended on trade with the agriculturalists for grain, cloth, metal tools, ceramics, and other items. In turn the agricultural peoples desired promises of peace from raiding parties, and demanded tribute in the form of horses, furs, gems, and other rarities from the steppe and forest nomads. In the course of diplomatic negotiations, Chinese states sometimes sent beautiful brides to far-off "barbarian" rulers on the steppe. One of the most famous was Wang Zhaojun of the Han dynasty, who lived many years among the Xiongnu. Her tomb mound lies near the city of Hohhot, Inner Mongolia.

(e)   In some cases, Chinese rulers attempted to play off rival groups of "barbarians" against each other; at other times, the border peoples created alliances to attack China. When the

---

6   Kaplan Robert 'The Revenge of Geography' page 3059 Kindle Edition.

Mongols invaded China they had to defeat the Jin, who had already conquered the northern part of the Song dynasty, as well as the Xixia kingdom in the northwest.

(f) At certain moments the nomadic peoples feared the strong Chinese armies, at other times the steppe people offered great enough challenges to the Chinese to stimulate the building of walls on the northern frontiers – culminating in the Great Wall. The wall, actually a series of smaller walls, reached its most advanced state during the Ming dynasty after the Mongols were driven from China.

Concept of Appointing Prefecture / Feudatories to Maintain Influence

(a) Faced with controlling what Mackinder calls 'the resources of the great continent'[7] – the Chinese rulers established a system of appointing Prefectures to govern politically less important areas. More often than not, the local war lords, rulers or over lords after their loss to the Chinese emperor or to avoid a war took on the role of the prefecture. This allowed them to retain their kingdoms while the Chinese emperor was able to increase his influence.

(b) The system was first reported during the Warring State Period at the end of the 5th century BC. Again the system is reported during the Eastern Han Dynasty whence it was also used to gain influence till across the Pamirs to the shores of the Caspian Sea thus opening the Silk Road. A combination of diplomatic overtures and military forays allowed Han emperors to establish feudatories among the Xiongnu i.e. the nomadic Huns in Outer Mongolia and East Turkestan (Xinjiang) as well as in Southern Manchuria and the northern part of Korea.[8] Under the second Tang emperor, military campaigns were launched to dissolve threats from nomadic tribes, and submit neighbouring states into a tributary system. Tang armies threaded their way through the space between Mongolia and Tibet to establish protectorates all over Asia as far as Khorasan in north eastern Iran.[9] The Ming Dynasty

---

7   Mackinder HJ 'The Geographical Pivot of History' The Geographical Journal volume 23 No 4, April 1904 page 437.

8   Kaplan Robert 'The Revenge of Geography' page 3099 Kindle Edition.

9   Ibid page 3109 Kindle Edition.

strenuously tried to extend China's influence beyond its borders by demanding other rulers send ambassadors to China to present tribute. They even used a large navy and a standing army conquering Vietnam sailing as far as the east coast of Africa. Qing dynasty again followed the system and extended it to Tibet and Xinjiang.

(c) The pattern which emerges is that 'China's settled agricultural civilisation had to constantly strive to create a buffer against the nomadic peoples of the drier uplands bordering it on three sides, from Manchuria counter clockwise around to Tibet'.[10] It was always a matter of manoeuvring amid the peoples of steppe land, rather than fighting them all at once.[11]

(d) China's internal dynamism, with all of its civil unrest and inefficiencies, to say nothing of an economic slowdown, creates external ambitions. Empires are often not sought consciously. Rather as states become stronger, they develop needs and – counter-intuitively – a whole new set of insecurities that lead them to expand in an organic fashion.[12]

Degree of Openness to the Outside

(a) Due to its geographical location, China could limit contact with the outside world. Aside from the northern nomads (who were not a cultural threat to the Chinese), the deserts and mountains of the west and the oceans of the east allowed the Central Kingdom relative (and often peaceful) insulation from entities such as the Roman Empire, which was at its height during the Han dynasty. The Silk Road was a narrow thread across the northwest barrens that allowed a limited but steady flow of goods and ideas across Central Asia between the high cultures of the Mediterranean, the Middle East, and India. During the Tang period, China was at its most open stance in antiquity. Elements from the cultures of the West, particularly India were welcomed and took root within China's borders.

(b) After the Mongol invasions of the 13th centuries, China was for the first time under complete foreign control. When the Mongols were finally driven out in the mid-14th century, the rulers of the new Ming dynasty were more wary of foreign

---

10 Kaplan Robert 'The Revenge of Geography' page 3019 Kindle Edition.

11 Ibid page 3109 Kindle Edition.

12 Ibid page 3161 Kindle Edition.

influences than emperors in the Tang period. By the mid-15th century the Chinese had made voyages to the coast of Africa, but in an inward turn the Chinese ships of exploration were ordered burned by the emperor and the Great Wall was refurbished.

(c)   As China began to lose ground technologically to the West, the Manchus invaded in 1644. Less than a century later, the British were warring with China over rights to peddle opium within China. By the turn of the 19th century, China was in danger of being cut to pieces by Western and Japanese imperialists. Over the centuries, ambivalence towards foreign contact developed. By the late 19th and early 20th centuries the principle of "taking what is best" from the outside was developed in an effort to import positive things from the West while keeping out influences thought to weaken or humiliate China.

(d)   The most recent expression of this **open/shut dynamic** was the near closing of mainland China to much of the outside world between 1949 and the late 1970s. Feelings derived from negative experiences with foreign contact still linger under the surface in China today.

Demographic Invasion

Faced with the challenge of maintaining and constantly improving the economic well being of their population, China has been encouraging population migration to areas of interest. **A policy which was started historically with Xinjiang, Tibet and Mongolia;[13,14] it is being increasingly noticed in other geographically adjacent areas.** The policy has an added advantage of securing these areas (Xinjiang, Tibet and Mongolia) under whose soil lies billions of tons of oil, natural gas and copper has meant populating them over the decades with Han Chinese immigrants from the nation's demographic heart land. It has also meant in the case of Xinjaing, an aggressive courting of independent ethnic Turkic republics of Central Asia, so that the Uyghurs will never have a political and geographical rear base with which to

---

13   Kaplan Robert 'The Revenge of Geography' page 3263 Kindle Edition.

14   Manchuria, Inner Mongolia, Xinjiang and Tibet are historically seen as buffer states for Han China. However, today two of these China's buffer regions are in flux. Elements within Tibet and Xinjiang adamantly resist Han Chinese occupation. China understands that the loss of these regions could pose severe threats to China's security -- particularly if such losses would draw India north of the Himalayas or create a radical Islamic regime in Xinjiang. In this regard see http://www.stratfor.com/weekly/state-world-assessing-chinas-strategy.

contest Beijing's rule. These immigrants take in their wake companies involved in garnering local resources for the main land. Export and employment of Chinese labour is an added advantage of the policy. 'It is not a question of an invading army or formal annexation, but of creeping Chinese demographic and corporate control over a region'.[15] 'Mongolia, the Russian Far East, Central Asia and South East Asia are all natural zones of Chinese influence and expansion'.[16] A policy which is causing tensions and raising eye brows in the region.

(a) **Mongolia.** Mongolia (geographic 'Outer Mongolia') to the North: a giant blob of territory that looks as though it has been bitten away from China which borders Mongolia to the south, west, and east. Mongolia, with one of the world's lowest population densities, is being threatened by the latest of Eurasia's great historical migration – that of an urbane Chinese civilisation with a tendency to move north. China has flooded its own Inner Mongolia with Han Chinese immigrants, and outer Mongolians worry that they are next to be demographically conquered. Having once conquered Outer Mongolia by moving the line of cultivation northward, China may be poised to conquer Mongolia through globalisation. China covets the oil, coal, uranium and other strategic minerals and rich, empty grasslands of its former Qing-Manchu possession.[17] Its building of access roads has to be seen in this light. Mongolia can provide China aluminium, copper, coal, lead, nickel, zinc, tin and iron all of which Mongolia has in abundance and of which China is world's largest consumer. China's mining companies have been seeking large stakes in Mongolia's underground assets. Mongolia will be a trip wire for judging future Chinese intentions.[18]

(b) **Russia Far East.** North of Mongolia, as well as north of China's three provinces of Manchuria, lies the Russian Far East, an interminable stretch of birch forest lying between Lake Baikal and Vladivostok. This numbing vastness, roughly twice the size of Europe, has a meagre population of 6.7 million that is in the process of falling further to 4.5 million people.

---

15 Kaplan Robert 'The Revenge of Geography' page 3216 Kindle Edition.

16 Ibid page 3355 Kindle Edition.

17 Spence Jonathan D, The Search for Modern China. New York Norton page 67.

18 Kaplan Robert 'The Revenge of Geography' page 3198 Kindle Edition.

Yet on the other side of the border are 100 million Chinese, a population density sixty-two times greater than in Eastern Siberia.[19] Chinese migrants have been filtering across this border. Resource acquisition is the principal goal of Chinese foreign policy, and Russia's demographically barren Far East is filled with large reserves of natural gas, oil, timber, diamonds and gold. 'Russia and China might operate a tactical alliance, but there is already tension between them over the Far East. Moscow is wary of large numbers of Chinese settlers moving into this region, bringing timber and mining companies in their wake.'[20]

(c) **South East Asia.** 'China dominated Vietnam during the first millennium of the modern era. China's Yuan Dynasty (of Mongol Descent) invaded Burma (now Myanmar), Siam and Vietnam in the late thirteenth century. Chinese migration to Thailand dates back many centuries. The lack of Great Wall in China's South East was not only because of the rugged forests and steep mountain folds between China and Burma (now Myanmar), but because Chinese expansion along this entire frontier from Burma (now Myanmar) in the west to Vietnam in the east was more fluid than in the north of China.'[21] The likely capital of a Mekong River prosperity sphere, linking all the countries of Indo-China by road and river traffic, is Kunming in China's Yunnan Province, whose dams will provide electricity consumed by the Thais and others in the demographic cockpit of the world.'[22] The corporate and demographic stresses being faced by the region have already been discussed earlier while discussing Chinese approach to dealing with natural resource deficiency.

(d) This trend has continued in the modern times too. 'An aspect not discussed widely is the settlement of the country's burgeoning population. Even Tibet and Xinjiang may not be able to contain the push as Beijing tends to ease its "one-child" policy to balance ageing population. There are some researches to

19 Kaplan Robert 'The Revenge of Geography' page 3216 Kindle Edition.

20 Blair David, 'Why the Restless Chinese Are Warming to Russia's Frozen East', Daily Telegraph, London, 16 July 2009.

21 Lattimore Owen 'Chinese Colonization in Manchuria', Geographical Review, London 1932 page 270.

22 Kaplan Robert 'The Revenge of Geography' page 3317 Kindle Edition.

suggest that China is acquiring long term mining contracts in African countries where Chinese workers can eventually settle down. The proverbial China towns. Population migration is a process since Man began his journey. But in today's age if such migration is a state policy, there is the fear of Trojan Horses being injected and much more.[23] 'To provide a safety valve for building pressures of unemployment, China is now exporting labour, some in slave form. It sent workers to Israel to replace barred Palestinians under conditions that they cannot marry Israeli women or use the services of Israeli prostitutes. It is sending farmers to sparsely populated Kazakhstan to farm excess fallow land. It is sending Chinese to perform odd jobs in the Russian Far East.'[24]

Trade

(a) Trade always played a big role in shaping the Chinese culture and civilisation. However, trade was more oriented inwards within the Chinese landmass than the sea faring type of the Europeans. Eastern Han Dynasty was reinstated with the support of the merchant families and undertook campaigns to secure the silk route for trade. During the Tang Dynasty, there was extensive trade with distant foreign countries, and many foreign merchants settled in China, boosting a vibrant cosmopolitan culture. The Ming Dynasty presided over a period in which urbanization increased and large urban centres, such as Nanjing and Beijing, contributed to the growth of private industry. In particular, small-scale industries grew up, often specializing in paper, silk, cotton, and porcelain goods. Also, relatively small urban centres with markets proliferated around the country. Town markets mainly traded food, with some necessary manufactures such as pins or oil.

(b) Today, international trade makes up a sizeable portion of China's overall economy. China's industrial base by design produces more than its domestic economy can consume, so China must export goods to the rest of the world while importing raw materials. Thus external trade is essential to maintain growth – which as we have seen earlier is critical to maintaining growth and in turn stability in the Chinese

---

23 http://www.southasiaanalysis.org/node/1089

24 http://www.southasiaanalysis.org/paper875

society.[25]

Oil Deficiency

There exists a big imbalance between supply and demand in oil for China. Its import requirement rose from 200 million metric tons of crude in 2010 to 271.02 million metric tons in 2012. Majority of this has to be transported on the sea.

---

25 See   http://timesofindia.indiatimes.com/world/china/Chinas-Xi-Jinping-calls-for-great-renais-sance/articleshow/19020759.cms for the stress being paid on the issue by the new Chinese leadership.

Chapter 6

CHINESE GEO-STRATEGY

NATIONAL STRATEGY

China's Security Problems[1]

From the consolidation of China as a unified state under the Han Dynasty (in the 3rd century B.C.) through the emergence of the present Communist government, Chinese regimes have faced a common set of security problems.

(a) First, China has an astonishingly **long border**– more than 10,000 miles in all—to defend against local and distant threats. During the imperial era (from the 3rd century B.C. until the mid-19th century), raids by nomadic tribes threatened the Chinese periphery. In the early modern era (from approximately 1850), the periphery was threatened by great imperialist powers, including Russia, Germany, Great Britain, and France. Since World War II, militantly strong, industrialized states--India, Russia, Japan, and the United States—have posed new security threats to the periphery.

(b) Second, China's domestic political system has always been marked by a personality-based pattern of rule in which ultimate authority comes from the power and beliefs of individual leaders, not from legal and organizational norms and processes. In such a system, policy content and behaviour--including external security policy—often become tools in the domestic power struggle among senior leaders. This tends to cause volatility within the government and internal political strife.

---

1   http://www.rand.org/pubs/research_briefs/RB61/index1.html

(c)   Third, no matter what its relative geopolitical strength at any time, China thinks of itself as a great power. This self-image is based on China's historical role as a central political player in Asia and on its tradition of economic self-sufficiency. During imperial times, Chinese regimes usually held a deep-seated belief in China's political, social, and cultural superiority over its neighbours. In modern times, Chinese regimes have aspired to economic, technological, and military equality with, rather than superiority over, the other major powers.

Viewed through the prism of time, the security strategies employed by various Chinese regimes converge into an overall "Grand Strategy" that strives for three interrelated objectives[2]: -

(a)   To control the periphery and ward off threats to the ruling regime.

(b)   To preserve domestic order and well-being in the face of different forms of social strife.

(c)   To attain or maintain geo-political influence as a major, or even primary, state.

Core Strategic Interests

Simply put, China has three core strategic interests.[3]

(a)   **Maintenance of Domestic Security.**

(i)   Historically, when China involves itself in global trade, as it did in the 19th and early 20th century, the coastal regions prosper, while the interior of China -- which begins about 100 miles from the coast and runs about 1,000 miles to the west -- languish. Roughly 80 percent of all Chinese citizens currently have household incomes lower than the average household income in Bolivia. Most of China's poor are located west of the richer coastal region; this disparity of wealth time and again has exposed tensions between the interests of the coast and those of the interior.

(ii)   Historically the perception of a Government not concerned about the well being of the citizens have led to revolts, upheavals and end of dynasty's. After a failed rising in Shanghai in 1927, Mao Zedong too exploited these

---

tensions by undertaking the Long March into the interior, raising a peasant army and ultimately conquering the coastal region. He shut China off from the international trading system, leaving China more united and equal, but extremely poor.

(iii) The current government has sought a more wealth-friendly means of achieving stability: buying popular loyalty with mass employment. 'Employment represents China's preferred tool to maintain social stability, and the Party sees stability as paramount to retaining its legitimacy as the unchallengeable and un-opposable leader of China.'[4,5] Plans for industrial expansion are implemented with little thought to markets or margins; instead, maximum employment is the driving goal. Private savings are harnessed to finance the industrial effort, leaving little domestic capital to purchase the output. China must export accordingly.

(b) **Ensuring Access to International Markets.** China's second strategic concern derives from the first. China's industrial base by design produces more than its domestic economy can consume, so China must export goods to the rest of the world while importing raw materials. The Chinese therefore must do everything possible to ensure international demand for their exports. This includes a range of activities, from investing money in the economies of consumer countries to establishing unfettered access to global sea-lanes.

(c) **Maintaining Control over Buffer States.**

(i) The population of the historic Han Chinese heartland is clustered in the eastern third of the country, where ample precipitation distinguishes it from the much more dry and arid central and western thirds. China's physical security therefore depends on controlling the four non-Han Chinese buffer states that surround it: Manchuria, Inner Mongolia, Xinjiang and Tibet. Securing these regions

4   http://www.stratfor.com/weekly/china-tests-japanese-and-us-patience?utm_source=freelist-f&utm_medium=email&utm_campaign=20130226&utm_term=gweekly&utm_content=read more&elq=3232f09271e74f758b80de4a322b60fb

5   See http://timesofindia.indiatimes.com/world/china/Chinas-Xi-Jinping-calls-for-great-renais-sance/articleshow/19020759.cms for the new Chinese leaderships stress on ever improving living standards.

means China can insulate itself from any attack from its neighbours.

(ii) Controlling the buffer states provides China geographical barriers -- jungles, mountains, steppes and the Siberian wasteland – that are difficult to surmount and creates a defence in depth that puts any attacker at a grave disadvantage.

(iii) 'However, two of these buffer regions are in flux. Elements within Tibet and Xinjiang adamantly resist Han Chinese occupation. China understands that the loss of these regions could pose severe threats to China's security -- particularly if such losses would draw India north of the Himalayas or create a radical Islamic regime in Xinjiang. The situation in Tibet is potentially the most troubling. Outright war between India and China – anything beyond minor skirmishes – is impossible so long as both are separated by the Himalayas. Neither side could logistically sustain large-scale multi-divisional warfare in that terrain. But China and India could threaten one another if they were to cross the Himalayas and establish a military presence on the either side of the mountain chain. For India, the threat would emerge if Chinese forces entered Pakistan in large numbers. For China, the threat would occur if large numbers of Indian troops entered Tibet. China therefore constantly postures as if it were going to send large numbers of forces into Pakistan, but in the end, the Pakistanis have no interest in de facto Chinese occupation -- even if the occupation were directed against India. The Chinese likewise are not interested in undertaking security operations in Pakistan. The Indians have little interest in sending forces into Tibet in the event of a Tibetan revolution. For India, an independent Tibet without Chinese forces would be interesting, but a Tibet where the Indians would have to commit significant forces would not be. As much as the Tibetans represent a problem for China, the problem is manageable.'[6]

(iv) So long as the internal problems in Han China are manageable, so is Chinese domination of the buffer states, albeit with some effort and some damage to China's reputation abroad.

---

6   http://www.stratfor.com/weekly/state-world-assessing-chinas-strategy

'The key for China is maintaining interior stability. If this portion of Han China destabilises, control of the buffers becomes impossible. Maintaining interior stability requires the transfer of resources, which in turn requires continued robust growth of the Chinese coastal economy to generate the capital to transfer inland. Should exports stop flowing out and raw materials in, incomes in the interior would quickly fall to politically explosive levels.[7] (China today is far from revolution, but social tensions are increasing, and China must use its security apparatus and the People's Liberation Army to control these tensions. The aspect of maintaining party's control over the Army has lately become an issue of importance in China. The new President Mr Xi Jinping in a speech in Dec 12 said 'the lesson for China from the disintegration of the Soviet Union is that "we must stand firm on the Party's leadership over the military". He pointed out, "In the Soviet Union, the military was depoliticised, separated from the Party and nationalized and the party was disarmed. A few people tried to save the Soviet Union; they seized Gorbachev, but within days it was turned around again, because they didn't have the instruments to exert power. Yeltsin gave a speech standing on a tank, but the military made no response, keeping so-called 'neutrality.' Finally, Gorbachev announced the disbandment of the CPSU. A big Party was gone just like that. Proportionally, the CPSU had more members than the CCP does, but nobody was man enough to stand up and resist).[8] Maintaining those flows is a considerable challenge. The very model of employment and market share over profitability misallocates scores of resources and breaks the normally self-regulating link between supply and demand. One of the more disruptive results is inflation, which

---

7   Gini coefficient is commonly used as a **measure of inequality of income or wealth**. It measures the inequality among values of a frequency distribution (for example levels of income). A Gini coefficient of zero expresses perfect equality, where all values are the same (for example, where everyone has an exactly equal income). A Gini coefficient of one (100 on the percentile scale) expresses maximal inequality among values (for example where only one person has all the income). A low Gini coefficient indicates a more equal distribution, with 0 corresponding to complete equality, while higher Gini coefficients indicate more unequal distribution, with 1 corresponding to complete inequality. (Seehttp://en.wikipedia.org/wiki/Gini_coefficient). It is believed by Social Scientists that a Gini coefficient higher than 0.4 and inching towards 0.5 can lead to social unrest and when it crosses 0.5 a major social upheaval may follow. **China has refused to allow calculation and publication of its Gini coefficient for the last eleven years** (see http://articles.marketwatch.com/2012-01-19/economy/30788275_1_income-gap-china-reform-foundation-gini-coefficient) however **unofficial commentators estimate that the Gini coefficient of China is already at a level of 0.47** (see http://www.chinadaily.com.cn/china/2010-05/12/content_9837073.htm and http://community.travelchinaguide.com/forum2.asp?i=43913).

8   http://www.southasiaanalysis.org/node/1170

alternatively raises the costs of subsidizing the interior while eroding China's competitiveness with other low-cost global exporters. For the Chinese, this represents a strategic challenge, a challenge that can only be countered by increasing the profitability on Chinese economic activity. This is nearly impossible for low value-added producers. The solution is to begin manufacturing higher value-added products (fewer shoes, more cars), but this necessitates a different sort of work force, one with years more education and training than the average Chinese coastal inhabitant, much less someone from the interior. It also requires direct competition with the well-established economies of Japan, Germany and the United States. This is the strategic battleground that China must attack if it is to maintain its stability'.[9]

Chinese Perusal of these Objectives.[10]

(a) Although the strategic approaches China employs to achieve these objectives have changed over time, certain general principles applied throughout China's imperial era. As a rule, imperial regimes were most likely to use: -

   (i) Military force to advance their security objectives when they were strongest, generally during the first one-third of the regimes' existence.

   (ii) As they matured, strong, stable regimes increasingly employed complex mixtures of force, diplomacy, and cultural norms.

   (iii) However, during the final one-third of their existence, waning regimes relied more on diplomatic manoeuvres, defensive or passive military stances, and other non-coercive strategies to advance their security objectives.

(b) Thus, "strong" regimes ruled by assertive coercive and non-coercive means, and "weak" ones largely by non-coercive and passive ones.

(c) Although China's basic security objectives have not changed substantially during the modern era, the challenges posed by the industrialized world have spawned new security strategies. China's modern regimes have been neither purely weak (nor therefore cooperative) nor wholly strong (and therefore assertive). Rather, in modern times China has adopted hybrid

---

9   http://www.stratfor.com/weekly/state-world-assessing-chinas-strategy

10 http://www.rand.org/pubs/research_briefs/RB61/index1.html

"weak-strong" strategies that use force and diplomacy selectively.

The Calculative Strategy[11]

In the last few decades, this hybrid strategy has coalesced into what Rand calls the "calculative" strategy--that is, a strategy calculated to protect China from external threats as it pursues its geopolitical ascent. *The purpose of the calculative strategy is to allow China to continue to reform its economy and thereby acquire comprehensive national power without having to deal with the impediments and distractions of security competition.* If successful, the strategy will buy China the breathing room it needs to improve domestic social conditions,[12] *increase the legitimacy of the governing regime,* expand the nation's economic and technological capabilities, *strengthen its military,* and enhance its standing and influence in the international political order--all of which are important elements in achieving its long-standing security objectives. The calculative strategy is designed to allow China to increase its power in a variety of issue areas in as non-provocative a fashion as possible. The RAND study traces the strategy in action through four issue areas: -

(a) **Policies toward the United States and other Powers.** The calculative strategy aims to win support for China's expansion, while preventing any efforts that may frustrate its growth. To this end, the strategy focuses on developing and maintaining friendly relations with the major powers and convincing them that the rise of China will be a stabilizing force in Asia. By garnering this cooperation, the strategy aims to forestall a U.S. defensive counter response that could widen the gap in power between China and the other major players. Continued friendly relations also improve China's access to the world's wealthiest economic markets.

(b) **Policies toward Military Modernization.** The calculative strategy aims to reduce China's existing vulnerabilities while increasing the ability of its military forces to secure diplomatic and political leverage. The modernization--in both nuclear and conventional forces--is going forward slowly and steadily because a rapid military build-up might alarm China's

---

11 http://www.rand.org/pubs/research_briefs/RB61/index1.html

12 Also see http://timesofindia.indiatimes.com/world/china/Chinas-Xi-Jinping-calls-for-great-renaissance/articleshow/19020759.cms.

neighbours and the major powers. Further, a sudden build-up would detract from China's current emphasis on civilian economic development.

(c) **Policies toward Territorial Claims.** The calculative strategy aims to avoid using force to settle territorial disputes. Rather, it dictates that China pursue a good-neighbour policy designed to strengthen or mend ties with its neighbours and to delay resolving disputes, at least until the regional balance of power shifts in favour of China.

(d) **Policies toward International Regimes.** The calculative strategy aims to secure advantages without incurring losses. Therefore, China's level of participation in international regimes--in such areas as economic development, trade, technology transfer, arms control, and the environment--is determined on a case-by-case basis.

Taken together, these policies display the "calculating" aspect of the calculative strategy. They illustrate how the strategy has encouraged foreign collaboration in underwriting China's rise to power, while temporarily removing external threats that could distract Beijing from its uninterrupted ascent.

Foreign Policy and Diplomacy

Deng Xiaoping around 1991-92 had given the dictum "hide your strength, bide your time". He crafted this policy, when China was isolated internationally following the June, 1989 Tiananmen Square incident. Deng decided to build an economically and militarily powerful China in a stable atmosphere. According to Li Wei, a lecturer at the Renmin University of China's School of International Studies, an intense debate is currently on in the country's foreign policy establishment examining whether it is still relevant. 'At least four elements of Deng's policies are currently under debate or changing: a shift from non-interference to creative involvement; a shift from bilateral to multilateral diplomacy; a shift from reactive to preventative diplomacy; and a move away from strict nonalignment toward semi-alliances.

(a) **Creative Involvement.** Creative involvement is described as a way for China to be more active in preserving its interests abroad by becoming more involved in other countries' domestic politics– a shift from non-interference to something more flexible. China has used money and other tools to shape domestic developments in other countries in the past, but an official change in policy would necessitate deeper Chinese involvement in local affairs.[13,14] However, this would undermine China's attempts to promote the idea that it is just another developing nation helping other developing nations in the face of Western imperialism and hegemony.[15] This shift in perception could erode some of China's advantage in dealing with developing nations since it has relied on promises of political non-interference as a counter to Western offers of better technology or more development resources that come with requirements of political change.

(b) **Multi Lateral Relations.** China has long relied on bilateral relations as its preferred method of managing its interests internationally. When China has operated within a multilateral forum, it has often shaped developments only by being a spoiler rather than a leader. For example, China can block sanctions in the U.N. Security Council but has rarely proffered a different path for the international community to pursue. Particularly through the 1990s, Beijing feared its relatively weak position left it little to gain from multilateral forums, and instead put China under the influence of the stronger members. But China's rising economic power has shifted this equation. China is pursuing more multilateral relationships as a way to secure its interests through the larger groups. China's relations with the Association of Southeast Asian Nations, its participation in the Shanghai Cooperation Organization and its pursuit of trilateral summits are all intended to help Beijing shape the policy direction of these blocs. By shifting to the multilateral approach, China can make some of the weaker countries feel more secure and thus prevent them from turning to the United States for support.

(c) **Preventive Diplomacy.** Traditionally, China has had a relatively reactive foreign policy, dealing with crises when they emerge but often failing to recognize or act to prevent

---

13 The problems of this nature are already being seen in Myanmar as it tries to end it's international isolation see http://www.c3sindia.org/southeastasia/2956

14 Also see http://www.c3sindia.org/southeastasia/3140 and http://www.southasiaanalysis.org/node/1028.

15 The problem is again being noticed in Myanmar see http://www.kdng.org/news/34-news/295-myanmar-china-relations-post-myitsone-suspension--analysis.html, http://www.eurasiareview.com/28012013-myanmar-china-relations-post-myitsone-suspension-analysis/ and http://strategicstudyindia.blogspot.in/2013/01/myanmar-china-relations-post-myitsone.html

the crises before they materialize. In places where Beijing has sought access to natural resources, it has often been caught off-guard by changes in the local situation and not had a response strategy prepared. (The division of Sudan and South Sudan is one recent example). Now, China is debating shifting this policy to one where it seeks to better understand the underlying forces and issues that could emerge into conflict and act alone or with the international community to defuse volatile situations. In the South China Sea, this would mean clarifying its maritime claims rather than continuing to use the vague nine-dash line and also more aggressively pursuing ideas for an Asian security mechanism, one in which China would play an active leadership role.

(d) **Semi Alliances.**

   (i) China's stance on alliances remains the same as that put forward by Deng in the 1980s: It does not engage in alliance structures targeted against third countries. This was both to allow China to retain an independent foreign policy stance and to avoid international entanglements due to its alliances with others. For example, Chinese plans to retake Taiwan were scuttled by its involvement in the Korean War, and thus its relations with the United States were set back by decades. The collapse of the Cold War system and the rise of China's economic and military influence have brought this policy under scrutiny as well. Beijing has watched cautiously as NATO has expanded eastward and as the United States has strengthened its military alliances in the Asia-Pacific region. Beijing's non-alliance policy leaves China potentially facing these groups alone, something it has neither the military nor the economic strength to effectively counter.

   (ii) The proposed semi-alliance structure is designed to counter this weakness while not leaving China beholden to its semi-alliance partners. China's push for strategic partnerships (even with its ostensible rivals) and increased military and humanitarian disaster drills with other nations are part of this strategy. The strategy is less about building an alliance structure against the United States than it is about breaking down the alliance structures that could be built against China by getting closer to traditional US partners, making them less willing to take strong actions against China. In its maritime strategy, Beijing is working with India, Japan and Korea in counter piracy operations and engaging in more naval exchanges and offers of joint exercises and drills'.[16]

Main Tasks of Chinese Foreign Policy

While some commentators feel that 'although China's relative power has grown significantly in recent decades, the main tasks of Chinese foreign policy are defensive and have not changed much since the Cold War era: to blunt destabilizing influences from abroad, to avoid territorial losses, to reduce its neighbours' suspicions, and to sustain economic growth. What has changed in the past two decades is that China is now so deeply integrated into the world economic system that its internal and regional priorities have become part of a larger quest: to define a global role that serves Chinese interests but also wins acceptance from other powers'.[17] Others feel that China is already in the process of discarding the policy of "hide your strength, bide your time". 'Contrarily, it appears that of late China has shown signs of discarding the time tested strategy of Deng Xiaoping as is well explained by his maxim "hide your strength, bide your time." Ever since the middle of the first decade of this century, especially the successful convocation of the Olympic Games in 2008, China started to take maximalist positions vis-à-vis conflicts with the neighbouring countries, be it the Diaoyu / Senkaku row with Japan in the East China Sea, or with Vietnam, Philippines and other smaller disputing countries in the South China Sea, or its dispute with South Asian neighbours'.[18]

'Accordingly to Li Wei's article, Professor Wang Yizhou, author of the book "Creative Involvement : a New Direction in China's Diplomacy", sees three basic issues that confronts China : -

(a) China's power growth leaves no room for vigorous development, and China is a source of growing concern and expectation in the international community. There are growing international responsibilities as per its power. If China fails to respond, it will fundamentally damage its "soft power".

(b) China faces a series of pressing diplomatic issues. Can it

---

16 http://www.stratfor.com/weekly/paradox-chinas-naval-strategy

17 http://www.foreignaffairs.com/articles/138009/andrew-j-nathan-and-andrew-scobell/how-china-sees-america?page=show

18 http://www.southasiaanalysis.org/node/1089

shelve disputes now with its current power?

(c)   The traditional diplomacy of hiding strength and biding time is proving incapable of protecting Chinese interests abroad.[19]

'The 18th congress of the Chinese Communist Party (CCP) mapped out the skeletal structure of China's foreign policy. Outgoing CCP General secretary Hu Jintao in his political report on 08 Nov 12 to the Congress expressed willingness to cooperate, but was also emphatic that not an inch will be given to outside pressures where China's sovereignty, security and development interests were involved. As the official *China Daily* (09 Nov 12) put it, Hu signalled the foreign policy for next five years when Beijing's influence on international affairs brings not only greater responsibility, but also frictions with neighbours and some developed economies due to their unease with China's rise and competition.[20] The major reason for the frictions is the introduction of the core interest principle post 2009. 'To suit to its grand strategy of achieving modernization of the country by middle of the century and convey to the outside word that its rise will be peaceful, the People's Republic of China (PRC) is implementing a foreign policy model which, as it visualizes, would create a 'win-win ' situation in international relations. However, with the introduction of the 'core interests' principle in external relations in the post-2009 period , which gives equal priority to the need for protection of the country's sovereignty, disallowing any compromise and even suggesting the use of force for the same, an assertive character is getting more and more pronounced in the model, somewhat diluting its original benevolent goal. As a result, the countries having land and sea territorial disputes with China are being subjected to a high degree of uneasiness.'[21]

Core Interest Concept

(a)   Core interests were first defined by the 'Chinese Vice- Foreign Minister Dai Bingguo who end July 2009) that "the PRC's first core interest is maintaining its fundamental system and state security, second is state sovereignty and territorial integrity and the third is the continued stable development of the economy and society." In specific terms, Tibet, Xinjiang and Taiwan stand officially listed under the 'core interest' category;

---

19 http://www.c3sindia.org/foreign-policy/3215 and http://www.tibettelegraph.com/2012/05/chinas-foreign-policy-debate.html

20 http://www.southasiaanalysis.org/node/1067

21 http://www.southasiaanalysis.org/node/987

state-controlled media have added South China Sea Islands as well as strategic resources and trade route to that list. They have also averred that the PRC will make no compromises on 'core interest' matters and never waive its right to protect them with military means. The obvious top priority given to the need for protecting the country's fundamental system, i.e. the rule of the Chinese Communist Party (CCP), coming at a time when the modernization process has given rise to a pluralistic society in China aspiring for deeper political reforms, looks politically very significant.'[22] Hence, the core interests of China can be listed as: -

(i) Protecting the rule of the Chinese Communist Party.[23]

(ii) Territorial Integrity including state sovereignty over: -

- ▶ Tibet.
- ▶ Xinjiang.
- ▶ Taiwan.
- ▶ South China Sea Islands.

(iii) Strategic resources.

(iv) Trade routes.

(b) The 'Core Interest Principle' apart from disallowing compromises and suggesting force to settle disputes also infuses a degree of nationalistic jingoism and assertiveness in the national behaviour. 'As China has started to define South China Sea as an area of core interest in addition to Taiwan and Tibet, it has taken the disputes to new stages by way of sending unmanned surveillance plane over disputed Diaoyu; *standoff with the Philippines over Scarborough Shoal*; Chinese fishing vessels cutting the cables of Vietnamese Oil & Gas Group seismic ship in Vietnam controlled waters; announcing new rules for the region that authorize its police in the southern province of Hainan to board and seize foreign ships in the South China Sea; raising threats of conflict by establishing Sansha on Yongxing Island in the southernmost province of Hainan; threats to disrupt ONGC Videsh exploration in South China Sea and reiterating China's 'indisputable sovereignty' in the region; initiating a new passport design containing a

---

22 http://www.c3sindia.org/eastasia/2590.

23 See http://timesofindia.indiatimes.com/world/china/Chinas-Xi-Jinping-calls-for-great-renais-sance/articleshow/19020759.cms for the new Chinese leadership's views on the need of avoiding political change which can loosen the party's grip over power.

map claiming the South China Sea and disputed areas along the Sino-Indian border; and even *flexing economic muscle against the smaller neighbours in the region by banning their exports on flimsy grounds*.[24] 'One of the proposed theories was that countries east of Suez including part of Africa to Asia Pacific Region (APR) should be under a kind of Chinese suzerainty. This swath includes south Asia and India. This was propounded from around 2004. The other more recent push was to make South China Sea an area of China's "Core" interest. This basically means China would control the South China Sea which is water for major international shipping.'[25]

(c) B Raman in his blog post 'Decoding China's Core Interests'[26] notes that an important statement on foreign policy for the year 2012 came from Mr. Xi himself during a visit he made to the US after it became clear that he would be taking over as the Party General Secretary and the State President. While addressing a luncheon hosted by the National Committee on U.S.-China Relations and the U.S.-China Business Council at Washington DC on 15 Feb 12, Mr. Xi said that China and the US should increase strategic trust and respect the core interests and major concerns of each other. In the overall statement while he tried to play down the tensions and suspicions that had arisen during the last two years following China's reported characterization of its sovereignty claims over the islands of the South China Sea as of core interest in addition to Taiwan and Tibet. Such a characterization was not made in any official document or policy statement of Beijing earlier. It did not refer to Xinjiang as a core interest though they included Tibet and "Tibet-related issues" as of core interest. The meaning of "Tibet-related" issues is not clear. Did they refer to China's sovereignty claims over Arunachal Pradesh? It needs to be noted that in their interactions with India, the Chinese have not referred to their sovereignty claims over Arunachal Pradesh as a core interest for them.[27] The Chinese

---

24 http://www.southasiaanalysis.org/node/1089

25 http://www.southasiaanalysis.org/node/1067

26 http://www.southasiaanalysis.org/node/1067

27 The new Chinese leadership has started referring to issues with India as 'Core Concerns'. While the definition of core concerns is not clear, China also talks of relations with Japan and ASEAN as core concerns. This is distinct from the Core Interests of sovereignty related issues of Taiwan and South & East China Sea. Analysts believe these implies a larger gambit than just the issue

definition of a core interest is one in which no concessions by them are possible. There were two other important statements indicating an inflexible line on territorial sovereignty issues on 20 and 21 Sep 2012. In a dispatch from Brussels, the "People's Daily" quoted Prime Minister Wen Jiabao as stating on the sideline of a China-EU summit that China would make no concession in affairs concerning the country's sovereignty and territorial integrity. The next day, when addressing the opening ceremony of the China-ASEAN Business and Investment Summit and Forum in Nanning, capital city of the Guangxi Zhuang Autonomous Region, Mr Xi said: "We are firm in safeguarding China's sovereignty, security and territorial integrity and are committed to resolving differences with neighbours concerning territorial land, territorial sea and maritime rights and interests peacefully through friendly negotiations." These two statements indicated that the non-confrontational line projected by Mr Xi in the US did not apply to China's sovereignty disputes with some ASEAN countries in the South China Sea and with Japan in the East China Sea. This hard line was reflected in an article carried by the "People's Daily" on November 2, 2012, a day after the final meeting of the 17th Central Committee started. The article was written by Mr. Wang Yusheng, Executive Director of the Strategic Research Centre of the China Institute of International Research Foundation. It said: "The parties concerned know clearly that China advocates building a harmonious neighbourhood, but has inviolable "red lines." If necessary, it will resort to force after trying peaceful means. The United States is just bluffing, and Japan and some other Asian countries are just taking advantage of U.S. influence to serve their own purposes. They may muddy the water in the Pacific, but cannot make big waves." While the statements related to China's territorial disputes with some ASEAN countries and Japan, the formulations clearly showed that the inflexible line applied to all territorial disputes with all neighbours. This should be a matter for added concern to India. Thus, the over-all Chinese line seems to be as follows: -

---

of sovereignty related issue of Arunachal – which is just one part of the issues which include the activities of Dalai Lama as also India's relations with US, Japan and Vietnam. While, China has been raising the issue of India's relation with these countries, it is not ready to discuss its relations with Pakistan or the activities of its troops in POK or Gilgit Pakistan or for that matter Gwadar. See http://southasiaanalysis.org/node/1209.

(i) It looks upon its sovereignty claims over Taiwan, Tibet and "Tibet-related issues" as of core interest and major concern. It has made this clear in formal official statements and is prepared for a military conflict if its interests are threatened, but it has not clarified what it means by Tibet-related issues.

(ii) Since May, 2010, it has informally indicated to the US its sovereignty claims in the South China Sea as of core interest, thereby not ruling out the use of force if its interests are threatened. However, there has been no formal declaration on this subject.

(iii) While continuing to reiterate its sovereignty claims in the East China Sea, it has refrained from characterizing them as of core interest to avoid a military conflict with Japan which enjoys the protection of the US-Japan Security Treaty in the East China Sea.

(d) Chinese emphasis on protecting 'core interests' appears to be driven in the main, by their perceived fears on internal security challenges and their external dimension (relating to 'Western anti-China forces' as being put by Beijing), with respect to issues of 'sovereignty' over Tibet, Xinjiang and Taiwan. Not to be missed is the fact that 'core interest' articulations have followed the ethnic unrest in Tibet (March 2008) and Xinjiang (July 2009). Experts point out that "a unique feature of Chinese leaders' understanding of their country's history is their persistent sensitivity to domestic disorder caused by foreign threats".[28]

(e) 'On the contrary, in the military, territorial and resources fronts, China's 'Core Interests"-based neighbourhood policy is giving rise to conflicts between it and regional nations. This has been despite China's "New Security Concept" aimed at reassuring neighbours that it is not an economic and security threat to them. Strategic issues dividing China and some ASEAN nations have become deeper as a result of China's growing territorial assertiveness. Through its unilaterally drawn U-shaped curve, called 'dotted line' by the Chinese side, the PRC claims vast territories in South China Sea. The result is emergence and continuation of serious sea territory conflicts between China on one hand and Southeast Asian nations on

---

the other. To buttress its claim, Beijing is projecting its force, causing fears in countries like the Philippines and Vietnam etc. In 2002, China signed the "Declaration of the Conduct of Parties in South China sea", which was not legally binding on the parties concerned; this apparent loophole appears to have given China an excuse to become regionally assertive. No doubt, the PRC joined with Southeast Asian nations at the ASEAN Regional Forum (ARF) meeting in Bali (23 July 2011) in accepting a set of "guidelines" to better implement the 2002 declaration, but that move only looked like Beijing's new temporary flexible approach, without signifying any shift in its fundamental Chinese position on the South China sea issue. Interestingly, some Chinese scholars (Professor Peng Zhongying of Renmin University) openly connect China's assertiveness abroad with the factor of domestic pressures."[29]

Middle Kingdom Approach[30,31]

The recent assertiveness which distinguishes China's foreign policy, especially with reference to South China Sea and Sino-Japan maritime border, has made many Sinologists conclude that the Middle Kingdom approach is again coming to the fore. This approach, according to Henry Kissinger, is the running theme throughout China's history. As mentioned earlier, Chinese consider their country to be the centre of the universe and those living outside China as barbarians. The relations between China and the outside world was an unequal relation, the neighbouring states had to pay regular tributes and kowtow (Kow Tow is the act of great respect displayed by kneeling and bowing so low as to have one's head touch the ground) before the Chinese emperor. As Henry Kissinger points out in his latest book, On China, the essence of Chinese approach to diplomacy have drawn on "methods handed over millennia". To quote Kissinger, "None equals China in persisting and persuading its neighbours to acquiesce – in such an elevated conception of its world role for so long and in the face

29 http://www.eurasiareview.com/30012012-us-china-and-developments-in-southeast-asia-analysis/

30 http://www.southasiaanalysis.org/node/995

31 Also see http://timesofindia.indiatimes.com/world/china/Chinas-Xi-Jinping-calls-for-great-re-naissance/articleshow/19020759.cmsas also http://timesofindia.indiatimes.com/world/china/Eye-on-future-president-sells-Chinese-dream/articleshow/19028057.cmsfor the views of the new Chinese leadership on what it calls the Chinese dream of China getting back its due in world politics and restoring its prosperity.

of so many historical vicissitudes. From the emergence of China as a unified country in the third century BC until the collapse of the Qing Dynasty in 1911, China stood at the centre of an international system of remarkable durability. The Chinese Emperor was conceived of (and recognized by most neighbouring states) as a pinnacle of a universal political hierarchy with all the other states' rulers theoretically serving as vassals".

Present Status[32]

(a) In the foreign policy front, China's concentration is on maintenance of a stable international situation, in the interest of its modernization programme. Accordingly, its diplomacy is more and more focusing now on adoption of an approach based on 'multilateralism' for addressing issues like global financial crisis, counter-terrorism, nuclear non-proliferation, energy security etc.

(b) At the same time, what is being witnessed now is China's mix of assertiveness and politico-economic cooperation in its strategy towards entire Asia-Pacific region. It is becoming clear that wherever China's 'core interests' are involved, Beijing's response is becoming assertive showing the complex nature of China's regional strategies; the reasons for China's unmistakable assertiveness need to be examined in a historical perspective.

(c) We should first look into the traditional mindset of the Chinese on the territorial aspects. The mindset is well-rooted in their "Tian Xia" (Under the Heaven) concept which views all territories as belonging to the Chinese Emperor, who is the son of heaven. Under its influence, the Chinese, traditionally, attach no sense to territory. In the modern era, the Tian Xia concept is manifesting in the Chinese not showing any hesitation to claim other territories which they believe as belonging to their country.

(d) In the current context, the following factors seem to be responsible for China's assertive external behaviour: -

  (i) Beijing's growing confidence internationally especially after its success in holding the Olympics and in maintaining high growth rates despite the global recession,

---

32 http://www.c3sindia.org/eastasia/2590

(ii) China's feelings that due to its enhanced position in the world, an opportunity has arisen for itself to increase its influence globally, at a time when the world balance of power is shifting from the West to East and a multi-polar world is emerging gradually.

(iii) The PRC's compulsions to protect land and sea trade routes in the interest of the much needed import of resources from abroad.

(iv) Beijing's perceptions on threats to internal security, making it to think that without China's assertive approach in this regard at this juncture, the task of finding a permanent solution to the sovereignty-related issues of Tibet, Xinjiang and Taiwan may get complicated in future.

East Asia[33,34]

It can be seen that since 2010 till today, Beijing's assertive behaviour in the region is being prominently witnessed on a variety of issues - US arms sales to Taiwan, US –South Korea joint military exercises in the Yellow Sea, ownership of Senkaku islands in East China Sea which are under Japan's control and sovereignty over the resources-rich South China Sea island chain. On its part, Beijing explains its stand by saying that all concerned nations should "accommodate each others' core interests and understand each others' strategic interests" and that the PRC stands for "shelving disputes and seek joint development" as well as pursuing bilateral cooperation and participation in regional and sub-regional cooperation. **Hidden in the term "Shelving" is the PRC's tactical line in favour of a temporary lull in the disputes, without indicating any change in its fundamental positions on territorial claims**; naturally this should merit the attention of those neighbours of China having land and sea boundary disputes with the PRC.

North and South East Asia[35]

(a) The changed US role in the region is an important factor playing in Beijing. Both the US Secretary of State Hillary Clinton and President Obama have declared that the 'US is

33 http://www.c3sindia.org/eastasia/2590

34 http://www.eurasiareview.com/30012012-us-china-and-developments-in-southeast-asia-analysis/

35 http://www.c3sindia.org/eastasia/2590

back in Asia'. It is evident that the US strategic focus is shifting from the Middle East to East Asia. Washington has been able to inject fresh vigour into its "alliance" relationship with Japan and South Korea; with other 'partners' like Singapore, the US has been successful in cementing strategic relations. The emerging US-Vietnam relations and Washington's growing interest in Indonesia are also worth noting.

(b) There are fundamental positional differences between the US and China, which affect the strategic situation in East Asia. The US stand that the case of the disputed Senkaku Island comes under the jurisdiction of US-Japan security treaty, is being considered as a serious challenge by Beijing, irrespective of the Obama regime's inclination of late 'not to explicitly mention the stand' in order not to anger Beijing. A second example is the US contention that the South China Sea islands dispute should be solved by multilateral efforts. China strongly opposes the same with its counter point that the issue should be solved bilaterally.

(c) Another point is that in the perceptions of China, the member states of ASEAN are not homogenous. The military junta in Myanmar is heavily dependent on China not only for military and economic support, but also for its legitimacy; Malaysia and Singapore would like the US and China to co-exist peacefully; but Vietnam, Indonesia and the Philippines are, in varying degrees, wary of the short term and long term consequences of the emergence of China as a major political, economic and military power.

(d) The PRC appears to be not happy about India's entrance into the East Asian scene. Its objection to India's cooperation with Vietnam on oil exploration in the South China Sea is an example. Beijing has also reservations on India playing a leading role in the East Asian integration process. It views India, Australia and New Zealand as "outsiders" to that process; the Chinese policy is that the leadership of that process should be in the hands of ASEAN plus 3.

South Asia[36]

(a) Like China's strategy in its other neighbouring regions, the one in South Asia is also based on Beijing's requirement

36 http://www.c3sindia.org/eastasia/2590

of a 'peaceful periphery' as a pre-requisite for the country's domestic development. Since end seventies, a recalibration of Beijing's attitude towards the region has been gradually taking place in pursuance of that pre-requisite.

(b) Authoritative experts in China visualized the visit of Premier Wen Jiabao to South Asia in 2005 as signifying Beijing's "Balanced South Asia Policy Under a New Situation" intended to develop relations with South Asian nations in a parallel manner and assure that China's strategic partnership with India and Pakistan is unprecedented in the sense that each relationship is not directed against any third country. As instances, the PRC started modifying its pro-Pakistan stand so far kept on Kashmir issue. China now says that that the Kashmir issue is one 'left over by history' and that 'India and Pakistan should properly solve the problem through dialogue and negotiations' (PRC Foreign Ministry Spokesperson, November 24, 2009). Beijing makes no references to 'self-determination' for the Kashmiri people and does not consider the 'Kashmiri people' as a third party to the dispute. Its official media (People's Daily, November 23, 2009) have declared that Beijing takes no sides on Kashmir issue. With the state-controlled media dropping references to 'India-occupied Kashmir' and using instead the terms 'India-controlled Kashmir' and 'Pakistan-controlled Kashmir'. Earlier, in December 1996, President Jiang Zemin favoured New Delhi - Islamabad 'consultations and negotiations' on Kashmir issue, during his speech to the Pakistan Senate. During the Kargil conflict in 1999, China refrained from taking sides and adopted a neutral position.

(c) Besides the 'peaceful periphery' factor, India's 'rise' also seems to have contributed to a change in China's South Asia approach. Indicative of this are the willingness of Beijing to stabilize ties with New Delhi through signing important agreements with India like Strategic and Cooperative Partnership for Peace and Prosperity and Political Parameters and Guiding Principles for Settlement of the Boundary Question' (2005) and 'Shared Vision for the 21st Century (2008). China has come to treat India not as a threat to it and the vice versa has also emerged true. Another point relates to Beijing's view that Sino-Indian ties have attained a global character. China seems to realize that cooperation with India is essential in tackling global issues like the WTO, climate change, reforms in global financial systems and revamping of UN. It can be seen without difficulty that congruence, to a good degree, of policy interests among China and India has emerged over the years; under its impact, in general, the comfort level in their relations has been increasing.

(d) It will not be out of place to mention about the existence of some other factors motivating China's South Asia policy. They include neutralizing the perceived US strategy to contain China with support of regional nations, developing economies in areas bordering China, cooperating with South Asian countries in exploitation of much needed energy resources, protecting oil transport security in the Indian Ocean, getting support to 'One China' policy and last but not least securing cooperation from the nations in the region in the matter of meeting terrorism threat to China's South West border coming from outside.

(e) Though at government levels, there is a tendency on the part of India and China to downplay their perceptional differences, Beijing has conveyed to New Delhi that it will take care of each other's "core interests and major concerns" during the visit to China made by the special envoy of the Indian Prime Minister in July 2010. Chinese Foreign Ministry has observed (Beijing, 16 September 2010) that exchanges between two sides will remain unaffected by disagreements over individual issues. As a sign that India also feels so, it has sent high level delegations to China.

(f) However, at top levels in India, a feeling persists that China is displaying its assertiveness in South Asia. There is no doubt that the assertiveness being shown by China since 2009 has raised questions on its 'balanced' South Asia policy. The PRC has taken harder positions on the issues of Sino-Indian border, Tibet and China-Pakistan nexus. Regarding the first, it is becoming more vociferous in claiming India's Arunachal Pradesh as part of its 'Southern Tibet' e.g. its objection to Indian Prime Minister's visit to Arunachal Pradesh. A solution to the boundary problem seems to be far way. Fourteen rounds of border talks held so far at the level of Special representatives have not resulted in any substantial result. Chinese experts close to the government treat the border issue as an 'imperialist' legacy reject McMahon line and expect India to make 'practical concessions' in the Eastern Sector (Professor Wang Hongwei of Centre for South Asia Studies, CASS). Both sides view the issue as a complex one requiring a long time for arriving at a solution and are keen to promote bilateral ties looking beyond the border Issue. The boundary problem has so far not been included by China under the 'core interest' category. Beijing may not do so, as 'core interests' involve no compromise, whereas it has been preferring to solve the border issue on the basis of 'mutual understanding and mutual accommodation' principle which provides for a compromise. This being so, New Delhi needs to carefully watch for any future movement of Beijing on this account.

(g) Tibet is not a bilateral **issue**, with New Delhi recognizing Tibet as part of China. But the two sides have differences on the Dalai Lama factor, which may sharpen as a result of China's growing assertiveness. No immediate breakthrough in talks between the Chinese and the Dalai Lama sides are likely in near future. China's campaign to prevent internationalization of the Tibet issue, while implementing its domestic strategy chalked out at a national conference linking Tibet's stability with development, may get further boost. On India's policy towards the Tibetan leader, despite New Delhi's assurances that he would not be allowed to engage in any anti-China activity from India's soil, Chinese suspicions in this regard are not going to disappear soon. Authoritative views in China (Prof Wang Hongwei) allege that India wants to play the Tibet 'card' against the PRC and as examples, point to the India's not banning the Tibet government in exile and the continuing support to the Dalai Lama coming from 'eminent' Indian personalities. New Delhi's nod for the visit of the Dalai Lama to Arunachal Pradesh has been looked at with concern by Beijing.

(h) China has further consolidated its 'all weather' partnership with Pakistan, especially by providing military assistance to the latter, knowing fully that Islamabad cannot guarantee the use of Chinese arms against India. Significant to note could be the PRC's peace treaty signed with Pakistan in 2005, unique in South Asia, providing for mutual support in protecting each other's national sovereignty and integrity. This treaty found a mention in the China-Pakistan Joint Statement issued at the end of Premier Wen's visit to Pakistan in December 2010. It is being viewed in China as a legal document providing for an 'alliance' between the two sides against any foreign threat.

(i) The PRC is taking up road and railway projects designed to link Pakistan and China via Pakistan Occupied Kashmir (POK) and is reportedly deploying Chinese troops for infrastructure building in the POK's Gilgit-Baltistan region. Fears are being expressed in India whether such projects could become strategically important to the Chinese military in the event of another conflict with India; in particular, the China-Pakistan project to modernize Karakorum Highway could be useful for the PRC as an overland route for moving Chinese missiles and spare parts to Pakistan.

(j) There appears to be a deeper meaning to the issuing of stapled visas by Beijing to Kashmiri Indians, indicating that China is shedding its traditional neutrality on the Kashmir issue. Indian analysts feel that this new nuanced position on Kashmir could be a dilution of China's past stand of accepting Kashmir as a de-facto part of India; the PRC at the same time appears to have started treating Pakistan Occupied Kashmir including Gilgit-Baltistan region as de-facto and de-jure parts of Pakistan. Questions arise- Is China's stand a quid pro quo for Pakistan's help to Beijing in fighting against Uighur separatism in Xinjiang? Is Beijing developing future options for questioning India's locus standi to negotiate with China on the territory in Ladakh ceded by Pakistan to the PRC.

(k) In addition, what many consider as a pressure tactic against India, Beijing is increasing its strategic presence in other countries in India's neighbourhood with its increased economic aid to the latter as foundation. It has been attempting to build maritime infrastructure in Gwadar (Pakistan) and other South Asia ports, ostensibly in the interest of its energy security. However, becoming visible are Beijing's moves to increase its strategic influence in Indian Ocean littorals including Maldives, Seychelles and Mauritius. China's official media have talked about "waters of China's interests", which may be intended to cover Indian Ocean also. With 'strategic resources' and 'trade routes', also coming, albeit unofficially, under 'core interests' category, China's profile in the Indian Ocean, the vital sea route for its energy import from the Middle East, has become more important. In this context, the real meaning of the bold views, but without official contradiction, being expressed by influential military and strategic experts in China on overseas naval bases to protect the country's energy supply routes need to be carefully analyzed; New Delhi may have reasons to fear over the future military potentials of China's port projects in India's neighbourhood, like Gwadar (Pakistan), Hambantota (Sri Lanka), Sittwe (Myanmar) and Chittagong (Bangladesh), which are ostensibly in the PRC's energy security interests.

(l) Overall, China appears to be showing two faces to India. On one hand, it is of the view that 'Sino-Indian cooperative partnership oriented towards 21st century', has entered into maturity and stability period and in this connection, points to the mechanism set up by the two sides to talk on border, contacts between two militaries, Chinese infrastructure projects in India covering sectors like power, telecom and steel, and cooperation between them in multilateral fora on issues of financial crisis, climate change, multi-polar world and North-South dialogue. On the other, Beijing is adopting a hard line position strategically vis-à-vis India. The net result therefore is the existing trust deficit between the two sides, for which there appears to be no early remedy.

Understanding Chinese Diplomacy[37]

(a) Coming to terms with the rapid rise of China and formulating and implementing a meaningful China policy pre-supposes a proper and balanced understanding of not only Chinese culture, but also its world view through the ages. China lays emphasis on the written word. Delivering the second K Subrahmanyam Memorial Lecture in New Delhi, Ambassador Shyam Sharan pointed out that "much of the Chinese discourse is conducted through historical analogies", some of which are explicit, while some are "artfully coded and the language lends itself easily to innuendo and ambiguity".

(b) Ambassador Shyam Saran stated that the Chinese will demand explicit formulation of their vital interests; however, they will scarcely concede clarity and finality in matters concerning the interests of others. As far Sino-Indian relations are concerned, there is persistent demand and India always agrees to reaffirm, time and again, the recognition of China's

37 http://www.southasiaanalysis.org/node/995

sovereignty over Tibet. But the reverse is not true. In 1962 RK Nehru met Zhou En-Lai and drew his attention to reports that China was leaning towards Pakistani position that Jammu and Kashmir was a disputed territory. RK Nehru recalled an earlier conversation with Zhou En-Lai on the subject when Zhou has said rhetorically, "Has China ever said that it does not accept India's sovereignty over J and K, or something to that effect". In the encounter in 1962, Zhou turned the same formulation on its head, to ask "Has China ever said that India has sovereignty over J and K?" Ambassador Shyam Saran concludes that much of the misunderstanding over India-China relations may be sourced to our failure to "be conversant with Chinese thought processes".

(c) Equally important, it is necessary to keep in mind that China's actions are governed by "contextualizing" the prevailing situation. Significant decisions are taken only after assessing the prevalent social, economic and political factors and their fallout on China. When Deng Xiao Ping consolidated his power and introduced the "four modernizations" for the speedy development of China, he concluded that an essential pre-requisite for attaining that objective was a "peaceful environment". Contentious issues, therefore, were shelved or relegated to the background and China embarked on a policy of winning friends and influencing people. What is more, on crucial occasions, it provided substantial economic assistance to those countries which required such aid. Thus during the economic crisis which engulfed Southeast Asia in the late 1990's and when there was considerable apprehension that China will devalue its currency to provide a boost to its exports, China refrained from doing so; in addition, it entered into long term trade agreements with many countries which enabled them to turn the corner.

(d) Another difference with India should be highlighted. As Ambassador Shyam Saran has pointed out while India considers the use of force as an option of the last resort, China considers the use of force "as an essential and accepted part of promoting national interests and war is not necessarily an unmitigated evil". No wonder China has used force to buttress its territorial claims – against India, Soviet Union, Vietnam and the Philippines. It may be recalled that when China attacked Vietnam in early 1979 to "teach Vietnam a lesson" it compared the attack on Vietnam with Chinese action against India in 1962.

Military Diplomacy[38]

(a) 'Reducing tensions' in the PRC's foreign relations, is being described in the Chinese State-controlled media as a thrust area for the country's current military diplomacy; to this, the official press is at the same time attaching a rider – there should be 'no compromise' on sovereignty related issues. China Radio International (5 September 2012) has been emphatic by assessing that 'under the current circumstances, apart from using diplomatic, economic and trade channels, there is a need for China to expand communication and coordination in the military and security realms'. With this mission in mind, the CMC and PLA officials visited 14 neighbouring nations in 2011 including Vietnam, Myanmar, Nepal, Singapore and the Philippines (Xinhua, 17 January 2012). The recent visits of Deputy Chiefs of General Staff Lt. Gen Cai Yingting to the US, Lt Gen Ma Xiaotian to Vietnam, Myanmar, Malaysia and Singapore and of China's Defence Minister Liang Guanglie to Sri Lanka, India and Laos, fall under the same category. The trend that China's military diplomacy is specially targeting nations in the Asia-Pacific region, where tensions are rising over sea territory disputes, is noticeable. While visiting Sri Lanka (from 29 Aug 12 to 02 Sep 12) stressed (at a speech to officers of Defence Services Command and Staff College) that China's national defence policy is peaceful and that South Asia, comprising five out of fourteen land bordering nations with China, is important in terms of China's foreign policy. The message coming out clear from the Chinese leader was that South Asia is becoming crucial in Beijing's formulation of foreign and security calculations. Similarly during his visit to India the Chinese Defence Minister's emphasized on resuming joint military exercises, apart from discussions on border dispute, 'sensitive' issues of situation in South Asia and Asia-Pacific, the US "Asia Pivot' policy and Afghanistan.

(b) Chinese 'military diplomacy' merits discussion in a wider context.

    (i) To some extent, it has been able to address the needs of non-traditional and maritime security (as evidenced

---

38 http://www.southasiaanalysis.org/node/981

by Beijing's participation in India-China-Japan joint piracy patrols in Gulf of Aden, joint services exercise by five South Asia nations, China's consensus with India on resumption of joint military exercises and the PRC's use of Shanghai Cooperation Organization for counter-terrorism purposes).

(ii) China's ability to persuade Seychelles to provide 'rest' facilities for China's naval vessels may perhaps also be counted as an achievement.

(c) This being so; the failures of China's 'military diplomacy' also need to be taken note of. It has been an ineffective part of the country's core-interests based foreign policy in general, which has so far failed to allay the fears of countries like the Philippines, Vietnam and Japan over, what they call China's military expansion.

'In China's Foreign Policy while the Party still holds the overriding final say. **But the PLA, as a party institution, is inseparably knit into foreign policy as it is not only responsible for the nation's physical security but also safeguarding resource centres abroad and retrieving claimed territories. The party, therefore, has to compromise with the PLA.** In the last three years it was evident that the PLA exercised a substantial say in not only threatening but exercising in small punitive measures against the Philippines, Vietnam and Japan on territorial issues. This is unlikely to diminish soon.'[39,40] 'The Chinese Defence White Papers of 2006, 2008 and 2010 also put forth their views about forward deployment, use of PLA Navy as a strategic force, trans-regional mobility and changes from a defensive mindset to usher in expeditionary capabilities.'[41]

Resource Access Policy[42]

(a) China's search for resource security has come under close international scrutiny in recent years. This is partly because of the economic impact on other countries – most notably changes in the price and availability of some key resources. But there are also important political dimensions to these

39 http://www.southasiaanalysis.org/node/1067

40 http://ramanstrategicanalysis.blogspot.in/2011/01/pla-barometer-of-us-china-relations.html

41 Commander Gurumurthy B 'A Case Study on Strategic and Geopolitical Impact of PLA-Pak Military Strategic Partnership and Security Implications for India' USI Journal Jan-Mar 2012 page 11.

42 http://www2.lse.ac.uk/IDEAS/publications/reports/pdf/SR012/breslin.pdf

debates. For example, supporters of a liberal global order are concerned that China is undermining attempts to pressure authoritarian states to reform.

(b) But at the same time, there is recognition in a number of developing countries that helping China meet its resource requirements is not always cost-free. Poor employment conditions in some Chinese-owned mines, the tendency to use Chinese workers rather than employ locals, the possibility of becoming dependent on Chinese demand, and the spectre of China buying up large tracts of land, have all generated complaints about Chinese activities in a number of states. In copper mines in Zambia – there have been complaints about low pay, poor (and illegal) work conditions and a lack of interest from Chinese managers when complaints are made. There has also been hostility towards the Zambian government for not insisting that the law is adhered to. Even when Chinese managers shot striking workers, prosecutions conspicuously failed to follow, with the fact that copper mining is the major source of exports and government income in Zambia thought to be no mere coincidence.

(c) While these issues point to problems, the increase in Chinese demand has been a positive force for many.

  (i) In a number of African states, trade relationships with China have been the catalyst for rapid economic growth over the last decade. As well as either directly buying locally produced resources, and/or investing in and buying mines, oil fields and land, China has also become a major source of development aid for many African states. This includes loans that help develop national infrastructures (some of which of course enables the efficient export of goods and resources), and loans from the China Development Bank that typically entail partial repayment through resources.

  (ii) As China tried to spend its way through the global economic crisis in 2009, increased demand for resources helped a number of Latin American countries offset the downturn in demand from the USA and Europe and rebound relatively quickly.

  (iii) Australian mining sectors have boomed on the back of increased Chinese demand, while China has now become the biggest export market for agricultural produce from the USA.

(d)   While other nations too, work towards their resource security the focus on China emerges from a feeling that Chinese actors aren't playing fairly and that China is not conforming to the interests of major Western powers. For example, by talking to and trading with people that are shunned by the West, China is able to take economic advantage of their political isolation. At the same time, by providing an alternative to dealing and trading with Western states and/or the international financial institutions, China is seen to weaken attempts to pressure more authoritarian states to liberalise and reform, and to accept liberal political and economic norms. This is reinforced by China's declared opposition to intervening in the domestic politics of sovereign nation states, and a willingness to oppose proposed interventions at the United Nations. Thus, for example, China's resource requirements are seen as being one reason behind the longevity of the Chavez regime in Venezuela, and a key obstacle to pressuring Iran to change its nuclear policy.

(e)   The idea, then, is that there is a grand strategy orchestrated by the Chinese state and enacted by giant State Owned Enterprises to corner markets and create monopolies that will be to the detriment of other global actors, and possibly even to the global economy as a whole.

(f)   'Though China's current borders encompass Manchuria, Inner Mongolia, East Turkestan and Tibet – all the surrounding plateaus and grasslands, that is – the very economic and diplomatic strategies of China's rulers today demonstrate an idea of China that reaches beyond the territorial extent of even the China of the eighteenth-century Hugh Qing, China, a demographic behemoth with the world's most energetic economy for the past three decades, is, unlike Russia, extending its territorial influence more through commerce than coercion.'[43]

Role of Chinese Companies in Foreign Policy[44]

(a)   The Chinese firms broadly are divided into three categories: the China International Investment Corps (CIC); the State

---

43   Kaplan Robert 'The Revenge of Geography' page 3148 Kindle Edition.

44   http://eprints.lse.ac.uk/44205/1/__Libfile_repository_Content_LSE%20IDEAS_Special%20 Reports_SR012%20China%27s%20Geoeconomic%20Strategy_China%27s%20Geoeconom- ic%20Strategy%20_Firms%20with%20Chinese%20Characteristics%20%28LSE%20RO%29.pdf

Owned Enterprises (SOEs); and large privately-owned companies. The most distinctive characteristic of all three types of companies are their close associations with the Chinese government, either in terms of funding or in terms of the strategic direction of their business activities.

(b) **The China International Investment Corps.**

(i) Set up in 2007, the China International Investment Corps is China's own sovereign wealth fund. As an investment institution it was tasked with generating higher returns on China's foreign reserves than those offered by the US Treasury. The CIC's formidable size, with a $200 billion seed fund and later $400 billion under its management, has attracted unprecedented attention around the world, and helped stimulate debate about the international role of SWFs more generally

(ii) The CIC has been particularly active in Europe and Africa, to the extent that it has become a representative of the Chinese government in conducting its economic statecraft. CIC has concentrated on industries such as civil aviation, civil nuclear technology, bio-tech, infrastructure and oil and gas, with a focus on high-technology portfolios in Europe and energy portfolios in Africa.

(iii) Its opaque management structure and its direct links with the State Council have caused great discomfort and at times outright hostility in hosting countries. The head of the CIC, and most of its senior management, are directly appointed and assessed by the Chinese Communist Party's Department of Organisation, and its investments are the subject of significant public political scrutiny.

(c) **The State Owned Enterprises.**

(i) The second category of the Chinese firms is the State Owned Enterprises (SOEs), which are mainly located in the energy, utilities, telecommunications, chemical, transportation and construction sectors. The firms constitute the main corporate tax-payers in China, and their activities and performance are supervised by the PRC State Owned Assets Supervision and Administration Commission (SASAC), which is currently responsible for 125 large SOEs. Like the CIC, the Chairmen of large SOEs are appointed and assessed by the CCP Department of

Organisation. They are also party secretaries of their respective companies, and their overall management performance is evaluated by SASAC and Department of Organisation. Most subsidiaries of large SOEs are publicly listed, on either or both of the Hong Kong and Shanghai stock exchanges depending on different types of stocks.

(ii) Unlike Western multinational companies, their non state shareholders play little role in determining their corporate strategies and overseas investments plans. Instead, their party secretaries usually possess final decision-making power to initiate corporate strategies. Given their direct ties to the government, it is difficult to judge whether SOEs' overseas investments plans are political decisions or based purely on commercial merit. Their close links with the state has become a double-edged sword for Chinese SOEs, providing support for overseas expansion but also hindering growth and profit-making in foreign markets, where their direct links with Beijing have often provoked suspicions and hostility.

(d) **Large Privately Owned Companies.** The final category of Chinese firms is the large privately owned companies. Many of these are the most well-known Chinese companies worldwide, including brands such as Huawei, Lenovo and Geely. Unlike the SOEs, they are private companies with powerful individual shareholders who decide corporate strategies. They are independently run but are supervised by Ministry of Commerce, and despite their operational independence, some of their senior management previously served in governmental institutions or the PLA. Doubts about the authenticity of their independence was emphasised by the deep suspicions in Western media (and among their potential clients) that marked a series of large scale overseas acquisitions were advertised yet necessarily supported by Beijing, which were seen as successes of Chinese companies 'Going Global'. This has hindered their business operations overseas, especially in OECD countries.

(e) **Assessment.**

(i) China's foreign economic policies have largely been directed to serve domestic economic and developmental interests. As Chinese growth has developed, those interests have become focused around the need for internal and external rebalancing of the economy. Over the past decade, the Chinese economy has been stimulated largely by ever-growing volumes of exports and major infrastructure investments.

(ii) Alongside this economic adventurism in the developed world, soaring energy demand has led Chinese firms to explore opportunities in resource-rich but politically unstable areas, particularly for new sources of oil and gas, as documented elsewhere in this report.

(iii) However, given the links on most of these companies with the government establishment will always raise a suspicion of their intentions and independence of their commercial decisions.

'The Chinese have more and more raw material equities to protect in sub-Saharan Africa at the Indian Ocean's opposite end: oil markets in Sudan, Angola and Nigeria; iron ore mines in Zambia and Gabon; and copper and cobalt mines in the Democratic Republic of Congo, all to be connected by Chinese-built roads and railways, in turn linked to Atlantic and Indian Ocean ports.'[45,46]

Economic War

(a) 'Even as China envelops Taiwan militarily, it does so economically and socially. Taiwan does 30 percent of its trade with China, with 40 percent of its exports going to the mainland. There are 270 commercial flights per week between Taiwan and the mainland. Two-thirds of Taiwanese companies, some ten thousand, have made investments in China in the last five years. There are direct postal links and common crime fighting, with half a million mainland tourists coming to the island annually, and 750,000 Taiwanese residing in China for half the year. In all there are five million cross-straits visits each year. There will be less and less of a need for an invasion when subtle economic warfare will achieve the same result. Thus, we have seen the demise of the Taiwan secessionist movement.'[47,48]

---

45 Kaplan Robert 'The Revenge of Geography' page 3562 Kindle Edition.

46 French Howard W 'The Next Empire' The Atlantic May 2010.

47 Kaplan Robert 'The Revenge of Geography' page 3504 Kindle Edition.

48 Ross, 'The Chinese Power and the Implications for the Regional Security Order'.

(b) In 2010 – after a collision between a Chinese fishing boat and two Japanese coast guard vessels in waters off the disputed Senkaku islands (called Diao Yu by the Chinese, now administered by Japan) – China[49]: -

    (i) Cancelled the scheduled visit to Japan by its senior parliamentarian, postponed bilateral talks over natural gas exploration in East China Sea, halted exports of rare earth metals essential for development of high technology goods in Japan (later denied by the Chinese Commerce Ministry), suspended plans to increase flights to each other nation and stopped a Chinese government-sponsored visit of 1000 Japanese to the Shanghai World Expo. (It has been estimated by some commentators that the ensuing economic war has set Japan behind by a few years – some even claim up to 20 years)[50].

    (ii) In apparent retaliation to Japanese detentions of Chinese crew, China's police arrested four employees of the Japanese firm, Fujita Corporation, in Shijiazhuang, Hebei province on charges of their entering a military zone without authorization.

    (iii) Massive 'anti-Japanese demonstrations were engineered by the authorities. This was for a limited purpose of warning Japan. The Japanese embassy in Beijing, consulates in other parts of the country, Japanese assets and even manufacturing factories have been (were) attacked by these nationalist demonstrators. Some of them even demanded that China should attack Japan militarily.'[51]

(c) 'In 2012, a year when tensions ran high due to Japan's decision regarding what it called the "purchase" of some of the disputed Senkaku / Diaoyu islands from a private Japanese citizen, anti-Japanese protests flared in China, as did unofficial boycotts of Japanese goods. Total trade between China and Japan fell 3.9 percent year on year, the first drop since the major financial crisis of 2009, with exports falling more than 10 percent. Japanese foreign direct investment, although rising slightly

49 http://www.c3sindia.org/eastasia/1722 also see http://www.eurasiareview.com/01102012-strategic-lessons-from-china-japan-stand-off-analysis/

50 http://www.eurasiareview.com/01102012-strategic-lessons-from-china-japan-stand-off-analysis/

51 http://www.southasiaanalysis.org/node/1001

for the year, saw a major falloff in the summer when tensions between the two countries ran high. Japanese firms in fact already are beginning to show an interest is shifting some of their manufacturing bases out of China even without the added incentive of anti-Japanese sentiment-driven protests and boycotts. In 2012, the gap between China and the United States as the top destination for Japanese exports narrowed further to just 0.6 percent.[52]

Military and Maritime Strategy

Historically, China has been a coastal and land focused power. 'The fundamental patterns and characteristics of the geo-strategies of coastal nations are:-

(a) Having a contiguous border with the vast ocean such that geo-strategy must take both land and sea into account.

(b) Having some space on land in which to operate, as well as maritime barriers and transport corridors that can be utilized.

(c) When engaged in war with maritime powers, coastal nations have been able to bring their strength to bear on land and limit the opportunities of their adversaries to occupy territory.

(d) When engaged in war with neighbouring land powers, they have had to concentrate forces on their land flanks, especially to avoid being attacked from the front and rear on land and sea and in this manner fall into the trap of being encircled by an alliance of sea and land powers.

(e) With respect to military structure, such powers have emphasized a balanced mix of land and sea forces and having a geo-strategy that comports with this balance.'[53]

Some believe that 'the most dangerous states in the international system are continental powers with large armies.'[54] However, China may not fully fit the bill for this. It's a rising land power and indeed PLA is perhaps one of the largest in the world. But, 'with the exception of

52 http://www.stratfor.com/weekly/china-tests-japanese-and-us-patience?utm_source=freelist-f&utm_medium=email&utm_campaign=20130226&utm_term=gweekly&utm_content=read more&elq=3232f09271e74f758b80de4a322b60fb

53 http://www.thefreelibrary.com/Maritime+geostrategy+and+the+development+of+the+Chin ese+navy+in+the...-a0156364589

54 Mearsheimer John J. 'The Tragedy of Great Power Politics', New York W.W. Norton 2001, page 135.

the Indian Sub Continent and the Korean Peninsula, China is merely filling vacuums more than it is ramming up against competing states. Moreover, as the events of 2008 and 2009 showed the PLA ground force will not have an expeditionary capability for years to come. In those years, the PLA had to respond to an earthquake emergency in Sichuan, to ethnic unrest in Tibet and Xinjiang, and to the security challenge of the Olympics in Beijing. What these "trans-regional mobility exercises" as the Chinese call them, indicated was an ability by the PLA to move troops from one end of continental China to another, but not an ability to move supplies and heavy equipment at the rate required.'[55]

'Of course, one might well argue that borders with so many troubled regions will constraint Chinese power, and thus geography is a hindrance to Chinese ambitions. China is virtually surrounded, in other words. But given China's economic and demographic expansion in recent decades, and its reasonable prospects of continued, albeit reduced, economic growth – with serious bumps mind you – into the foreseeable future, China's many land borders can also work as a force multiplier: for it is China encroaching on these less dynamic and less populated areas, not the way around. Some explain that the presence of failed and semi-failed states on China's borders – namely Afghanistan and Pakistan – is a danger to Beijing. They are in the remotest terrain at exceedingly high elevations. Few live there. Pakistan could completely unravel and it would be barely be noticed on the Chinese side of the border. China's borders are not the problem: the problem is Chinese society, which, as it becomes more prosperous, and as China's economic growth rate slows, raises the spectre of political upheaval of some sort. And serious upheaval could make China suddenly vulnerable on its ethnic peripheries.'[56]

China is using all forms of its national power – political, diplomatic, economic, commercial, military and demographic – to expand virtually beyond its legal land and sea borders in order to encompass the borders of imperial China at its historical high points.'[57] 'Beijing has the aim of creating a disposition so favourable to PRC (People's Republic of China) that it will not actually have to use force to secure its interests.'[58]

---

55 Kaplan Robert 'The Revenge of Geography' page 3192 Kindle Edition.

56 Ibid page 3308 Kindle Edition.

57 Ibid page 3542 Kindle Edition.

58 Newmyer Jacqueline 'Oil, Arms and Influence: The Indirect Strategy Behind Chinese Military Modernisation' Orbis Philadelphia, Spring 009.

'Chinese diplomats have been busy in recent years settling remaining border disputes with the Central Asian republics and with its other neighbours (India being a striking exception).'[59] Most of these accords have not been on China's terms and they therefore do suggest a strong strategic direction. China has already signed military agreements with Russia, Kazakhstan, Kyrgyzstan and Tajikistan. 'The stabilisation of China's land borders maybe one of the most important geopolitical changes in Asia in the last few decades.'[60] The 'Chinese way is characterised to go for half boils which reaps imponderable gains. It does concede to the other side but only when the long term gains and / or losses are clearly in sight. The latest in the row are the cases of Russia and Vietnam. There are then, big power – small power considerations while giving concessions to the other side. A case in point is the border consideration with the Russian Federation along the Heilongjiang River, where China gave out half of the Heixiazi Island while it could have held the full in terms of agreed thalweg principle. In contrast, China entered into a settlement to demarcate 1350 km long border with Vietnam only after the latter conceded China's right to use and operate railways on 300 meters stretch on its soil at the junction of Guangxi Zhuang Autonomous Region (GZAR) of China and Lang Son province of Vietnam, occupied by China in 1979 war. Concessionary approach, applied in the case of Myanmar (October 01, 1961), Nepal (October 05, 1961), Mongolia (December 26, 1962) and Pakistan (March 2, 1963) carried enormous hidden costs to their detriment.'[61] However, the significance of this is that China for the first time in history is secure on its land borders.[62] Hence, building a great Navy and including the Pacific and maybe the Indian Ocean is the next logical step for China.

'Two factors contributed to China's experiments with naval development: a shift in warfare from northern to southern China and periods of relative national stability. During the Song dynasty (960-1279), the counterpart to the horse armies of the northern plains was

59 Fravel M Taylor, 'Regime Insecurity and International Co-operation: Explaining China's Compromises in Territorial Disputes' International Security, Fall 2005.

60 Grygiel, 'Great Powers and Geopolitical Change' page 170.

61 Dr Pandey Sheo Nandan and Professor Kusum Hem, 'Sino-Indian Border Talks and the Shifting Chinese Stance', USI Journal Jan-Mar 2012 page 35.

62 As Kaplan Robert in 'The Revenge of Geography' page 3401 Kindle Edition points out 'The Great Wall of China was built in the third century B.C. ostensibly to keep out Turkic invaders. It was the Mongol invasion from the North that led to the end of the Ming forays in the Indian Ocean in the fifteenth century'.

a large inland naval force in the riverine and marshy south. The shift to river navies also spread to the coast, and the Song rulers encouraged coastal navigation and maritime trade by the Chinese, replacing the foreign traders along the coast. While still predominately inward-looking during the Yuan dynasty (1271-1368) under the Mongols, China carried out at least two major naval expeditions in the late 13th century -- against Japan and Java -- both of which ultimately proved unsuccessful. Their failure contributed to China's decision to again turn away from the sea. The final major maritime adventure occurred in the early Ming dynasty (1368-1644), when Chinese Muslim explorer Zheng He undertook his famous seven voyages, reaching as far as Africa but failing to use this opportunity to permanently establish Chinese power abroad. Zheng He's treasure fleet was scuttled as the Ming saw rising problems at home, including piracy off the coast, and China once again looked inward. At about the same time that Magellan started his global expedition in the early 1500s, the Chinese resumed their isolationist policy, limiting trade and communication with the outside and ending most consideration of maritime adventure. China's naval focus shifted to coastal defence rather than power projection. The arrival of European gunboats in the 19th century thoroughly shook the conventional maritime logic of Chinese authorities, and only belatedly did they undertake a naval program based on Western technology.[63] Both the factors – shift from North to South and period of relative national stability – are present in today's China.

China's coastline is quite extensive, but its land-sea orientation was powerfully influenced by the special circumstances of its neighbours; for a time, the sea was viewed as a solid barrier and so was neglected. In modern times, the sea became a springboard for foreign invaders. While the great powers were smashing in China's maritime gate, China simultaneously confronted the expansionist Czarist Russia and dared not let down its guard on its land flank. In modern times China has attempted to settle its border disputes with most of its land neighbours – India being a notable exception. At the same time it has sought to assure its maritime neighbours of China's peaceful rise – albeit with India and its maritime neighbours China has sought to shelf the disputes without compromising on its claims. However, events in the last few years have raised some suspicions that the policy of shelving disputes for some other generation was an alibi to gain military strength.

---

63 http://www.stratfor.com/weekly/paradox-chinas-naval-strategy

Nine Dash Line

The nine dash line forms the basis of Chinese maritime claims and hence needs to be understood in perspective. 'The nine-dash line was based on an earlier territorial claim known as the eleven-dash line, drawn up in 1947 by the then-ruling Kuomintang government without much strategic consideration since the regime was busy dealing with the aftermath of the Japanese occupation of China and the ongoing civil war with the Communists. After the end of the Japanese occupation, the Kuomintang government sent naval officers and survey teams through the South China Sea to map the various islands and islets. The Internal Affairs Ministry published a map with an eleven-dash line enclosing most of the South China Sea far from China's shores. This map, despite its lack of specific coordinates, became the foundation of China's modern claims, and following the 1949 founding of the People's Republic of China, the map was adopted by the new government in Beijing. In 1953, perhaps as a way to mitigate conflict with neighbouring Vietnam, the current nine-dash line emerged when Beijing eliminated two of the dashes. The new Chinese map was met with little resistance or complaint by neighbouring countries, many of which were then focused on their own national independence movements. Beijing interpreted this silence as acquiescence by the neighbours and the international community, and then stayed largely quiet on the issue to avoid drawing challenges. Beijing has shied away from officially claiming the line itself as an inviolable border, and it is not internationally recognized, though China regards the nine-dash line as the historic basis for its maritime claims.'[64]

'The complications from the nine-dash line, the status of domestic Chinese developments and the shifting international system have all contributed to shape China's evolving maritime strategy. Under former leader Mao Zedong, China was internally focused and constrained by a weak navy. China's maritime claims were left vague, Beijing did not aggressively seek to assert its rights and the independence struggles of neighbouring countries largely spared China from taking a stronger maritime stance. China's naval development remained defensive, focused on protecting its shores from invasion. Deng Xiaoping, in concert with his domestic economic reforms in the late 1970s and early 1980s, sought the more pragmatic joint economic development of the East and South China seas, putting aside claims of territorial sovereignty for another time. China's

---

64 http://www.stratfor.com/weekly/paradox-chinas-naval-strategy

military expenditures continued to focus on land forces (and missile forces), with the navy relegated to a largely defensive role operating only in Chinese coastal waters. To a great degree, Deng's policies remained in place through the next two decades. There were sporadic maritime flare-ups in the South China Sea, but in general, the strategy of avoiding outright confrontation remained a core principle at sea. China's navy was in no position to challenge the dominant role of the U.S. Navy or to take any assertive action against its neighbours, especially since Beijing sought to increase its regional influence through economic and political means rather than through military force. But joint development proposals for the South China Sea have largely failed. China's expanded economic strength, coupled with a concomitant rise in its military spending -- and more recently its focus on naval development -- has raised suspicions and concerns among neighbouring countries, with many calling on the United States to take a more active role in the region to counterbalance China's rise.'[65]

'China faces a concentration of strategic power in the Asia-Pacific region on its maritime flank. The geostrategic tendency is dangerously uncertain. Since this maritime strategic region and, more broadly, the strategic region of the periphery of the Eurasian landmass constitute points of contention, they are also important arenas for global great-power competition. From a geostrategic perspective, China's heartland faces the sea, the benefits of economic development are increasingly dependent on the sea, and security threats come from the sea.'[66]

In General Douglas MacArthur's words, Taiwan is 'an unsinkable aircraft carrier that dominates the centre point of China's convex seaboard, from which an outside power like the United States can radiate power along China's coastal periphery.'[67] 'Beneath Taiwan on the map looms the South China Sea, framed by the demographic cockpit of mainland South East Asia, the Philippines and Indonesia, with Australia further afield. A third of all seaborne commercial goods worldwide and half of all the energy requirements for North East Asia pass through here. As the gateway to the Indian Ocean – the worlds hydrocarbon interstate, where China is involved in several port development projects – the South China Sea must in some future

---

65 http://www.stratfor.com/weekly/paradox-chinas-naval-strategy

66 http://www.thefreelibrary.com/Maritime+geostrategy+and+the+development+of+the+Chinese+navy+in+the...-a0156364589

67 See. Holmes and Yoshihara, 'Command of the Sea with Chinese Characteristics

morrow be virtually dominated by the Chinese Navy'.[68] Hence, 'China is intent on access denial in its coastal seas'.[69]

'China depends on the high seas to survive. Geographically the configuration of the South China Sea and the East China Sea render China relatively easy to blockade. Beijing's single greatest strategic concern is that the United States would impose a blockade on China, not by positioning its Fleet inside the two island barriers but outside them. From there, the United States could compel China to send its naval forces far away from the mainland to force an opening -- and encounter US warships -- and still be able to close off China's exits. That China does not have a navy capable of challenging the United States compounds the problem. China is still in the process of completing its first aircraft carrier; indeed, its navy is insufficient in size and quality to challenge the United States. But naval hardware is not China's greatest challenge. The United States commissioned its first aircraft carrier in 1922 and has been refining both carrier aviation and battle group tactics ever since. Developing admirals and staffs capable of commanding carrier battle groups takes generations. Since the Chinese have never had a carrier battle group in the first place, they have never had an admiral commanding a carrier battle group. China understands this problem and has chosen a different strategy to deter a U.S. naval blockade. This includes: -

(a) Anti-ship missiles capable of engaging and perhaps penetrating US carrier defensive systems, along with a substantial submarine presence. While China has a robust land-based missile system, (a land-based missile system is inherently vulnerable to strikes by cruise missiles, aircraft, unmanned aerial vehicles currently in development and other types of attack), China's ability to fight a sustained battle is limited. Moreover, a missile strategy works only with an effective reconnaissance capability. You can't destroy a ship if you don't know where it is.

(b) This in turn necessitates space-based systems able to identify U.S. ships and a tightly integrated fire-control system. That raises the question of whether the United States has an anti-satellite capability. We would assume that it does, and if the United States used it, it would leave China blind.

---

68 Kaplan Robert 'The Revenge of Geography' page 3522 Kindle Edition.

69 Ibid page 3542 Kindle Edition.

(c) China is further supplementing this strategy by acquiring port access in countries in the Indian Ocean and outside the South China Sea box. Beijing has plans to build ports in Myanmar, which is flirting with ending its international isolation, and Pakistan. Beijing already has financed and developed port access to Gwadar in Pakistan, Colombo and Hambantota in Sri Lanka, Chittagong in Bangladesh, and it has hopes for a deepwater port at Sittwe, Myanmar. In order for this strategy to work, China needs transportation infrastructure linking China to the ports. This means extensive rail and road systems. The difficulty of building this in Myanmar, for example, should not be underestimated.

(d) But more important, China needs to maintain political relationships that will allow it to access the ports. Pakistan and Myanmar,[70] for example, have a degree of instability, and China cannot assume that cooperative governments will always be in place in such countries. In Myanmar's case,[71,72] recent political openings could result in Naypyidaw's falling out of China's sphere of influence. Building a port and roads and finding that a coup or an election has created an anti-Chinese government is a possibility. Given that this is one of China's fundamental strategic interests, Beijing cannot simply assume that building a port will give it unrestricted access to the port. Add to this that roads and rail lines are easily sabotaged by guerrilla forces or destroyed by air or missile attacks.

(e) In order for the ports on the Indian Ocean to prove useful, Beijing must be confident in its ability to control the political situation in the host country for a long time. That

---

70 The issue is best reflected by the Chinese concerns for the spreading violence in the Rakhine State of Myanmar. In this regard see http://www.c3sindia.org/southeastasia/3140.

71 http://www.kdng.org/news/34-news/295-myanmar-china-relations-post-myitsone-suspen-sion--analysis.html,
http://www.eurasiareview.com/28012013-myanmar-china-relations-post-myitsone-suspen-sion-analysis/ and
http://strategicstudyindia.blogspot.in/2013/01/myanmar-china-relations-post-myitsone.html

72 The Chinese pursuit of minerals in Maynmar is also being resisted by the local population. See http://www.canberratimes.com.au/world/burmas-suu-kyi-heckled-over-copper-mine-20130315-2g4kr.html and http://www.watoday.com.au/world/burmas-suu-kyi-heckled-over-copper-mine-20130315-2g4kr.html

sort of extended control can only be guaranteed by having overwhelming power available to force access to the ports and the transportation system.'[73]

(f)   These states, hence are developing into the new buffer states for China; control over these would be critical for China in the future.

'China is developing asymmetric and anti-access niche capabilities, designed to deny US Navy easy entry to the East China Sea and other coastal waters. Analysts are divided over the significance of this. Robert S Ross of Boston college believes that until China develops situational awareness capability and can degrade US counter surveillance technologies, it possess only a limited credible access-denial operations. Andrew F Krepinevich of the Centre for Strategic and Budgetary Assessments believes that whatever technical difficulties China may momentarily be encountering, it is on the way to Finlandising East Asia. Thus, while it has modernised its destroyer fleet, and has plans for an aircraft carrier or two, China is not buying naval platforms across the board. Rather, China has been building four new classes of nuclear and conventional powered attack and ballistic missile submarines.'[74]

'China could field a submarine force larger than the US Navy's within the foreseeable future. The Chinese Navy plans to use over-the-horizon radars, satellites, seabed sonar networks and cyber warfare in the service of the anti-ship ballistic missiles with manoeuvrable re-entry vehicles, which along with its burgeoning submarine fleet, will be part of its effort to rebuff US Naval access to large portions of the Western Pacific. This is not to mention China's improving mine warfare capability, the acquisition of Russian Su-27 and Su-30 fourth generation jet fighters, and 1500 Russian surface to air missiles deployed along China's coast. Moreover, the Chinese are putting their fibre-optic systems underground and moving defence capabilities deep into Western China, out of naval missile range – all the while developing an offensive strategy designed to be capable of striking that supreme icon of American wealth and power – the aircraft carrier.'[75] 'China likely has no intention of ever attacking a US aircraft carrier.

---

73   http://www.stratfor.com/weekly/state-world-assessing-chinas-strategy

74   Kaplan Robert 'The Revenge of Geography' page 3457 Kindle Edition.

75   Ibid page 3467 Kindle Edition.

China is not remotely capable of directly challenging the US militarily. The aim here is dissuasion: to amass so much offensive and defensive capability along its seaboard that the US Navy will in the future think twice and three times about getting between the first Island Chain and the Chinese coast. That, of course, is the *essence of power: to affect your adversary's behaviour'*.[76]

---

76   Ibid page 3476 Kindle Edition.

Chapter 7

CHINA'S INTERNATIONAL BEHAVIOUR

Pattern of Chinese Behaviour.[1] A study of patterns of China's assertiveness with regard to the various island disputes,[2] reveals that in its application, there are five dimensions – administrative, military, economic, diplomatic and policy support. The Chinese official media call them as "combination punches" (People's Daily, 13 August 2012).

(a) **Administrative.**

    (i) What is striking is that China's assertiveness is assuming certain new forms. The PRC's major thrust has so far been on gathering historical evidences to strengthen its territorial claims. It is now using it as an additional mean – taking administrative measures intended to gain jurisdiction over the claimed regions. Notable are legal steps now being taken by China to " select and protect base points" of islands under dispute under the 'China Islands Protection Law', passed by the China State Oceanic Administration (Xinhua, 13 September 2012).

       ▶ Sansha city in Yongxiung island of Hainan province is one such base point selected. The administrative status of Sansha city, so far ranking as a County, was upgraded to the level of a Prefecture on 24 July 2012; the responsibilities assigned by the PRC Ministry of Civil Affairs to the

---

1 http://www.southasiaanalysis.org/node/987

2   They involve four island chains, all with resource-rich surroundings. Three of them, contested by China and several ASEAN nations, are in South China Sea – Paracel (now under China's control), Spratlys (reefs and shoals with China) and Macclesfield Bank (China-the Philippines stand off point), called respectively by Beijing as Xisha, Nansha and Zhongsha. The fourth, claimed by China and Japan, is in the East China Sea - the Senkakus islands as Japan calls them (now under Tokyo's control), Diaoyu as the PRC calls it.

status-updated Sansha city are " further strengthening of China's administration and development" of the three South China sea island groups – Xisha, Nansha and Zhongsha.[3]

▸ In such situation, the dispatch by authorities of Chinese trawlers and escort vessels to the disputed islands in South China Sea in June-July 2012 appears to have been a step to justify that action on legal grounds.

▸ Also not to be missed is the establishment of a military garrison in Sansha city on 26 July 2012, with the stated charter of 'military mobilisation'; to prevent any misgiving abroad naturally arising out of this measure, Beijing is giving adequate media publicity to its defence that the Sansha city garrison is not for 'combat' purposes, which are being handled by the Xisha (Paracels) garrison (China Daily, 27 July 2012).

(ii) The Sansha city example, when subjected to a closer scrutiny, may have relevance to studies on future trends in China's land border dispute with India. Chinese official literature[4] has described Tawang in India's Arunachal Pradesh as "the birth place of the Sixth Dalai Lama belonging to Cuona county of Shannan prefecture in the Tibet Autonomous Region". Also, in some unofficial media coverage in the PRC, the Chinese occupied Aksai Chin is being termed as an area under "Hotan County of Hotan Prefecture" in Western China. In such context, following questions may be of interest to India: -

▸ Whether China can assert its claims over Tawang and Aksai Chin through issuing Sansha-type notifications formally bringing the two areas under the administrative controls of Shannan and Hotan Prefectures respectively ?

▸ Whether such notifications have already been issued by China?

▸ Will China chose to provoke India by taking such

---

3   Analysts also believe that the military garrison on Sansha on the Yongxing Island would be a virtual Diego Garcia for China in the South China Seas see http://idsa.in/idsacomments/Yongx-ingIslandChinasDiegoGarciaintheSouthChinaSea_ssparmar_070812

4   http// eng.tibet.cn/2010/home/news/201204/t2012 dated 15 April 2012

measures?

> Does India have adequate mechanisms to monitor such notifications if issued?

(iii) China's assertiveness with respect to East China Sea island issue is manifesting in a form, not seen before- domestic channels of the PRC's National TV have begun to broadcast from end August 2012 weather reports for Senkakus, as a firm message to the Japanese side that Senkakus is China's internal part. How about the possibility of Tibet domestic TV broadcasting weather reports on 'Southern Tibet', i.e. Arunachal Pradesh? Or, is this already being done? These points should not be missed by India.

(iv) China has opened Xisha islands (Paracel) under its control for tourism – marking another indirect way of asserting territorial sovereignty. Will China object to India's launching of tourism projects in Arunachal? New Delhi should be alive to any indication to this effect, as Beijing even contested Indian PM's official visit to Arunachal.

(v) The PRC is apparently encouraging its nationals to go to Senkakus, in attempt to signal its intention to assert its territorial rights over that island. 'Grass roots' activists from Hongkong have also gone to Senkakus. Tokyo, a claimant to Senkakus, has arrested 14 Chinese nationals on charges of intrusions. These developments may be relevant to India. There have been Chinese troop intrusions into Indian border. It is however not clear whether Chinese civilians were found entering Indian boundaries. In any case, New Delhi may have to be careful over China using intrusions as a mean to assert its claims.

(b) **Military.**

(i) What can be seen without difficulty is Beijing's tendency of applying strategic pressure on contesting nations under a belief that the same may indirectly strengthen its negotiating position on sea and land border disputes with the latter.

> There were island landing drills by Chinese troops around Huangyan island (Scalborough Shoal, under dispute with the Philippines).

> Combat-ready Chinese patrols were in operation in

the disputed areas in South China Sea in June 2012.

- ▶ A Chinese Naval exercise was held in the Yellow sea.

- ▶ China's Marine Corps has conducted amphibious combat training operations.

- ▶ A sixth Type 052C Luyang-class destroyer was added so as to augment naval capabilities for enforcing claims over South and East China Seas.

- ▶ New civilian ships capable of carrying out maritime transportation of military troops are being launched by the Chinese Navy.

(ii) Through increasing its military profile across the Indian border, Beijing seems to be intent on applying strategic pressure on New Delhi also, with a view to gaining a position of strength during border negotiations with India. Military infrastructure building in Tibet is in full swing, about which details are already known. Notable are the reported deployment of missiles and the trend to conduct integrated ground-air operations in Tibet. Such operations with live ammunition were organised 'over Himalayas' by a mountain infantry brigade under Tibet Military Command on 13 August 2012. Use of Air Force in Tibet has an external dimension; Beijing does not need Air Force to suppress civilian unrest in Tibet; definitely, it has an external target – India. New Delhi is reacting to this situation by taking steps to develop its own border infrastructure. Notwithstanding such signs of India-China strategic competition, their common border is now quiet and as a result of resumption of high-level military exchanges between the two sides, the military trust-deficit between them seems to have subsided. However, it would be in India's interests to develop a long term view of Chinese strategic pressures.

(c) **Economic.** Looking at the economic dimension, China's assertiveness can be seen in relation to the competition that has erupted between contesting powers in South and East China Seas over the rights to exploit the offshore oil and gas deposits. The Chinese decision to open nine offshore areas in South China Sea for commercial joint exploration and similar actions by Vietnam, are exacerbating the crisis in the region. This factor needs to be given a careful consideration by India which has signed an agreement with Vietnam on oil exploration in areas being contested by China and Vietnam in South China Sea. Overall, New Delhi's challenge will be on how to strengthen its position globally on exploration of off-shore energy conducive to its development, without getting sucked into any regional territorial dispute.

(d) **Diplomatic**. China is taking diplomatic initiatives to improve relations with ASEAN nations and Japan with the objective of reducing the levels of present sea territory tensions in the region. "Shelving the disputes and working for common development", is China's formula being applied in this regard. Beijing's charm offensive, is however, not leading to desired results. The diplomatic visits of Chinese Foreign Minister Yang Jiechi to Indonesia, Brunei and Malaysia in August 2012 provided an opportunity for the PRC to explain its position on the maritime issues in East Asia – that need to be solved bilaterally between the concerned nations. The US, also an Asia-Pacific player, on the other hand, wants a multilateral solution. The ASEAN opinion on code of conduct in South China Sea is also divided. Under the circumstances, the Chinese diplomacy seems to be operating with a limited aim-reducing tensions, leaving solutions to a later date. China's diplomatic initiatives in the case of India also, need to be seen from this angle. The Indian External Affairs Minister has paid a visit to China in February 2012, followed by that the PRC Defence Minister to India in September that year. The good atmosphere notwithstanding, it looks certain that a long way awaits the two nations in solving strategic issues dividing them, like the border problem. A firm indicator one sees in the current Chinese flexing of military muscles on South and East China Seas is that Beijing's basic 'uncompromising' attitude towards all sovereignty-related issues, including the India-China boundary question, will remain forever.

(e) **Policy Support.** It cannot be denied that Beijing's territorial assertiveness is a result of policy formulations made at high levels. Statements being made at leadership levels reflect the agreed policies.

(i) One such example relates to expressions of China's unambiguous commitment to the need for not giving any 'concession' on issues concerning its sovereignty and territorial integrity. Premier Wen Jiabao has himself declared it (10 September 2012). China's Defence Minister Liang Guanglie has stated in an interview (December 2010) that "in the coming five years, China's military will push forward preparations in every strategic direction".

▶ The editorials in the PRC's official press including in the PLA Daily, are also making repeated stress on the need for the country's diplomacy to maintain 'uncompromising' territorial positions.

▶ China's last Defence White Paper has found 'local conflicts' possible. It may be wrong to take such statements as only rhetoric; on the contrary, they seem to reflect a leadership consensus on directions of Beijing's foreign policy.

(ii) In other such examples, stamping of Chinese map on passports that show India's Arunachal Pradesh and disputed Aksai Chin as Chinese territories; including South China Sea with the nine dashed lines to claim Chinese sovereignty; including Taiwan as China's territory, which is not unusual; a major omission in this map was non-inclusion of the Diaoyu/Senkaku island.[5]

(iii) Another instance of the policy was the law enacted by China's Hainan province in November which empowers the police of this island province to board and control foreign ships which enter the province's waters without permission. Hainan province, which is located at the eastern mouth of the South China Sea, is responsible for protecting and administrating China's claims in this huge water body.[6] 'The ordinance mentions six occasions[7] in which the Public Security Border Defence Authority could take action

▶ Stopping or anchoring.

▶ Exit and entry to ports without approval or inspection.

▶ Landing on Islands.

---

5   http://www.southasiaanalysis.org/node/1089

6   Ibid

7   These 'occasions' apparently are intended to cover the passage of ships that are not 'innocent', hence the use of the word 'illegally' in the regulation. UNCLOS, as per Articles 17 to 19, covers the right of innocent passage.

▶ Destruction of coastal defence/production/living facilities on the Islands.

▶ Implementation of promotional activities (could be equated to propaganda) that infringe national sovereignty.

▶ Violation of other laws and regulations that threaten the coastal border public security management'.[8]

(iv) Hainan's issuance of the ordinance has invited the ire of several nations, with Vietnam responding by planning to send its own naval patrols to safeguard its interests in the region. The ordinance also raises questions about the freedom of navigation and specifically passage rights of ships in disputed areas not internationally recognised as belonging to any nation. The issue as to who will decide if the passage is innocent has always remained a grey area. Therefore, nations could reserve the right to employ rules of engagement to thwart an 'illegal' boarding or not to comply with an 'illegal' request to alter course out of such disputed waters.[9]

(v) The issuance of these ordinances will not only add to the growing tensions in the disputed areas, specifically the South China Sea, but also add to the growing suspicions about Chinese intent. The moot question is "who will stand up to China if it adopts strong arm tactics and enforces the ordinances in disputed areas?" As former US President Dwight D Eisenhower said, "History does not long entrust the care of freedom to the weak or the timid."

(f) Turning to India, suffice to say that it would be essential for it to correctly understand the practical meaning of China's present 'core interests' based foreign policy – China may not be willing to give up its option to use force at an opportune time, if it considers necessary, to settle territorial issues, including the one with India.

Chinese Actions in Senkaku. The Chinese behaviour following a collision between a Chinese fishing boat and two Japanese coast guard vessels in waters off the disputed Senkaku islands (called Diao

---

8 http://www.idsa.in/idsacomments/TrespasserswillbeProsecutedChinaslatestBillboardintheS-outhChinaSea_ssparmar_081212.

9 Ibid .

Yu by the Chinese, now administered by Japan) on 8 September 2010 is a case in point: -

(a) The Chinese actions included[10]: -

(i) Warnings to Japan over release of Chinese boat captain have coming from top leadership in China, which rather look unusual. For e.g., Premier Wen Jiabao has himself cautioned that Beijing would take 'unspecified actions' if Tokyo does not correct its mistake.

(ii) The Chinese Foreign Ministry summoned the Japanese Ambassador to the PRC five times for lodging protests.

(iii) The PRC cancelled the scheduled visit to Japan by its senior parliamentarian, postponed bilateral talks over natural gas exploration in East China Sea, halted exports of rare earth metals essential for development of high technology goods in Japan (later denied by the Chinese Commerce Ministry), suspended plans to increase flights to each other nation and stopped a Chinese government-sponsored visit of 1000 Japanese to the Shanghai World Expo. (It has been estimated by some commentators that the ensuing economic war has set Japan behind by a few years – some even claim up to 20 years).[11]

(iv) In apparent retaliation to Japanese detentions of Chinese crew, China's police arrested four employees of the Japanese firm, Fujita Corporation, in Shijiazhuang, Hebei province on charges of their entering a military zone without authorization.

(v) Massive 'anti-Japanese demonstrations were engineered by the authorities. This was for a limited purpose of warning Japan. The Japanese embassy in Beijing, consulates in other parts of the country, Japanese assets and even manufacturing factories were attacked by these nationalist demonstrators. Some of them even demand that China should attack Japan militarily.'[12]

(vi) Assertions that China has undisputed sovereignty over

10 http://www.c3sindia.org/eastasia/1722 also see http://www.eurasiareview.com/01102012-strategic-lessons-from-china-japan-stand-off-analysis/

11 http://www.eurasiareview.com/01102012-strategic-lessons-from-china-japan-stand-off-analysis/

12 http://www.southasiaanalysis.org/node/1001

the Senkakus have come from high political and official levels in the PRC, adding a new sharpness and urgency to the dispute; this may stand in contrast to the advice given by veteran leader Deng Xiaoping in 1978 to leave the issue in the hands of 'wiser' next generations. Notably such assertions include Wen's claim of sovereignty over Senkakus during his talks with Naoto Kan at Brussels and the PRC Foreign Ministry's demand for an official apology from Japan for its "severe infringement of China's territorial sovereignty and personal rights and interests of Chinese citizens".

(vii) Subsequently, China raised its presence in the region from fishing boats to PLA Navy.[13]

(viii) While such actions were being undertaken with reference to East China Sea, the ante was simultaneously raised in the South China Sea too.

▶ 'The aggression also coincides with the China National Offshore Oil Corporation's acquisition of its first deepwater drilling rig and announcement of plans to operate in the South China Sea. The Chinese drilling rig, the CNOOC 981, was first deployed in May and sited some 200 miles southeast of Hong Kong, in an area also claimed by Taiwan and Vietnam. As the energy company's chairman, Wang Yilin, put it, "Large deepwater drilling rigs are our mobile national territory and strategic weapon for promoting the development of the country's offshore oil industry." The firm also chose the occasion to auction off to foreign and domestic corporations a number of exploration blocks in areas of the South China Sea situated close to Vietnam. Needless to say, the move infuriated Hanoi.'[14]

▶ In the similar time frame China objected to joint Indo-Vietnam oil exploration of similar nature and even went to the extent to threaten India. 'In a front-page commentary published on October 16, the "China Energy News" said: "India is playing with fire by agreeing to explore for oil with Vietnam in the disputed South China Sea. India's energy strategy is slipping into

---

13 http://www.southasiaanalysis.org/node/1001

14 http://www.foreignaffairs.com/articles/138093/michael-t-klare/island-grabbing-in-asia

an extremely dangerous whirlpool. On the question of cooperation with Vietnam, the bottom line for Indian companies is that they must not enter into the disputed waters of the South China Sea. Challenging the core interests of a large, rising country for unknown oil at the bottom of the sea will not only lead to a crushing defeat for the Indian oil company, but will most likely seriously harm India's whole energy security and interrupt its economic development. Indian oil company policy makers should consider the interests of their own country, and turn around at the soonest opportunity and leave the South China Sea.'[15]

▶ 'In April 2012, Chinese ships blocked efforts by the Philippine Navy to combat illegal fishing by Chinese ships in Philippine-claimed waters.'[16]

(b)   Analysts have attributed this behaviour to: -

(i) An assertiveness and nationalism linked to the Core Interest Principle which has been noticed since China started proclaiming the concept.[17]

(ii) Chinese view of the US being an inhibiting factor for it in the disputed areas.

(iii) Chinese internal politics in the run up to the leadership change.

(c)   The first two are and have been issues of continuing concern for the international community.

Chinese Actions in Spartly Islands. Almost similar trends can be seen in the Chinese actions in its row with Vietnam over Spartly Island[18]: -

(a)   As Chinese analysts see, to defend its strategic interests in South China Sea, China may have to deal with, what they consider as, two 'unfavourable' factors

(i) China has actual control over only a small number of disputed islands and lacks channels that give connection to the ocean.

---

15   http://ramanstrategicanalysis.blogspot.in/2011/10/india-vietnam-oilgas-cooperation-sparks. html

16   http://www.foreignaffairs.com/articles/138093/michael-t-klare/island-grabbing-in-asia

17   Also see http://www.foreignaffairs.com/articles/138093/michael-t-klare/island-grabbing-in-asia

18   http://www.c3sindia.org/eastasia/2427

    (ii) The country has 'no formidable' Navy to protect its maritime interests.

(b) **History.** China-Vietnam clashes over Paracels and Spratlys are not new.

    (i) In 1974, the two fought in Paracels.

    (ii) Since 1979 Sino-Vietnam War, occasional conflicts between them have taken place.

    (iii) The nineties saw no major confrontation between the two nations, with China in that period opting more for a political approach towards the islands issue; the then Chinese Prime Minister Li Peng proposed in 1990 that the territorial issue may be put aside, to enable the two sides to indulge in 'common development'.

    (iv) Two years later, China passed its "Law on Territorial Waters and Adjacent Areas" which reiterated its claim over Paracels and Spratlys.

    (v) In April and July 2007, Chinese patrol boats captured some Vietnamese fishermen and boats operating close to Spratlys.

(c) **26 May 11 Incident.**

    (i) On 26 May 2011, a Chinese fishing boat, escorted by two Chinese patrol vessels, rammed into and disabled the cables of a Vietnamese seismic survey ship owned by 'Petro Vietnam'. China, alleged that the Vietnamese ship was illegally exploring in the area of its jurisdiction and explained that the ship's cable was cut in the 'turmoil' that resulted from the chasing of Chinese vessels by Vietnamese ships.

    (ii) This was followed by the holding of "Live Fire Drills" by both Vietnam and China involving their respective civilian coastal security units and also military forces.

    (iii) The venue for Vietnam's drills (13 June 2011), which took place with Hanoi's prior-publicity for the first time, was Hon Ong Island, 40 kms off its central coast, 250 kms away from Paracels and 1000 kms away from Spratlys. The drills were close to land territory and no anti- ship missiles were fired. Thus, Vietnam appeared to have acted with some degree of caution, possibly with intention not to jeopardize the otherwise positive climate prevailing in its political ties with China.

(iv) China chose to respond quickly and rather aggressively. It sent the country's maritime surveillance forces, responsible for 'defending islands and meeting any crises' to the vicinity of Spratlys for conducting a 3- day long "live fire drills." Taking part in the exercise, which began on 17 June 2011, were 14 Chinese patrol boats, landing craft, submarine-hunting boats and two Chinese fighter aircraft, along with 'naval forces'. (Chinese TV broadcast, 17 June 2011).

(d) **Assessment.**

(i) No doubt, both held drills, but China's exercise, by its scale and timing, definitely appears to be a bigger show of strength against Vietnam. Beijing, at the same time, in an effort taken prior to its exercise with the apparent aim of preventing a loss of image internationally, made an official statement containing seemingly benign inputs (Chinese foreign ministry spokesperson, Beijing, 14 June 2011). It blamed Vietnam for provocation, but at the same time pledged that China "will not resort to use or threat of force" in South China Sea disputes.

(ii) Question arises – why then China clashed with Vietnam now? The answer is simple – Beijing utilized the clash to reassert its claims over Spratlys. In broader terms, the 'reassertion' at this juncture is very much linked to China's current 'core interests' concept, which disallows compromise and even permits use of force while addressing all sovereignty related issues including the South China Sea. In fact, the concept has now come to override every other Chinese diplomatic principle governing territorial issues.

This pattern is not limited to the disputes of East and South China seas but has been noticed in China's dealing with other nations too. 'In November 2006, a Chinese submarine stalked the USS Kitty Hawk and provocatively surfaced within torpedo firing range. In November 2007, the Chinese refused entry to Kitty Hawk Carrier Strike Group into Hong Kong Harbour, despite building seas and deteriorating weather (the Kitty Hawk did make a visit to Hong Kong in early 2010). In March 2009, a handful of Chinese ships harassed the American surveillance ship the USNS Impeccable while it was conducting operations outside

China's twelve mile territorial limit in South China Sea. The Chinese ships blocked passage and pretended to ram the Impeccable, forcing the Impeccable to respond with fire hoses.'[19]

These along with the policy of demographic invasion, economic and cyber warfare activities discussed above not only affects the other claimants, but the international community as a whole.

(a) 'The United States is not a passive bystander to China's escalated brinkmanship over the South China Sea conflict. Even before it enunciated the Obama Doctrine of strategic pivot to Asia Pacific, the United States had already put into motion a southward realignment of US Forces to Guam with the aim of swift responses to any outbreak of conflict in the South China Sea region. The global responses are best illustrated from a reading of speeches given at the Shangri La Dialogue June 2013 deliberations at Singapore. The common thread running through these speeches was that the global community and major powers were committed to the security of the "global commons" and to the "freedom of the high seas" and that no country had a right to declare them as national territories. The United States, UK, and the new French Foreign Minister emphasised that all of them stood committed to the security and stability of South East Asia. The new French Government through its Foreign Minister made clear that France and European nations had a stake in South East Asia and the stability and security of the region was their strategic concern. He further emphasised that France would support any regional security grouping in the region.'[20]

(b) 'Japanese Prime Minister Shinzo Abe has warned Beijing that Tokyo is losing patience with China's assertive maritime behaviour in the East and South China seas, suggesting China consider the economic and military consequences of its actions. His warning followed similar statements from Washington that its patience with China is wearing thin ... In an interview The Washington Post published just prior to Abe's meeting with U.S. President Obama in Washington, Abe said China's actions around the disputed Senkaku / Diaoyu islands and its overall increasing military assertiveness have already resulted in a major increase in funding for the Japan

---

19 Kaplan Robert 'The Revenge of Geography' page 3448 Kindle Edition.

20 South China Sea: China Escalates Brinkmanship To Dangerous Levels by By Dr. Subhash Kapila

Self-Defence Forces and coast guard.'[21]

(c) 'His (Japanese Prime Minister Shinzo) warning followed similar statements from Washington that its patience with China is wearing thin, in this case over continued Chinese cyber espionage and the likelihood that Beijing is developing and testing cyber sabotage and cyber warfare capabilities. Together, the warnings are meant to signal to China that the thus-far relatively passive response to China's military actions may be nearing an end. Though not mentioning China by name in his 2013 State of the Union address, Obama said, "We know foreign countries and companies swipe our corporate secrets. Now our enemies are also seeking the ability to sabotage our power grid, our financial institutions, our air traffic control systems." Obama's comments, and the subsequent release of a new strategy on mitigating cyber theft of trade secrets, coincided with a series of reports highlighting China's People's Liberation Army backing for hacking activities in the United States, including a report by Mandiant that traced the activities to a specific People's Liberation Army unit and facility. The timing of the private sector reports and Obama's announcement were not coincidental.'[22]

(d) 'Both Tokyo and Washington are reaching their limits for tolerating aggressive Chinese behaviour. The United States is pivoting toward Asia, seen by China as a constraining action. Japan is strengthening ties with Russia, Australia, India and Southeast Asia, something China regards as containment.'[23]

The pattern of application of Chinese assertiveness in the form of administrative, military, economic, diplomatic and policy support seems to be repeating against India too. Instances of these include: -

(a) Repeated Chinese assertion of Arunachal Pradesh as South Tibet.

(b) Chinese opposition to international financial assistance to developmental projects in Arunachal Pradesh.

---

21 http://www.stratfor.com/weekly/china-tests-japanese-and-us-patience?utm_source=freelist-f&utm_medium=email&utm_campaign=20130226&utm_term=gweekly&utm_content=read more&elq=3232f09271e74f758b80de4a322b60fb

22 Ibid

23 Ibid. Also see http://www.eurasiareview.com/20062012-france-reaffirms-commitment-to-asia-pacific-security-analysis/

(c) Objecting to the visit of India's Prime Minister to Arunachal Pradesh.

(d) Denial of visa to an IAS officer from Arunachal Pradesh in May 07.

(e) Issue of stapled visas to Indian citizens from Jammu and Kashmir and denial of visa to Indian Northern Army Commander.

(f) China's attempts to undermine the India-US civil nuclear initiative at the Nuclear Suppliers Group in 2008 and later extending similar cooperation to Pakistan.[24]

(g) Beijing's reluctance to support India's permanent membership of the United Nation's Security Council.[25]

(h) Unwillingness to condemn Pakistan's support of cross border terrorism against India.

(i) Building military infrastructure in Tibet while protesting India's infrastructural improvements in Uttrakhand, Sikkim and Arunachal Pradesh.[26]

(j) Cyber attacks.[27]

A common precursor to all these actions has been their quite reversal /burial on being confronted. However, their resurrection cannot be ruled out as China as the actions themselves reflect the strategic vision of China.

As was noted by The Economist, 'China and India, repositories of 40% of the world's people, are often unsure what to make of each other. Since re-establishing diplomatic ties in 1976, after a post-war pause, they and their relationship have in many ways been transformed. The 1962 war was an act of Chinese aggression most obviously springing

---

24 China has recently signed a deal to provide a third nuclear reactor to Pakistan in contravention of the Nuclear Suppliers Group rules. See http://www.deccanherald.com/content/321148/china-pak-seal-secret-nuclear.html.

25 Also see http://timesofindia.indiatimes.com/world/china/After-Wen-new-China-rulers-seal-their-lips-on-India/articleshow/19028963.cms.

26 An editorial in the Global Times, an English-language tabloid in Beijing, warned that "India needs to consider whether or not it can afford the consequences of a potential confrontation with China." See http://www.economist.com/node/16843717

27 Early this year India's outgoing national security adviser and special envoy to China, M.K. Narayanan, accused Chinese hackers of attacking his website, as well as those of other Indian government departments. See http://www.economist.com/node/16843717

from China's desire for western Aksai Chin, a lofty plain linking Xinjiang to Tibet. But its deeper causes included a famine in China and economic malaise in both countries. China and India are now the world's fastest-growing big economies, however, and in a year or two, when India overtakes Japan on a purchasing-power-parity basis, they will be the world's second- and third-biggest. And as they grow, Asia's giants have come closer. Their two-way trade is roaring: only $270m in 1990, it is expected to exceed $60 billion this year. They are also tentatively co-operating, for their mutual enrichment, in other ways: for example, by co-ordinating their bids for the African oil supplies that both rely on. Given their contrasting economic strengths—China's in manufacturing, India's in services—some see an opportunity for much deeper co-operation. There is even a word for this vision, "Chindia". On important international issues, notably climate-change policy and world trade, their alignment is already imposing. Their leaders naturally talk up these pluses: at the summit of the BRICs (Brazil, Russia, India, China) in Brasília in April, for example, and during celebrations in Beijing earlier this year to commemorate the 60th anniversary of India's recognition of the People's Republic. "India and China are not in competition," India's sage-like prime minister, Manmohan Singh, often says. "There is enough economic space for us both." China's president, Hu Jintao, says the same. And no doubt both want to believe it. The booms in their countries have already moved millions out of poverty, especially in China, which is far ahead on almost every such measure of progress (and also dismissive of the notion that India could ever rival it). A return to confrontation, besides hugely damaging the improved image of both countries, would plainly jeopardise this movement forward. That is why the secular trend in China-India relations is positive. Yet China and India are in many ways rivals, not Asian brothers, and their relationship is by any standard vexed—as recent quarrelling has made abundantly plain. If you then consider that they are, despite their mutual good wishes, old enemies, bad neighbours and nuclear powers, and have two of the world's biggest armies—with almost 4m troops between them—this may seem troubling.[28,29]

---

28 http://www.economist.com/node/16843717

29 Chinese public opinion also seems to be turning against India, a country the Chinese have been wont to remark on fondly, if at all, as the birthplace of Buddhism. According to a recent survey of global opinion released by the BBC, the Chinese show a "distinct cooling" towards India, which 47% viewed negatively. See http://www.economist.com/node/16843717

The reflection of this is visible in that despite efforts to downplay any mutual rivalry, declarations of adequate space for peaceful rise of both India and China and their cooperation being essential for the emergence of the Asian century – China's strategic partnership with Pakistan now extends to Nepal, Bhutan, Bangladesh, Burma (now Myanmar) and Sri Lanka.[30,31]

---

30 Dr C Raja Mohan 'Rising Power and Enduring Paradox: India's China Challenge', USI Journal Jan-Mar 2012, page 25.

31 Hawkish Indian commentators are meanwhile up in arms. "China, in my view, does not want a rival in Asia," says Brajesh Mishra, a former national security adviser and special envoy to China. "Its main agenda is to keep India preoccupied with events in South Asia so it is constrained from playing a more important role in Asian and global affairs." Senior officials present a more nuanced analysis, noting, for example, that India has hardly been alone in getting heat from China: many countries, Asian and Western, have similarly been singed. Yet they admit to heightened concern over China's intentions in South Asia, and foresee no hope for a settlement of the border. Nicholas Burns, a former American diplomat who led the negotiations for an America-India nuclear co-operation deal that was concluded in 2008, and who now teaches at Harvard University, suspects that over the past year China has supplanted Pakistan as the main worry of Indian policymakers. He considers the China-India relationship "exceedingly troubled and perturbed" and thinks that it will remain "uneasy for many years to come". See http://www.economist.com/node/16843717

Chapter 8

LESSONS AND HANDLING CHINA

How India can respond to the evolving China's approach towards South Asia? It will be important for India to realise that China's new assertiveness could be meant to redefine the boundaries of its economic and diplomatic clout and military influence in the present international scenario. In such circumstances, it will be desirable for India to get closer to its neighbours through measures like extending economic aid. Countries like Pakistan, Nepal, Bangladesh and Sri Lanka have developed proximity- induced mistrust of India and intend to hedge their ties with India with some kind of balancing act with China. New Delhi's aim should be to eradicate such mistrust and that will be possible if India is prepared to share its new prosperity with its weaker neighbours. At the same time, it would be necessary for India to 'engage' China on the basis of its assessment that 'there is enough space for both to pursue their ambitions of economic development'. No doubt, while doing so, New Delhi should evolve an effective approach to counter the evolving China's overall postures in South Asia, which can impinge on India's long-term interests. It can be said that there is a deep contradiction between the two basic elements in China's strategy towards Asian neighbours- the aim for a 'win-win' bilateral relationship on one hand and adoption of assertive positions on the territorial issues on the other. In short, assertiveness hurts China's diplomatic interests in the region. Beijing cannot but be aware of the same, but will it abandon its assertive path? When seen against China's consistent position that it cannot compromise on matters of 'core interests', the answer can be taken as 'no'. For India, other Asian powers and also the US, all of which have a stake in the region's stability, there seems to be only one choice – be prepared to face China's rise, peaceful or non-peaceful'.[1]

---

1 http://www.c3sindia.org/eastasia/2590.

As India expands her horizons, the two giants are beginning to rub shoulders in different parts of Asia, Africa and Latin America. New economic prosperity and military strength is reawakening nationalistic pride in India, which could bring about a clash with Chinese nationalism. In the power competition game, China has surged ahead by acquiring economic and military capabilities underpinned by a clear policy to achieve broader strategic objectives. Any attempt by India to challenge or undermine China's power and influence or to achieve strategic parity is strongly resisted through a combination of military, economic and diplomatic means.[2] 'Basically, India's strategic challenges in Southeast Asia come from China. Beijing's strong objection to India's collaboration with Vietnam on oil exploration in South China Sea, is a prominent example. Beijing has also reservations on India playing a leading role in the East Asian integration process. We have to remove China's doubts, may be through bilateral dialogue. We should understand the nature of economic, political and security perceptions of China which motivate Beijing to look upon India, Australia and New Zealand as "outsiders" to formation of an East Asian order. Our second option should be to build firm bridges with ASEAN nations which all welcome India's participation. The ASEAN-China free trade pact provides more advantageous terms to the regional nations than the similar pacts signed by India. The "services" sector is still outside the purview of India-ASEAN FTA. India needs to bridge this gap. Also, India can offer assistance to East Asian nations in building capabilities to protect the sea lanes of communication. There is also tremendous scope for India's cooperation with Southeast Asian nations in non-traditional security fields.'[3]

Overall, China appears to be showing two faces to India. On one hand, it is of the view that 'Sino-Indian cooperative partnership oriented towards 21st century', has entered into maturity and stability period and on the other, Beijing is adopting a hard line position strategically vis-à-vis India. The net result therefore is the existing trust deficit between the two sides, for which there appears to be no early remedy.

China's approach to India may be on the following lines: -

(a) Boundary/border/territorial issues are separate.

---

2 Commander Gurumurthy B 'A Case Study of Strategic and Geopolitical Impact of PLA-Pak Military Strategic Partnership and Security Implications for India', USI Journal Jan-Mar 2012 page 9.

3 http://www.eurasiareview.com/30012012-us-china-and-developments-in-southeast-asia-analysis/

(b)   Trade and economic exchanges, as long as they are in China's favour, should not be influenced by Boundary/border/territorial issues.

(c)   Delink India-US relations that can counter China. There will be many buyers in India for this approach.'[4]

Similarities

'For analysts in India, a look into the similarities or otherwise in the Chinese attitudes towards Senkaku dispute and the Sino-Indian border question, may be useful.

(a)   Both Senkakus and Arunachal Pradesh (called Southern Tibet by China) are important to the PRC in terms of national sovereignty and regional strategy.

(b)   Beijing sees a US angle in the East and South China Sea issues. It does not see the same in China-India boundary question, but in general continues to nurture suspicions of US-India collusion.

(c)   Presence of resources in Senkakus and Arunachal – oil and gas in East China seas and minerals, coal, zinc etc in Arunachal. Beijing may like to exploit them which is possible only when the PRC exercises sovereignty over them.

(d)   The PRC does not have a fixed formula to settle the Senkakus problem; it only demands Japan 'to take real actions to add to the content of the mutually beneficial and strategic relationship'. It holds a hawkish position in favour of forcibly throwing out any foreign ship operating off the Senkakus islands as per its Territorial Waters Law adopted in 1992. On the other hand, China supports the principle of 'mutual understanding and mutual accommodation' as basis for solution to the Sino-Indian boundary question.

(e)   China views the border dispute with India as a colonial legacy; in the case of Senkakus, Beijing seems to find a similar US legacy against the fact that it was the US which handed over the administration of Senkakus to Japan in 1971.'[5]

---

4   http://www.southasiaanalysis.org/node/1001

5   http://www.c3sindia.org/eastasia/1722

Lessons for India

(a) Striking first is China's postponement of talks with Japan on reaching a pact providing for joint development of the gas fields in East China Sea, in the wake of Senkakus developments. A Sino-Japanese agreement concluded in June 2008, had provided the basis for such talks. The emerging point is **that Beijing can go back on its past commitments if the situation warrants,** which should be noted by New Delhi. Chinese position on Sikkim is a classic example. As per information available so far, despite a Sino-Indian basic understanding, de jure recognition of Sikkim as India's state is yet to come.

(b) The PRC's **use of civilians to assert its sovereignty** over Senkakus, should be another point of interest for India. Chinese fishing vessels are armed, indicating closeness between the PRC Navy and the fishing industry. The cases of Chinese border intrusions into India, similarly intended for asserting sovereignty, need to be examined from this perspective.

(c) Chinese blogs suggest that a particular motive for Chinese action in Senkakus is to monitor Japan's reported increase in the recent period of Ground Self Defence Personnel in that island, and of active roles to the country's coast guards to defend the area and augmentation of air cover level for the island. This could be relevant to India's case. Beijing has strong reservations on India's plans to dispatch two mountain divisions and position advanced Su-37 fighter aircraft to defend Arunachal Pradesh. Will there be an increased surveillance from the PRC over **India's defence preparedness** in the Sino-Indian border, can be a moot question for India.

(d) Japan's economy is dependent on China. The PRC has become Japan's biggest trading partner. Among the countries which export to China, Japan occupies No.1 position now, replacing the US. On the Senkaku issue, Beijing seems to have used its **economic leverage** against Tokyo. It will be a useful exercise for New Delhi to study the possibilities of China doing the same at times of conflict with India.'[6]

(e) 'India should realize that the **'core interests'** concept which China uses against Vietnam, can also influence Beijing's policy behaviour with respect to the Sino-Indian border issue (though not so far included by China in the 'core interests' list).

(f) India should take note of the **contradiction between China's "not to use force" declaration** with respect to settlement of South China Sea disputes **and its ground level actions** of confronting Vietnamese boats and carrying out a Navy-involved exercise to warn Vietnam. The contradiction was also visible in the case of China's approach towards Japan on Senkakus issue. Not long time back, Beijing bullied Tokyo on the issue. Can China, which in theory stands for a peaceful dialogue on the Sino-Indian boundary issue, indulge in limited, but offensive border actions against India in practice at any point of time from now? New Delhi should ponder over this question especially with reference to the "Chinese intrusions" into Indian border being frequently noticed.

(g) China is applying the 'diplomatic' formula of **"shelving the disputes and seeking common development"** to its stand on territorial issues with Vietnam. **This line may turn into an aggressive one**, as and when China becomes a 'maritime' power, leaving no necessity for 'shelving'. In the case of India also, Beijing is in favour of 'shelving' the 'difficult' border issue and improving ties in other areas. Will China gain assertiveness on territorial issues with India once its defence modernization programme is complete, say by the middle of the century as being projected? India should deeply examine this aspect too.

(h) The US factor has emerged as an irritant in China's dealing with the islands issue with Vietnam. There is a parallel case with respect to India with Chinese opinions doubting Washington-New Delhi collusion to strategically 'encircle' China. New Delhi should therefore handle the **US-China-India triangular** relations with finesse.

(i) New Delhi should look closely at the implications of **China's aim to become a "maritime power"** for the situation **in the Indian Ocean**, a region of strategic importance to India.[7]

India and China 'have repeatedly found themselves at odds in reshaping regional and international institutions. India has been wary of China's increasing influence in the South Asian Association of

---

7   http://www.c3sindia.org/eastasia/2427

Regional Cooperation. Beijing in turn has sought to limit India's role in East Asian Institutions. Delhi and Beijing have also clashed over the reform of the global nuclear and United Nations Security council. The world is watching very closely the unfolding rivalry between the rising Asian Giants. If the rivalry ends up in war or conflict, it is bound to diminish both China and India. While the talk of a grand eastern alliance between Beijing and Delhi was always farfetched, the big question is whether the two can manage their competition by keeping it limited and peaceful.'[8]

---

8   Dr C Raja Mohan, 'Rising Power and Enduring Paradox: India's China Challenge', USI Journal Jan-Mar 2012 page 26.

Chapter 9

OVERALL ASSESSMENT

East (Han) China is the Chinese heartland. Defined South and East of the 15 inch isohyet line, it is the region where the vast majority of the population lives. Availability of water due to adequate rain, three major rivers and vast irrigation network centred around the Great Canal makes the region – the bread basket of China. Emergence of modern industrial infrastructure and access to the coast has made the region the economic hub of modern China. The region is home to the ethnic Han, whom the world regards as the Chinese. More than a billion people live in this area. The rest of China has water shortages and is not conducive to sustained agriculture throughout the year. As such China has about one-third the arable land per person as the rest of the world. This pressure has defined modern Chinese history — both in terms of living with it and trying to move beyond it. The rest of the China however, is rich in minerals and act as important buffer regions to the Chinese heartland. Historically these regions have been under Chinese control whenever China is strong.

The Wall of islands East of Chinese coast has the potential to choke sea borne trade (both import and export) as also allow foreign power to radiate power inwards. Hence, the Chinese efforts to gain a foothold on the islands in East and South China Seas are not just about increase of its 'Exclusive Economic Zone' and minerals in the region; but also to secure its oceanic access. Failure to gain a foothold would keep China insecure. The insecurity would be compounded by lack of an adequate Navy and force the Chinese Government to invest more and more in Naval infrastructure.

A highly centralised bureaucratic system has been the hall mark of Chinese governance throughout its history. It is believed by many that the present Communist regime is just the latest of some twenty five dynasties. Hence, even if at some stage the control of the Communist Party of China (CPC) reduces, any new regime or system of governance is likely to be as centralized as the present system with a strong central bureaucracy focussing on stability and with goals similar to those of the present regime.

Historically China has cycled between opposites: either isolation combined with relative poverty or an openness to trade combined with social instability.[1] Historically, social instability in China unless controlled has the potential of both regime overthrow and fragmentation of China. The present regime has tried to balance the two extremes and has experimented with openness while maintaining social stability – albeit the latter by use of both the carrot and the stick. Hence, the two pillars of the Chinese system are: -

(a)   Social stability through 100% employment.

(b)   Control over the Armed Forces.

For this following are essential: -

(a)   Transfer of prosperity from the more prosperous regions to the less prosperous ones. This entails taxing the prosperous regions and investing in physical and social infrastructure of the less fortunate areas. In modern day China this would imply transferring prosperity from Coastal Han regions to West including non-Han China.

(b)   Import and export economy which can import adequate raw material, leverage the cheap labour[2] to manufacture volumes beyond local consumption levels and export the surplus. This however is dependent on the market forces, health of the markets to which the goods are being exported and the ability to keep labour cheap.

The system however, has come under strain in the economic crisis which engulfed the world post 2007. As the world economies cut down their imports the Chinese export dependent economy was forced to try and raise the domestic consumption as well as quality of their products. This required salary increases and replacement of

---

1   Friedman George – The Next Decade Doubleday publications Random House, page 2431 Kindle Edition.

2   It is believed by some that China's Primary economic asset is cheap labour in this regard see George Friedman – The Next Decade Doubleday publications Random House, page 2439 Kindle Edition.

unskilled labour with skilled ones.[3] On the one hand while this has created a scarcity of skilled labour (putting further upward pressure on their wages) on the other, employment opportunities for the unskilled labour have rapidly shrunk. Overall, this has resulted in China no longer having a wage advantage[4,5] and consequently its ability to export goods competitively in large enough numbers has come under pressure. Some indicators have started appearing of how this is adversely affecting the economy – these can be seen in terms of downgrading of growth forecasts,[6] drop in the stock market,[7] crisis in the banking and financial system[8,9,10,11,12,13,14] crisis in the construction sector,[15] emergence of ghost cities,[16] health care[17] or rising unemployment.[18,19] Views vary on the quantum of the drawback – however, all agree that

---

3   See Shaun Rein 'The End of Cheap China' John Wiley and Sons Inc. page 493 Kindle Edition.

4   http://www.news.com.au/business/worklife/china-labour-costs-like-us-within-years/story-e6frfm9r-1226438065496#ixzz22K62hsDt

5   http://knowledgetoday.wharton.upenn.edu/2013/07/as-china-changes-so-do-global-supply-chains/

6   http://www.globaltimes.cn/content/785391.shtml#.UabOeNLlvYo

7   http://english.peopledaily.com.cn/90778/8334764.html

8   http://business.time.com/2012/06/05/chinas-antiquated-financial-system-the-creaking-grows-louder/

9   http://www.reuters.com/article/2012/10/03/us-economy-global-currencies-idUS-BRE8920Q820121003

10 http://cinemarasik.com/2013/05/04/chinahandle-with-care.aspx

11 http://knowledge.wharton.upenn.edu/article.cfm?articleid=3313

12 http://www.globaltimes.cn/content/790733.shtml#.UcUyhfnI3Lk

13 http://english.peopledaily.com.cn/90778/8297840.html

14 http://news.xinhuanet.com/english/indepth/2013-07/20/c_125039658.htm

15 http://www.foreignaffairs.com/articles/138449/lynette-h-ong/indebted-dragon?page=show

16 Due to inability of builders to find buyers for the apartments see http://www.globaltimes.cn/content/800201.shtml#.UfiY8Y3I3Ys

17 http://knowledgetoday.wharton.upenn.edu/2013/06/health-care-in-china-is-there-a-doctor-in-the-house/

18 http://economictimes.indiatimes.com/news/international-business/china-labour-ministry-says-faces-big-pressure-on-employment/articleshow/21325086.cms

19 http://www.globaltimes.cn/content/796936.shtml#.Uedj3dlwffl

the era of fast growth is nearing to an end.[20,21,22,23] This is not to say that the Chinese economy would collapse or go into a depression – albeit it will continue to remain an economic power at the world stage.

Other nations (notably Japan and SE Asia in the 90s and US and EU in the 2000's) too have passed through similar downturns as more will in the future – however, what distinguishes the crisis in China is the high level of inequality[24] and the expectations of complete employment and prosperity promised by the Chinese Communist Party. The dilemma that China faces is that while externally it would be viewed as a rich developed economic powerhouse, internally it would still be a poor country. This is increasingly leading to social tensions. China so far has managed these tensions by focusing them at the local government level (issues like family planning officials[25,26] corruption,[27] Chengguan system. etc),[28,29,30] appealing to the population for more patience[31] and use of force.[32] However, the Chinese Communist Party realises that the key to social stability lies in: -

20 http://knowledge.wharton.upenn.edu/article.cfm?articleid=2962

21 http://www.stratfor.com/weekly/recognizing-end-chinese-economic-miracle?utm_source=freelist-f&utm_medium=email&utm_campaign=20130723&utm_term=Gweekly&utm_content=readmore&elq=ed0c59a49ae34fc1ae653be09b16d701

22 http://www.stratfor.com/weekly/us-foreign-policy-room-regroup

23 http://www.foreignaffairs.com/articles/139295/evan-a-feigenbaum-and-damien-ma/the-rise-of-chinas-reformers?page=show

24 Symbolized by a Gini Coefficient of over 0.47 (see http://www.chinadaily.com.cn/china/2010-05/12/content_9837073.htm and http://community.travelchinaguide.com/forum2.asp?i=43913) and the fact that over a 100 million people live in Sub Saharan poverty (see http://articles.economictimes.indiatimes.com/2012-06-21/news/32352617_1_sustainable-development-wen-jiabao-countries).

25 http://www.globaltimes.cn/content/798567.shtml#.Ue9Rztlwffl

26 http://www.globaltimes.cn/content/798547.shtml#.Ue9R-Nlwffl

27 http://www.globaltimes.cn/content/801460.shtml#.Uf8iltlwffl

28 http://www.globaltimes.cn/content/797396.shtml#.UejPRdlwffl

29 http://www.globaltimes.cn/content/797375.shtml#.UejPYdlwffl

30 http://www.globaltimes.cn/content/797634.shtml#.Uet6YY3I3Lk

31 http://www.globaltimes.cn/content/785711.shtml#.UagkMdLIvYo

32 It needs to be reiterated that the protests against the Chengguan System were similar to the outcry in Tunisia which led to the initiation of the Arab Spring. However, China was able to control the fallout by judicious use of the security forces and measures like ban on carriage of knives.

(a) Keeping the protests focussed away from the Central Government.

(b) Transferring prosperity to the less prosperous regions.[33]

(c) Complete control over the Armed Forces.[34]

This however has two significant obstacles – **one**, to transfer prosperity inwards, China will have to tax higher, the coastal regions and the well-off Chinese residents – who are likely to resist the central government. Attempts to transfer wealth thus either weakens the central government or forces it to become dictatorial.[35] On the other hand for the poor even a small contraction in living standards is likely to be catastrophic. This is where the small decline in growth is a problem and will generate resistance to the central government. This slowing down of economy, increased unemployment and resistance to increased taxation would test the Government's skills who may have to resort to an increased use of security forces to maintain stability. And **two**, this is likely to lead to a more assertive PLA (as the umbrella under which all the security forces function) as its importance in maintaining rule of the Communist Party increases. This rise of assertiveness (which some believe is already visible)[36] is unlikely to go down well with the world and may affect the market access of China.

However, in all this it needs to be noted that China possesses enough mineral resources so that loss of imported raw material is not an existential threat to China in the short term. Even energy as a component of overall trade and the reserves capability built up by the nation makes it a suspect target in a short war. In addition with the efforts to operationalise the new technologies (including Shale deposits of which it has substantial reserves), opening of Arctic

---

33 The Government has been attempting to link the interiors with the more prosperous coastal regions by developing industrial corridors along the river valleys like the Yangtze River Corridor see http://www.stratfor.com/analysis/geopolitics-yangtze-river-developing-interior?utm_source=freelist-f&utm_medium=email&utm_campaign=20130412&utm_term=Yagntze&utm_content=readmore&elq=a07b5dd9de0a4f7ca34c859e2627a6fc

34 The party often cities the example of USSR in which they believe that a depoliticised armed forces were a major reason for the collapse of the Soviet Union and Warsaw Pact.

35 Friedman George – The Next Decade Doubleday publications Random House, page 2449 Kindle Edition.

36 http://www.c3sindia.org/foreign-policy/3670

route[37,38] diversification and pipelines would further reduce the risk and dependence on sea based energy import.

China, will continue its efforts to gain, retain and defend its international market share for both exports and imports. For this it is likely to resort to at least three non-conventional tools.

(a) **Use of Money Power.**

    (i) With its large foreign exchange reserves and perception of being an economic power house, China has been using and will continue to use money power to buy influence and access to resources and international markets. This would take the route of both loans and grants to governments[39] as well as political leaders. However, all these are **linked to a quid pro quo of an increased access to natural resources and market** for the Chinese government and/or the Chinese companies.

    (ii) In this the role of the Chinese companies is increasingly coming under the global scanner. The Chinese system ensures close linkages between the Communist party and the Chinese business. Many believe that the latter cannot exist without the approval of the first. Even if this belief is some distortion of the truth, the government efforts to help them gain market access, perhaps obligates business to help the government. While allegations of **electronic espionage** have been documented by the US and EU forcing them to stop trade with some Chinese companies,[40] their role in other fields has come under the scanner in

---

37 http://www.stratfor.com/analysis/growing-importance-arctic-council?utm_source=freelist-f&utm_medium=email&utm_campaign=20130528&utm_term=FreeReport&utm_content=readmore&elq=8e2c531f02544925a37ee5b8c3f073d6

38 http://www.foreignaffairs.com/articles/139456/scott-g-borgerson/the-coming-arctic-boom?page=show

39 These loans and grants are more often than not used for building infrastructure however, mostly, only that infrastructure is supported which would enable access to the mineral wealth of the host nation.

40 http://www.globaltimes.cn/content/781627.shtml#.UZLb57XI3Lk

Africa,[41] Central Asian Republics[42] and Latin America.[43,44] Most recently, they have come under the scanner for funding Robert Mugabe in the Zimbabwe general elections.[45,46,47] Simultaneously their role in subverting the national laws to their advantage has been cause of the latest outcry. In Africa they are being blamed for a threat to the African wildlife.[48] Other alleged transgressions include ill treatment of local labour and land hoarding. Characteristically at times the Chinese Government has responded by seeking **preferential treatment and exemption from local laws**. Typically, while dealing with a host of allegations of environment violations it has called for the right to set the standards which its companies would have to implement,[49] thereby indicating its unwillingness to follow the local environment regulations.

(b) **Economic War.** While the actions by China to target Japan when the Senkaku Islands dispute escalates have already been documented, the use of this tool by China to retain its market share has also been recorded. In the recent days, a dispute with EU over export of Solar Panels,[50] China used the

---

41 http://www.iol.co.za/business/international/china-s-role-in-africa-under-scrutiny-1.1529528#. UgcWrJLI3Ys

42 http://www.universalnewswires.com/centralasia/security/viewstory.aspx?id=13991

43 http://online.wsj.com/article/SB10000872396390443696604577647102203290514.html

44 http://thediplomat.com/china-power/china-and-latin-america-big-business-and-big-compe-tition/

45 http://www.diamonds.net/News/NewsItem.aspx?ArticleID=40453&ArticleTitle=Global+Witne ss+Ties+Diamond+Business+with+Funding+Mugabe's+Military+

46 http://africajournalismtheworld.com/tag/mugabe-diamond-funds-for-election/

47 http://www.mining.com/chinese-diamond-mogul-funding-zimbabwes-mugabes-military-re-port/

48 http://english.peopledaily.com.cn/90882/8353272.html

49 http://www.globaltimes.cn/content/781566.shtml#.UZLcCLXI3Lk

50 The complete incident can be sequentially understood by
http://www.globaltimes.cn/content/785093.shtml#.UaWES9LIvYo,
http://news.xinhuanet.com/english/business/2013-06/04/c_132430788.htm,
http://news.xinhuanet.com/english/business/2013-06/05/c_124811764.htm,
http://www.globaltimes.cn/content/787104.shtml#.UbAGAtLIvYo,
http://english.peopledaily.com.cn/90778/8282812.html,
http://www.globaltimes.cn/content/799516.shtml#.UfS1S43I3Ys,

threat of sanctions against EU wine exports and forced the EU to a compromise on Chinese terms. Hence, even while the intellectuals talk of increased trade relations to diffuse inter-state tensions, **China uses trade as a tool not only during a confrontation but also in peace to safeguard its interests.**

(c) **Demographic Invasion.** The policy has been part of the Chinese rulers discourse since historical times. While Tibet and Xinjiang have been the historic targets, more recently Mongolia, Russian Far East and South East Asia have been the targets. **The pattern normally starts with immigrants, followed by companies, workers labour and slowly control over the local resources.** Complaints of the pattern are being heard from Africa, Central Asia, even Israel and Palestine. Apart from control over resources and export of labour the policy has the advantage of injecting Trojan horses where desired.

This policy of **resource and market access are increasing become a defining feature of Chinese foreign policy.** The foreign policy is likely to have the following highlights: -

(a) It would continue to strive to gain maximum advantages from international regimes.

(b) Semi alliances and multilateralism would be used to maintain a stable international situation favourable to China.

(c) It is likely to have different approaches to different countries guided only by self interest.

(d) Would get involved in affairs of other nations under the policy of preventive diplomacy. This is already visible in Myanmar and Zimbabwe.

(e) China would like to keep nations in the neighbourhood either under own influence or in a state of internal strife and thus limiting their influence and actions to the region. This would be aimed to ensure stability of Chinese border regions.

(f) While maintaining own strategic alliances would continue to question others.

http://news.xinhuanet.com/english/indepth/2013-07/28/c_132580690.htm,
http://news.xinhuanet.com/english/indepth/2013-07/28/c_132580396.htm and
http://www.globaltimes.cn/content/801948.shtml#.UgHFpNlwffl.

(g) Diplomacy would be aimed at not giving clarity while seeking complete clarity from others.

Deng's principle of 'keeping a low profile' in international affairs has undergone a revision. The new message that it is seeking to convey is that China is peacefully rising and hence the world must respect its core interest – as such the **peaceful rise is being seen as conditional to achieving the desired respect on the issues of core interest.**[51] The infusion of the core interest concept in its foreign policy has itself injected a **level of assertiveness** not seen before. Its features, of ruling out compromises and suggesting use of force, infuse a degree of nationalistic jingoism and assertiveness in its international behaviour. For India, vaguely defined core interests (what China calls Tibet related issues but does not define them) are a red flag which not only keeps it uncomfortable but allows China an excuse to use military force as and when it so desires.

It must be noted that China **considers the use of force "as an essential and accepted part of promoting national interests and war is not necessarily an unmitigated evil** and that China has already used force to buttress its territorial claims – against India, Soviet Union, Vietnam and the Philippines. Even today China is not hesitating to adopt aggressive postures on sovereignty issues. Beijing's ongoing sabre rattling with respect to South China Sea and East China sea issues, e.g. establishment of a PLA garrison in Sansha city in Hainan province; conduct of a training exercise in South China Sea and Western Pacific Ocean during March 2013 of the Chinese Navy's South Fleet, reaching up to Zeng Mu reef, contested by Malaysia, symbolizing demonstration of the PRC's determination to claim entire South China Sea; locking of fire control radar by a Chinese frigate at a Japanese destroyer on the high seas near the Senkaku Islands in January 2013 and the PLA's repeated intrusion into India's Ladakh in 2013.[52] Seen alongside its declared policy of military modernisation and development of infrastructure to support it; can anyone be sure about Beijing not using the force option? Perhaps the answer is 'no'.[53]

This also gets reiterated by the developments post the ascendance of the new leadership. In a report adopted in the 18th CCP congress in November 2012, it was said, "Peaceful development is China's basic state policy, and win-win cooperation is a banner for China's friendly

---

51 http://www.c3sindia.org/foreign-policy/3670

52 Ibid

53 Ibid

relations with other countries. To realise 'China dream', we must have a peaceful international environment. At the same time, the country will resolutely safeguard its national sovereignty, security, and core interests. The two policies are two pillars of Chinese diplomacy, and do not conflict with each other". For the first time in a party congress report, references to "never yielding to outside pressure" and "protecting legitimate rights and interests overseas' found a place. Strongly echoing the Congress guideline, Xi Jinping in his speech at a party politburo session held in January 2013 stated that China would remain on a path of peaceful development, yet it will "never give up" legitimate rights or sacrifice 'core interests'. Observing that China would adhere to an "open, cooperative and win-win" development model, Xi cautioned that "no country should presume that we will engage in trade involving our 'core interests' or that we will swallow the 'bitter fruit' of harming our sovereignty, security or development interests" [54].

Hence, it is safe to assume that **China's diplomatic formulae of shelving the disputes and seeking common development may turn into an aggressive one as and when it suits China.** It in effect seeks to postpone negotiations on territorial claims but would not give up any. They would only **negotiate from a position of strength and strike bargains, only where the bargains allow them access / protection to their trade routes.** This approach has already been seen in their border settlements accords with Vietnam, Myanmar and Mongolia. Most recently, their border settlement with Tajikistan is being viewed similarly where the Chinese forego claims of over 28,500 sq kms for 1100 sq kms in the Gorno-Badakhshan Autonomous region. The region lies immediately to the North of the strategic Wakhan Corridor which in turn provides the sole Chinese link to Afghanistan – one of the last unexplored regions for minerals and an area where the Chinese companies are already active. Hence, the pact enabled China to secure the North flank of the strategic link to an area which can soon emerge as a possible source for natural resources for China. Some commentators even view the Chinese incursions into Ladakh as attempts to secure the southern flank of the Wakhan Corridor.

With slowing down of economy and unemployment becoming a problem, **use of security forces to maintain stability would increase.** This is likely to lead to a more assertive PLA as the umbrella under which all the security forces function. PLA already holds the

54 http://www.c3sindia.org/foreign-policy/3670

responsibilities for physical security of China and resource centres abroad as also retrieving claimed territories. They thus already have a major say in the Chinese foreign policy. Reportedly the PLA has also started foraying into the realm of diplomacy.[55] As yet the effort is limited to its Island disputes and anti piracy operations, **however an effort seems to be underway by the PLA to take over the foreign policy of China or at the minimum increase its influence even further on the issue.** When seen in light of its policy of 'not attacking till attacked, but counter attacking if attacked' as also of use of force as an essential and accepted part of policy – it does raise suspicions of an increased assertiveness as also Chinese attempts to undermine its neighbours.

The pattern of assertiveness which emerges from the Chinese actions is that

(a) China uses **a combination of the following** measures

(i) **Administrative support** including collecting historical evidence to justify claims, notifying legal steps to claim jurisdiction, movement of its population to the claimed areas and other measures which can help fortify its claims.

(ii) Applying **strategic military coercion** by military exercises, patrols and sometimes even live firing.

(iii) **Economic pressure** in terms of denying exploration rights to competitors while going ahead and granting the same on its own, stoppage of trade with competitors and harming the economic interests of the adversary in China.

(iv) **Diplomatic offensive** in support of its claims both directly with the adversary as also through multi lateral agencies where it suits China and / or refusal to accept multilateral arrangements where it does not.

(v) **Policy support** in terms of suitable policy formulations at the highest level supported by statements from the top leadership to both buttress its own claims as also to undermine those of the other claimants / adversary.

(b) However on being confronted China does step back but the overall aim is to **two steps forward and one step back.** Hence,

---

55 http://articles.timesofindia.indiatimes.com/2013-07-30/china/40894205_1_south-china-sea-pla-navy-indian-ocean

the **confrontation needs to be swift and encompassing all the measures** that China uses.

In what specific areas, China's assertiveness is going to be felt in the future? In his article , now believed to a study material for the PLA, Lt Gen Qi Jianguo, China's Deputy Chief of General Staff of the PLA has identified the following 'risks and challenges' for the country[56]: –

(a) The long term danger coming from **Western** subversive strategy of penetration and subversion, including use of military 'hard strikes'.

(b) Domination of 'rightists' in **Japanese** politics, Japan's changing self-defence policy into an 'outside oriented' policy, which would affect stability in East Asia.

(c) Involvement of great powers in **South China Sea**.

(d) **Neo-interventionaism**, i.e. "neo- colonialism waving the banner of human rights" having implications for national sovereignty.

(e) **Non-traditional security** factors including cyber security, terrorism and energy security, also impacting on national sovereignty.

(f) **Financial and 'outer space'** threats.[57]

It must be remembered that the list above **is in addition to the Core Interests** (protecting the rule of the Communist party, territorial integrity including Tibet, Xinjiang, Taiwan and South and East China Seas Islands, strategic resources and Trade routes) enumerated earlier. It would suggest that **China's assertiveness, now centring around 'core interests', may expand to include issues that adversely affect China like human rights, energy security etc.** As the list expands, so is the world likely to see an expansion in the tools that China may deploy in support. Issues like water (China controls the source of many trans-border rivers), nuclear / missile proliferation etc may raise their head in the future.

Overall, the inequities in the Chinese society have got exposed as China struggles with the effects of the world economic crisis. The Chinese heartland already under pressure due to the economic slowdown is likely to see further tensions as the government

---

56 http://www.c3sindia.org/foreign-policy/3670

57 http://www.thehindu.com/news/international/world/china-doesnt-want-unexpected-border-incident-says-pla-general/article4857683.ece

intensifies its efforts to transfer prosperity to the inner regions. So far the government has managed to contain these by focussing the dissatisfaction at the local level however, an increased use of force cannot be ruled out in the future. This would lead to a more assertive PLA and in turn a more assertive Chinese foreign policy approach to the world. For securing its interests, China had already been using non-conventional tools like money power, economic war and demographic pressures; these would further be bolstered by its determination of breaking out of the last vestiges of isolationism and an assertiveness of not compromising on its interests. This assertiveness has a pattern wherein all the tools of the nation state are brought to bear in favour of an issue. The specific tools and measures may increase in the future, as China seeks to exploit the vulnerability of its opponents.

Chapter 10

RECOMMENDATIONS

While China has settled most of its border disputes, India[1] and the maritime boundaries are an exception, it is not a pure coincidence that most of these directly or indirectly have been included in the 'Core Interests'. Hence, India would have to keep a close watch on China's motivations for being assertive. It cannot afford to lag behind in the matter of protecting its strategic interests, but should at the same time engage China. As correctly pointed out by former Indian Foreign Secretary Mr Shyam Saran, India should diversify its relations with other major powers and expand its diplomatic options in order to manage relations with friends and adversaries alike. 'India should continue with its 'engagement policy' towards the PRC, while simultaneously working towards securing its own strategic interests.'[2] While the tasks of managing the complex Indo-China relationship are

---

1   The Chinese attitude towards India can be ascertained by the five point formulae proposed for Indo-Chinese relations by the new Chinese President on taking over and prior to his first meeting with the Indian Prime Minister. The agenda include; first, to keep **strategic communication** and bilateral relation on the right track; second, harness each other's comparative strength and expand win-win **cooperation in infrastructure**; third, strengthen **cultural ties and increase mutual understanding** and friendship; fourth, expand **cooperation and collaboration in multilateral affairs** to jointly safeguard the legitimate rights and interests of developing countries, and; fifth, accommodate each other's **core concerns**. An analysis of the proposal shows that the **Chinese concerns and interests have all been included even as the Chinese seek additional access in Indian Infrastructure.** However, the Indian concerns of **trade deficit, river water sharing and diversions by China, accommodation** for Indian Global aspirations in multilateral forums and **Chinese Cyber Offensive Capabilities** have been ignored. In this regard see http://blogs.timesofindia.indiatimes.com/Globespotting/entry/china-s-new-president-must-go-beyond-platitudes-to-address-india-s-concerns.

2   http://www.c3sindia.org/strategicissues/992

well understood, the widening strategic-economic gap between the two is an issue of concern.

- (a) States in a position similar to India have the following options.[3]

    - (i) Adjust itself to the power differential, eschew rivalry, and tailor its policies towards greater accommodation.

    - (ii) Persist in balancing the greater power. This can be done either internally or externally or simultaneously both internally and externally.

        ▶ Internal balancing involves the full mobilisation of domestic economic and military resources to maintain a measure of strategic equity if not full parity.

        ▶ External alliances involve alliances and partnerships.

    - (iii) Asymmetric strategy towards the greater power as Pakistan has been doing with India.

- (b) India needs to look at these options not as alternatives but rather as simultaneous paths to balance China.

Securing Required Resources

With China making concerted efforts to secure the resources it feels essential for its future growth – some of the world's last untapped resources are getting committed. A long term view therefore needs to be developed of the **resources that India would need and action taken to secure them** by using all possible means.

Foreign Policy

- (a) China with its multi event history of following only it's self interest – at best is a selfish neighbour. Hence, even while we may cooperate with it on specific international issues and forums, the **national foreign policy must hedge its bets with multiple additional powers.**

- (b) Understand the **semi alliance structure** being created by China in our neighbourhood and take action to counter the same.

---

3   Dr C Raja Mohan, 'Rising Power and Enduring Paradox: India's China Challenge', USI Journal Jan-Mar 2012 page 28.

(c) Understand the China's **Core Interest Concept** and its implications in the various dealings and discussions. Notifying own core interests and / or inviolable lines may be considered.

(d) Understand **China's diplomatic proposal of shelving disputes and seeking joint development as a temporary lull** without any change in its fundamental position. In practice it seems to imply an excuse for building China's military capability.

(e) **Move of civilians** including sponsored tourism needs close monitoring as China has been using these as basis of and in support of their claims.

Diplomacy

(a) India needs to seek explicit clarity on what China and its leaders imply by **'Tibet related issues'** and whether China considers the border dispute with India under the 'Core Interest Concept' which implies no compromise.

(b) **Monitor and challenge** all efforts by China which seem to use **administrative or policy measures to challenge India's territorial integrity or interests.** These maybe major issues like China's protest against the Prime Minister visit to Arunachal or mundane issues like stapled visas and maps on passports. Reciprocity on such issues may be considered lest China cites them as a basis in the future.

(c) The **principle of reciprocity** also needs to be employed when issuing and seeking clarity on various issues and claims.

Dealing with Chinese Companies and Commercial Entities

China does not shy from using economic war when required. It **prepares for it by creating monopolies and dependencies in target nations** as also by planting Trojan horses in the labour that it exports. These are issues which need to be guarded against. Also at the macro level adequate alternatives need to be available so that any abrupt interruptions / blockade do not adversely affect either the economy or any segment of it.

(a) Considering its own population size and unemployment problem – it should be ensured that the **Chinese companies and commercial entities do not import their own labour.** This would ensure that Trojan horse activity too is limited.

(b) Further it should be ensured that they **comply with all the local labour regulations**. This would ensure that the problems which emerged in certain African countries are not repeated in India.

(c) **Monopolies of China and Chinese entities need to be very closely monitored** to ensure that they cannot be used as a pressure tactics in a potential economic war. At no stage a situation should emerge wherein a Chinese monopoly is allowed to emerge in any trade / territorial segment of the nation. These especially need monitoring in the: -

   (i) Exports from India.

   (ii) Imports by India and Indian industry.

   (iii) Local markets at the lowest level.

(d) While being permitted to carry out their commercial activity, Chinese companies and commercial entities **should not be allowed to purchase land** (if required it may be leased to them with a provision that the government may take it back).

(e) Activities of Chinese International Investment Corps need to be monitored against their either **taking over strategic industries or creating monopolies**.

(f) Adequate precautions need to be taken against **cyber espionage, sabotage and warfare related activities**.

Internal Strife in China

(a) Internal strife remains the most potent threat for China. It can lead to turmoil in our neighbourhood as also affect our commercial interests and the alliances that the nation forms in the various international forums. Due to the historical perception of a good and legitimate government being one which looks after the well being of the population, social parameters like the Gini Coefficient, the unemployment ratios etc need to be monitored closely. The situation may be exacerbated by the highly centralised nature of the regime.

(b) Also the ability of the secessionist forces in the buffer states (Tibet, Xinjiang and Inner Mongolia) to harm Han China – the Chinese heartland – would raise the spectre of unravelling of China. It would be the trigger for increased repression and connected population displacement issues. The same needs to be closely monitored.

Military Threat

Some believe that as the Indo-China trade increases,[4] the chances of a military conflict reduces. However, the notion is not supported with historical evidence. 'In 1914, when the World War I was imminent, Germany and France were the two largest trading partners.'[5,6] It must always be kept in mind, that, unlike India China does not consider use of force as an option of last resort but rather as an essential and accepted part of promoting national interest. As a nation therefore we need to be forever prepared for military action from China despite their assurances of peaceful settlement. Hence, **military preparations and the allied infrastructure development must match the Chinese capability enhancements.** While, China may not be able to sustain large scale multi-division operations South of the Himalayas, border skirmishes or operations to secure what it calls its core interest are a distinct possibility for which the nation needs to be forever ready. Explicit circumstances under which the possibility of a military threat is most likely, would be: -

(a) When China is secure on the coast enabling it to transfer both prosperity and military forces towards the west and especially Tibet.

---

4 Trade between the two countries has galloped from barely $2billion in 1998 to nearly 70 billion in 2011. See Dr C Raja Mohan, 'Rising Power and Enduring Paradox: India's China Challenge' USI Journal Jan-Mar 2012 page 24.

5 Joll James, 'The origins of the First World War', London: Longman 1992, Chapter 7.

6 Trade is also fast emerging as a bone of contention. As The Economist noted '**Over 70% of India's exports to China by value are raw materials, chiefly iron ore**, bespeaking a colonial-style trade relationship that is hugely favourable to China'. See http://www.economist.com/node/16843717. Further balance of trade is also becoming an issue **as Indian exports are roughly half of its imports from China**. See http://busienomics.wordpress.com/2012/03/07/india-looks-to-balance-china-trade/. As business week noted 'India's growing trade deficit with China—an estimated $27 billion in 2011—has become a source of anguish in Indian policy circles. Bilateral trade between the two emerging giants grew to $73 billion in 2011, up from $63 billion in 2010 and less than $3 billion in 2000. The Indian side, though, is becoming increasingly alarmed over the growing trade balance in China's favour, which amounted to a Chinese surplus of $23.9 billion last year'. See http://www.businessweek.com/articles/2012-03-21/indias-misguided-china-anxiety.

(b)　**Tibet.** When China feels that either: -

(i)　The 'threat from' or 'actions of' India can lead to secession of Tibet from China.

(ii)　The integration of Tibet with Han China is complete and therefore, to ensure its security, there is a need of a buffer state to its south.

(c)　When China establishes a military base / foothold south of the Himalayas. China's all weather partnership with Pakistan and it's 2005 peace treaty with it and the subsequent actions thereafter to operationalise it, need close monitoring.

SLOCs

With China taking aggressive action to build capacity for securing and protecting its SLOCs – it also achieves the capacity to interfere in our SLOCs. The much touted string of pearls strategy may be interpreted both as action by China to protect its own SLOCs or to contain India. As a nation therefore we need to take action to **protect our SLOCs** in the long term.

Deterrence

With its population and development concentrated along the east of country – **effective deterrence would only be achieved once it is possible to target China's East Coast.**

CONCLUSION

China is a rising continental power, and as Napoleon famously said, the policies of such states are inherent in their geography. The one overriding theme in Chinese history is the search for stability. A stability that comes from a Government which is responsive to, and was concerned with the welfare of the population. This population often gauged this concern through an improvement – or at least not deterioration – in their living conditions. To achieve this, successive regimes have therefore maintained a system of centralised bureaucracatic control which made massive infrastructure investments while protecting Han China by controlling the neighbouring areas. Simultaneously, internal peace was ensured by transferring prosperity from the wealthier regions to the less fortunate. These were mostly geographically defined factors.

The present regime – the current one in a series of Chinese dynasties – has sought to legitimise its existence through the tool of mass employment. However, to maintain that unfettered access to world markets, ability to secure cheap resources and space for its burgeoning population is essential. While it has managed to subjugate and attempts to integrate its neighbourhood[1] (the access to the natural resources there being a major bonus) its attempts of securing unfettered market access and cheap resources is increasingly bringing it in focus of the rest of the world. The perceived demographic

---

1   As was noted by Kaplan Robert 'The question now becomes whether the dominant Huns who comprise more than 90 percent of China's population and live mainly in the arable cradle of China, are able to permanently keep the Tibetans, Uighur Turks and Inner Mongolians who live on the periphery under control. The ultimate fate of the Chinese state will hinge on this fact, especially as China undergoes economic and social disruptions'. Kaplan Robert 'The Revenge of Geography' page 3129 Kindle Edition.

invasion further raises the concerns of its neighbours and client states. To secure these goals China does not come armed with any moral or missionary approach; rather its policies are aimed at securing these without seeking any approbation or appreciation. If need be, to secure its interests and investments it keeps its options open to get involved in the local affairs – a policy of creative involvement, preventive diplomacy and semi-alliances; a policy which is currently being hotly debated as essentials of its foreign policy. China's core interest policy essentially reflects these concerns of regime stability, market access, resource mobilisation and maintaining buffers in the neighbourhood. However, what is of concern to the international regime is the fact that the policy disallows compromises on the issues and advocates force for settling them in China's favour. China's international behaviour in recent years too reflects the same.

On one side, where China speaks of shelving disputes for joint development – a policy which many perceive as building its national and military strength prior to settling disputes favourably – on the other it uses a policy of what the Chinese official media calls the Combination Punches. The latter entails administrative, military, economic, diplomatic and policy measures to assert its claims. Cyber actions – which have recently been issues of concern for the western world – when used in addition can form a potent cocktail against an adversary.

Despite assertions of not being in competition and of adequate economic space for rise of both China and India – the two nations are essentially rivals for resources, market access and trade surpluses. Lack of clarity on whether the border dispute is part of the core interests does not help in mitigating the rivalry. The unresolved dispute provides adequate excuse for action – whether to create a buffer zone or to secure Tibet or even to discredit India in the eyes of potential allies. Further military hostilities may just be one of the many actions as part of China's combination punches, it may well be the last or may even be conspicuous in its absence even as the other measures take effect. Hence, a holistic approach to secure own national interests and simultaneously ensuring that there are no dependencies which infuse lethality to the Chinese combination punches, is recommended.

APPENDIX

CHINA'S EXPORTS AND IMPORTS 2010 AND 2011[2]

Chinas Imports 2010

	North America	South & Central America	Europe	CIS	Africa	Middle East	Asia	Total	% of Total
Manufactures	20.74	1.66	33.91	0.61	0.67	5.22	326.41	389.21	26.62%
Machinery and transport equipment	11.90	1.17	12.54	0.05	0.22	1.48	220.50	247.86	16.96%
Office and telecom equipment	7.74	1.05	4.88	0.03	0.19	0.83	167.01	181.73	12.43%
Integrated circuits	3.50	0.87	1.47	0.02	0.14	0.13	75.21	81.34	5.56%
Other machinery	3.07	0.11	5.75	0.01	0.01	0.41	51.18	60.55	4.14%
Other manufactures	3.16	0.04	10.00	0.15	0.01	0.37	45.39	59.13	4.04%
Telecommunications equipment	2.36	0.07	2.43	0.01	0.05	0.65	52.31	57.88	3.96%
EDP and office equipment	1.88	0.11	0.97	0.00	0.00	0.05	39.48	42.51	2.91%
Electrical machinery	1.73	0.11	1.62	0.01	0.01	0.06	38.41	41.93	2.87%
Miscellaneous manufactures	2.05	0.02	6.62	0.15	0.01	0.30	31.00	40.15	2.75%
Other semi-manufactures	2.57	0.39	4.23	0.10	0.37	2.63	17.75	28.03	1.92%
Chemicals	2.75	0.04	4.55	0.11	0.04	0.73	14.98	23.21	1.59%
Fuels and mining products	0.68	0.16	1.07	0.40	0.24	0.09	20.42	23.07	1.58%
	North America	South & Central America	Europe	CIS	Africa	Middle East	Asia	Total	% of Total

Continued...

2 http://www.wto.org/english/res_e/statis_e/its2012_e/its12_appendix_e.htm

Continued...

Other chemicals	2.47	0.04	3.25	0.11	0.04	0.72	14.42	21.05	1.44%
Agricultural products	3.91	2.06	4.00	0.04	0.42	0.46	9.74	20.62	1.41%
Food	3.32	2.01	2.96	0.02	0.35	0.45	8.91	18.01	1.23%
Clothing	0.11	0.01	1.52	0.00	0.01	0.00	15.00	16.64	1.14%
Fuels	0.02	0.03	0.05	0.22	0.00	0.07	14.97	15.35	1.05%
Other food products	2.98	1.87	2.74	0.01	0.17	0.39	6.80	14.97	1.02%
Non-electrical machinery	0.78	0.01	2.31	0.01	0.00	0.03	9.12	12.26	0.84%
Textiles	0.21	0.01	0.87	0.00	0.00	0.00	10.17	11.27	0.77%
Personal and household goods	0.12	0.02	2.16	0.00	0.00	0.00	7.92	10.23	0.70%
Scientific and controlling instruments	0.99	0.00	1.22	0.00	0.00	0.07	6.47	8.74	0.60%
Non-ferrous metals	0.37	0.12	0.93	0.17	0.22	0.01	4.89	6.70	0.46%
Power generating machinery	0.56	0.00	1.82	0.00	0.00	0.32	3.65	6.35	0.43%
Transport equipment	1.09	0.00	1.92	0.00	0.02	0.24	2.31	5.59	0.38%
Automotive products	0.48	0.00	1.46	0.00	0.02	0.22	1.33	3.52	0.24%
Iron and steel	0.04	0.01	0.19	0.19	0.02	0.00	2.63	3.08	0.21%
Fish	0.33	0.14	0.22	0.00	0.18	0.06	2.11	3.04	0.21%
Raw materials	0.60	0.05	1.04	0.02	0.07	0.01	0.82	2.61	0.18%
Pharmaceuticals	0.28	0.01	1.31	0.00	0.01	0.00	0.56	2.16	0.15%
Other transport equipment	0.61	0.00	0.46	0.00	0.00	0.02	0.98	2.07	0.14%
Ores and other minerals	0.30	0.02	0.10	0.01	0.02	0.01	0.56	1.02	0.07%
Total merchandise	83.70	12.19	120.57	2.46	3.51	16.03	1223.41	1461.87	

China's Imports 2011

	North America	South & Central America	Europe	CIS	Africa	Middle East	Asia	Total	% of Total
Manufactures	24.36	1.93	43.21	0.61	0.71	7.37	353.89	432.09	26.55%
Machinery and transport equipment	14.37	1.37	15.21	0.05	0.24	2.09	238.62	271.96	16.71%
Office and telecom equipment	8.71	1.25	6.19	0.04	0.19	1.13	180.86	198.36	12.19%
Integrated circuits	3.82	1.09	1.68	0.01	0.14	0.18	77.83	84.74	5.21%
Other manufactures	3.72	0.05	13.99	0.35	0.01	0.72	51.40	70.25	4.32%
Telecommunications equipment	2.91	0.10	3.55	0.02	0.04	0.89	59.73	67.25	4.13%
Other machinery	3.35	0.12	6.85	0.01	0.02	0.63	55.07	66.06	4.06%
Miscellaneous manufactures	2.55	0.03	9.53	0.35	0.01	0.66	35.67	48.78	3.00%
EDP and office equipment	1.98	0.06	0.96	0.00	0.01	0.07	43.30	46.38	2.85%
Electrical machinery	1.89	0.12	1.77	0.01	0.01	0.07	41.84	45.70	2.81%
Other semi-manufactures	2.88	0.42	5.71	0.12	0.40	3.74	20.78	34.04	2.09%
Fuels and mining products	0.89	0.04	1.40	0.20	0.36	0.04	24.55	27.47	1.69%
Chemicals	3.03	0.05	4.91	0.04	0.04	0.82	15.57	24.47	1.50%
Agricultural products	4.50	2.52	5.29	0.05	0.52	0.32	11.03	24.23	1.49%
Other chemicals	2.72	0.05	3.52	0.04	0.04	0.81	14.94	22.12	1.36%
Food	3.96	2.46	4.12	0.03	0.43	0.31	10.00	21.30	1.31%

Continued...

Continued...

	North America	South & Central America	Europe	CIS	Africa	Middle East	Asia	Total	% of Total
Fuels	0.05	0.00	0.04	0.17	0.00	0.03	18.50	18.78	1.15%
Other food products	3.56	2.27	3.89	0.02	0.22	0.24	7.59	17.78	1.09%
Clothing	0.12	0.02	2.18	0.00	0.01	0.00	14.91	17.25	1.06%
Non-electrical machinery	0.88	0.00	2.65	0.00	0.01	0.04	9.14	12.72	0.78%
Personal and household goods	0.11	0.03	3.04	0.00	0.00	0.00	8.29	11.47	0.70%
Textiles	0.21	0.01	0.93	0.00	0.00	0.00	9.89	11.05	0.68%
Scientific and controlling instruments	1.06	0.00	1.43	0.00	0.00	0.06	7.45	10.00	0.61%
Power generating machinery	0.59	0.00	2.43	0.00	0.00	0.52	4.09	7.64	0.47%
Transport equipment	2.31	0.00	2.17	0.00	0.04	0.33	2.69	7.53	0.46%
Non-ferrous metals	0.55	0.02	1.25	0.02	0.32	0.01	5.36	7.53	0.46%
Automotive products	0.69	0.00	1.42	0.00	0.04	0.27	1.43	3.85	0.24%
Other transport equipment	1.63	0.00	0.74	0.00	0.00	0.05	1.26	3.68	0.23%
Fish	0.40	0.19	0.23	0.00	0.21	0.06	2.41	3.51	0.22%
Iron and steel	0.03	0.01	0.26	0.04	0.01	0.00	2.73	3.08	0.19%
Raw materials	0.53	0.07	1.17	0.03	0.09	0.01	1.03	2.93	0.18%
Pharmaceuticals	0.31	0.01	1.39	0.00	0.01	0.00	0.63	2.35	0.14%
Ores and other minerals	0.30	0.02	0.10	0.00	0.04	0.01	0.69	1.16	0.07%
Total merchandise	98.95	14.29	153.25	2.24	4.15	21.50	1333.14	1627.52	

China's Exports 2010

	North America	South & Central America	Europe	CIS	Africa	Middle East	Asia	Total	% of Total
Manufactures	47.20	4.06	46.33	1.78	2.29	5.04	266.28	372.98	27.96%
Machinery and transport equipment	19.83	2.59	19.59	1.11	1.47	2.25	187.98	234.82	17.60%
Office and telecom equipment	13.47	2.09	12.97	0.95	1.25	1.55	140.47	172.75	12.95%
Telecommunications equipment	9.15	1.57	8.61	0.77	1.01	0.98	42.77	64.87	4.86%
Integrated circuits	1.42	0.17	1.54	0.03	0.05	0.06	60.89	64.16	4.81%
Other manufactures	14.56	1.05	14.62	0.47	0.40	0.93	29.06	61.09	4.58%
Other machinery	6.17	0.49	6.42	0.16	0.21	0.68	45.42	59.54	4.46%
Electrical machinery	5.06	0.36	5.15	0.14	0.13	0.24	33.29	44.38	3.33%
EDP and office equipment	2.90	0.35	2.82	0.16	0.18	0.51	36.80	43.72	3.28%
Miscellaneous manufactures	9.53	0.79	11.18	0.38	0.31	0.75	18.56	41.50	3.11%
Clothing	9.70	0.23	8.86	0.13	0.18	0.36	4.57	24.03	1.80%
Other semi-manufactures	2.63	0.07	2.87	0.05	0.07	1.37	14.44	21.49	1.61%
Chemicals	0.27	0.03	0.20	0.01	0.03	0.04	17.77	18.35	1.38%
Other chemicals	0.25	0.03	0.19	0.01	0.03	0.04	16.11	16.65	1.25%
Textiles	0.21	0.08	0.19	0.01	0.13	0.08	10.60	11.31	0.85%
Personal and household goods	4.12	0.21	2.60	0.07	0.07	0.15	3.97	11.20	0.84%

Continued...

Continued...

	North America	South & Central America	Europe	CIS	Africa	Middle East	Asia	Total	% of Total
Non-electrical machinery	0.58	0.07	0.50	0.01	0.04	0.07	8.90	10.17	0.76%
Fuels and mining products	0.11	0.01	0.84	0.00	0.03	0.01	7.48	8.47	0.63%
Scientific and controlling instruments	0.91	0.05	0.83	0.03	0.02	0.03	6.52	8.39	0.63%
Agricultural products	0.27	0.01	0.12	0.01	0.02	0.06	7.54	8.03	0.60%
Non-ferrous metals	0.10	0.01	0.57	0.00	0.02	0.00	5.91	6.61	0.50%
Food	0.24	0.01	0.10	0.01	0.02	0.06	5.69	6.12	0.46%
Other food products	0.17	0.01	0.10	0.01	0.02	0.06	5.31	5.67	0.43%
Power generating machinery	0.53	0.06	0.77	0.00	0.03	0.37	3.22	4.99	0.37%
Transport equipment	0.20	0.02	0.20	0.00	0.01	0.02	2.09	2.54	0.19%
Raw materials	0.03	0.00	0.02	0.00	0.00	0.00	1.85	1.90	0.14%
Iron and steel	0.00	0.00	0.02	0.00	0.00	0.00	1.86	1.88	0.14%
Pharmaceuticals	0.01	0.01	0.01	0.00	0.00	0.00	1.66	1.70	0.13%
Automotive products	0.07	0.00	0.07	0.00	0.01	0.01	1.39	1.55	0.12%
Ores and other minerals	0.01	0.00	0.27	0.00	0.01	0.00	0.89	1.17	0.09%
Other transport equipment	0.12	0.01	0.13	0.00	0.00	0.01	0.71	0.99	0.07%
Fuels	0.00	0.00	0.00	0.00	0.00	0.00	0.69	0.69	0.05%
Fish	0.07	0.00	0.00	0.00	0.00	0.00	0.38	0.45	0.03%
Total merchandise	**149.88**	**14.44**	**148.68**	**6.30**	**8.05**	**15.74**	**991.08**	**1334.17**	

China's Exports 2011

	North America	South & Central America	Europe	CIS	Africa	Middle East	Asia	Total	% of Total
Manufactures	47.45	5.11	49.42	2.17	2.46	6.51	294.75	407.89	27.87%
Machinery and transport equipment	19.72	3.42	20.71	1.36	1.60	2.57	206.89	256.27	17.51%
Office and telecom equipment	13.23	2.88	13.51	1.16	1.33	2.11	155.48	189.69	12.96%
Telecommunications equipment	8.47	2.28	8.66	0.90	1.14	1.40	48.65	71.50	4.89%
Integrated circuits	1.61	0.18	1.73	0.03	0.06	0.08	64.90	68.58	4.68%
Other manufactures	14.96	1.18	16.01	0.54	0.43	1.09	33.09	67.30	4.60%
Other machinery	6.28	0.52	6.98	0.19	0.25	0.45	49.26	63.94	4.37%
EDP and office equipment	3.15	0.43	3.12	0.22	0.14	0.63	41.94	49.61	3.39%
Electrical machinery	5.14	0.40	5.33	0.17	0.14	0.21	35.78	47.18	3.22%
Miscellaneous manufactures	10.03	0.85	12.36	0.43	0.33	0.88	20.88	45.77	3.13%
Other semi-manufactures	2.69	0.07	3.71	0.05	0.09	2.34	17.85	26.80	1.83%
Clothing	9.52	0.28	8.46	0.20	0.16	0.37	5.50	24.49	1.67%
Chemicals	0.34	0.04	0.30	0.01	0.04	0.07	19.10	19.90	1.36%
Other chemicals	0.32	0.04	0.29	0.01	0.04	0.07	17.34	18.10	1.24%
Personal and household goods	3.98	0.28	2.76	0.09	0.09	0.18	4.65	12.03	0.82%
Fuels and mining products	0.16	0.01	1.20	0.01	0.03	0.15	9.80	11.36	0.78%

Continued...

Continued...

Textiles	North America	South & Central America	Europe	CIS	Africa	Middle East	Asia	Total	% of Total
	0.22	0.11	0.21	0.01	0.14	0.08	10.51	11.28	0.77%
Non-electrical machinery	0.61	0.07	0.59	0.02	0.06	0.07	9.72	11.14	0.76%
Scientific and controlling instruments	0.94	0.05	0.88	0.03	0.02	0.03	7.56	9.50	0.65%
Agricultural products	0.27	0.02	0.13	0.01	0.02	0.06	8.70	9.21	0.63%
Non-ferrous metals	0.15	0.01	0.92	0.01	0.03	0.14	7.87	9.12	0.62%
Food	0.23	0.02	0.09	0.01	0.02	0.06	6.66	7.09	0.48%
Other food products	0.17	0.02	0.09	0.01	0.02	0.06	6.18	6.55	0.45%
Power generating machinery	0.53	0.05	1.06	0.00	0.05	0.16	3.76	5.62	0.38%
Transport equipment	0.21	0.01	0.22	0.01	0.02	0.02	2.14	2.63	0.18%
Raw materials	0.03	0.00	0.04	0.00	0.00	0.00	2.04	2.12	0.15%
Iron and steel	0.00	0.00	0.02	0.00	0.00	0.00	1.82	1.85	0.13%
Pharmaceuticals	0.01	0.01	0.01	0.00	0.00	0.00	1.76	1.80	0.12%
Automotive products	0.07	0.00	0.08	0.01	0.01	0.00	1.26	1.44	0.10%
Ores and other minerals	0.01	0.00	0.28	0.00	0.00	0.01	1.00	1.29	0.09%
Other transport equipment	0.13	0.01	0.14	0.00	0.01	0.02	0.88	1.20	0.08%
Fuels	0.00	0.00	0.00	0.00	0.00	0.00	0.94	0.94	0.06%
Fish	0.06	0.00	0.00	0.00	0.00	0.00	0.48	0.54	0.04%
Total merchandise	150.71	18.36	159.32	7.67	8.73	19.81	1099.14	1463.74	

BIBLIOGRAPHY

1. HJ Mackinder 'The Geographical Pivot of History' The Geographical Journal volume 23 No 4, April 1904.
2. Pascal Venier 'The Geographical Pivot of History and the Early Twentieth Century Geopolitical Culture' The Geographical Journal volume 170 No 4, December 2004.
3. Robert Kaplan 'The Revenge of Geography'.
4. George Friedman – The Next Decade Doubleday publications Random House, page 2439 Kindle Edition.
5. Shaun Rein 'The End of Cheap China' John Wiley and Sons Inc. page 493 Kindle Edition.
6. Jakub J Grygiel 'Great Powers and Geopolitical Change' Baltimore: John Hopkins University Press.
7. Owen Lattimore, 'Inner Asian Frontiers: Chinese and Russian Margins of Expansion', The Journal of Economic History, Cambridge, England May 1947.
8. Owen Lattimore 'Chinese Colonization in Manchuria', Geographical Review, London 1932 page 270.
9. Uttam Kumar Sinha, 'Tibet's Watershed Challenge', Washington Post 14 June 2010.
10. Holmes and Yoshihara, 'Command of the Sea with Chinese Characteristics'.
11. Jonathan D Spence, The Search for Modern China. New York Norton page 67.
12. David Blair, 'Why the Restless Chinese Are Warming to Russia's Frozen East', Daily Telegraph, London, 16 July 2009.
13. Maj Gen Vinod Sehgal, 'Global Security Paradoxes' Manas Publications New Delhi.
14. Ashley J Tellis, 'Stability in South Asia' Rand Report, Natraj Publishers Dehradun.
15. Zalmay Khalizad and Ian O. Lesser, 'Sources of Conflict in the 21st Century' Rand Report, Natraj Publishers Dehradun.
16. Howard W French 'The Next Empire' The Atlantic May 2010.
17. Ross, 'The Chinese Power and the Implications for the Regional Security Order'..
18. John J. Mearsheimer, 'The Tragedy of Great Power Politics', New York W.W. Norton 2001.
19. Jacqueline Newmyer 'Oil, Arms and Influence: The Indirect Strategy Behind Chi-

nese Military Modernisation' Orbis Philadelphia, Spring 009.

20. M Taylor Fravel, 'Regime Insecurity and International Co-operation: Explaining China's Compromises in Territorial Disputes' International Security, Fall 2005.

21. Grygiel, 'Great Powers and Geopolitical Change'.

22. James Joll, 'The origins of the First World War', London: Longman 1992.

23. Brahma Chellaney 'Asia's Water Crisis and the New Security Risks' USI Journal Jan-Mar 2012 page 55.

24. Commander B Gurumurthy 'A case study on Strategic and Geopolitical Impact of PLA-Pak Military Strategic Partnership and Security Implications for India', USI Journal Jan-Mar 2012.

25. David Zweig and Bi Jianhai, 'China's Global Hunt for Energy' Foreign Affairs 84, Volume No 5 (Sep-Oct 2005).

26. Dr Sheo Nandan Pandey and Professor Hem Kusum, 'Sino-Indian Border Talks and the Shifting Chinese Stance', USI Journal Jan-Mar 2012 page 35.

27. http://idsa.in/idsacomments/YongxingIslandChinasDiegoGarciaintheSouthChinaSea_ssparmar_070812.

28. http://www.idsa.in/idsacomments/TrespasserswillbeProsecutedChinaslatestBillboardintheSouthChinaSea_ssparmar_081212.

29. Dr C Raja Mohan 'Rising Power and Enduring Paradox: India's China Challenge', USI Journal Jan-Mar 2012.

30. http://en.wikipedia.org/wiki/Geography_of_China.

31. http://en.wikipedia.org/wiki/Geography_of_Tibet.

32. http://en.wikipedia.org/wiki/Yellow_Sea.

33. http://en.wikipedia.org/wiki/File:Bar-tailed_Godwit9may.gif.

34. http://en.wikipedia.org/wiki/East_China_Sea.

35. http://en.wikipedia.org/wiki/South_China_Sea.

36. http://en.wikipedia.org/wiki/History_of_China.

37. http://en.wikipedia.org/wiki/File:Shang_dynasty.svg.

38. http://en.wikipedia.org/wiki/File:Zhou_dynasty_1000_BC.png.

39. http://en.wikipedia.org/wiki/File:Chinese_plain_5c._BC-en.svg.

40. http://en.wikipedia.org/wiki/File:Streitende-Reiche2.jpg.

41. http://en.wikipedia.org/wiki/File:Qin_empire_210_BCE.png.

42. http://en.wikipedia.org/wiki/File:Han_map.jpg.

43. http://en.wikipedia.org/wiki/File:%E6%96%B0%E8%8E%BD%E6%97%B6%E6%9C%9F%E7%96%86%E5%9F%9F%E5%9B%BE%EF%BC%88%E7%B9%81%EF%BC%89.png.

44. http://en.wikipedia.org/wiki/File:China_5.jpg.

45. http://en.wikipedia.org/wiki/File:Northern_and_Southern_Dynasties_560_CE.png.

46. http://en.wikipedia.org/wiki/File:Cheui_Dynasty_581_CE.png.

47. http://en.wikipedia.org/wiki/File:Tang_Dynasty_circa_700_CE.png.

48. http://en.wikipedia.org/wiki/File:Five_Dynasties_Ten_Kingdoms_923_CE.png.

49. http://en.wikipedia.org/wiki/Economy_of_the_People%27s_Republic_of_China.

50. http://en.wikipedia.org/wiki/Petroleum_industry_in_China.
51. http://afe.easia.columbia.edu/china/geog/M_Wall.htm.
52. http://afe.easia.columbia.edu/china/geog/M_rivr.htm.
53. http://afe.easia.columbia.edu/china/geog/M_Mt.htm.
54. http://english.ts.cn/topic/content/2008-01/11/content_2389669.htm.
55. http://www.china.org.cn/english/MATERIAL/139230.htm.
56. http://www.lhassa.org/en/geography-of-tibet/mineral-resources-of-tibet.php.
57. http://www.apcss.org/Publications/Ocasional%20Papers/OPSloc.htm.
58. http://unctad.org/en/Docs/rmt2011ch4_en.pdf.
59. http://www.bbc.co.uk/news/world-asia-20730880.
60. http://www.japanfocus.org/-Reinhard-Drifte/3156.
61. http://www.wto.org/english/res_e/statis_e/its2012_e/its12_appendix_e.htm.
62. http://www.kdng.org/news/34-news/295-myanmar-china-relations-post-myit-sone-suspension--analysis.html.
63. http://depts.washington.edu/chinaciv/1xarshang.htm.
64. http://depts.washington.edu/chinaciv/1xarzhou.htm.
65. http://depts.washington.edu/chinaciv/1xarhan1.htm.
66. http://depts.washington.edu/chinaciv/1xarsui1.htm.
67. http://depts.washington.edu/chinaciv/1xartang.htm.
68. http://depts.washington.edu/chinaciv/1xarfive.htm.
69. http://depts.washington.edu/chinaciv/1xarsong.htm.
70. http://depts.washington.edu/chinaciv/1xaryuan.htm.
71. http://depts.washington.edu/chinaciv/1xarming.htm.
72. http://depts.washington.edu/chinaciv/1xarqing.htm.
73. http://www.foreignaffairs.com/articles/138597/aviezer-tucker/the-new-power-map?page=show.
74. http://www.foreignaffairs.com/articles/138093/michael-t-klare/island-grabbing-in-asia.
75. http://www.foreignaffairs.com/articles/138009/andrew-j-nathan-and-andrew-scobell/how-china-sees-america?page=show.
76. http://www.foreignaffairs.com/articles/138449/lynette-h-ong/indebted-dragon?page=show
77. http://www.foreignaffairs.com/articles/139295/evan-a-feigenbaum-and-damien-ma/the-rise-of-chinas-reformers?page=show
78. http://www.foreignaffairs.com/articles/139456/scott-g-borgerson/the-coming-arctic-boom?page=show
79. http://www.reuters.com/article/2013/03/10/us-china-shale-idUSBRE-9290GR20130310.
80. http://www.reuters.com/article/2012/10/03/us-economy-global-currencies-idUSBRE8920Q820121003
81. http://www.stratfor.com/weekly/state-world-assessing-chinas-strategy.
82. http://www.stratfor.com/weekly/china-tests-japanese-and-us-patience?utm_source=freelist-f&utm_medium=email&utm_campaign=20130226&utm_

term=gweekly&utm_content=readmore&elq=3232f09271e74f758b80de4a322b
60fb.

83. http://www.stratfor.com/weekly/paradox-chinas-naval-strategy.

84. http://www.stratfor.com/weekly/china-tests-japanese-and-us-patience?utm_
source=freelist-f&utm_medium=email&utm_campaign=20130226&utm_
term=gweekly&utm_content=readmore&elq=3232f09271e74f758b80de4a322b
60fb.

85. http://www.stratfor.com/analysis/growing-importance-arctic-council?utm_
source=freelist-f&utm_medium=email&utm_campaign=20130528&utm_
term=FreeReport&utm_content=readmore&elq=8e2c531f02544925a37ee5b8c
3f073d6

86. http://www.stratfor.com/analysis/geopolitics-yangtze-river-devel-
oping-interior?utm_source=freelist-f&utm_medium=email&utm_
campaign=20130412&utm_term=Yagntze&utm_content=readmore&elq=a07b
5dd9de0a4f7ca34c859e2627a6fc

87. http://www.stratfor.com/weekly/recognizing-end-chinese-eco-
nomic-miracle?utm_source=freelist-f&utm_medium=email&utm_
campaign=20130723&utm_term=Gweekly&utm_content=readmore&elq=ed0c
59a49ae34fc1ae653be09b16d701

88. http://www.stratfor.com/weekly/us-foreign-policy-room-regroup

89. http://www.c3sindia.org/afganistan/3090.

90. http://www.c3sindia.org/eastasia/3222.

91. http://www.c3sindia.org/southeastasia/2956.

92. http://www.c3sindia.org/southeastasia/3140.

93. http://www.c3sindia.org/foreign-policy/3215.

94. http://www.c3sindia.org/eastasia/2590.

95. http://www.c3sindia.org/eastasia/1722.

96. http://www.c3sindia.org/eastasia/2427.

97. http://www.c3sindia.org/strategicissues/992.

98. http://www.c3sindia.org/foreign-policy/3670

99. http://www.southasiaanalysis.org/node/1072.

100. http://www.southasiaanalysis.org/paper875.

101. http://www.southasiaanalysis.org/node/1089.

102. http://www.southasiaanalysis.org/node/1170.

103. http://www.southasiaanalysis.org/node/1028.

104. http://www.southasiaanalysis.org/node/1067.

105. http://www.southasiaanalysis.org/node/987.

106. http://www.southasiaanalysis.org/node/1041.

107. http://southasiaanalysis.org/node/1209.

108. http://www.southasiaanalysis.org/node/995.

109. http://www.southasiaanalysis.org/node/981.

110. http://www.southasiaanalysis.org/node/1067.

111. http://www.southasiaanalysis.org/node/1001.

112. http://www.southasiaanalysis.org/node/987.
113. http://timesofindia.indiatimes.com/world/china/Chinas-Xi-Jinping-calls-for-great-renaissance/articleshow/19020759.cms.
114. http://timesofindia.indiatimes.com/world/china/Eye-on-future-president-sells-Chinese-dream/articleshow/19028057.cms.
115. http://timesofindia.indiatimes.com/world/china/After-Wen-new-China-rulers-seal-their-lips-on-India/articleshow/19028963.cms.
116. http://blogs.timesofindia.indiatimes.com/Globespotting/entry/china-s-new-president-must-go-beyond-platitudes-to-address-india-s-concerns.
117. http://articles.economictimes.indiatimes.com/2012-06-21/news/32352617_1_sustainable-development-wen-jiabao-countries).
118. http://economictimes.indiatimes.com/news/international-business/china-labour-ministry-says-faces-big-pressure-on-employment/articleshow/21325086.cms
119. http://www.thehindu.com/news/international/world/china-doesnt-want-unexpected-border-incident-says-pla-general/article4857683.ece
120. http://www.rand.org/pubs/research_briefs/RB61/index1.html.
121. http://ramanstrategicanalysis.blogspot.in/2011/01/pla-barometer-of-us-china-relations.html.
122. http://ramanstrategicanalysis.blogspot.in/2011/10/india-vietnam-oilgas-cooperation-sparks.html.
123. http://www.eurasiareview.com/30012012-us-china-and-developments-in-southeast-asia-analysis/.
124. http://www.eurasiareview.com/01102012-strategic-lessons-from-china-japan-stand-off-analysis/.
125. http://www.eurasiareview.com/28012013-myanmar-china-relations-post-myit-sone-suspension-analysis/.
126. http://www.eurasiareview.com/20062012-france-reaffirms-commitment-to-asia-pacific-security-analysis/.
127. http://www.paulnoll.com/China/Dynasty/dynasty-Song.html.
128. http://www.paulnoll.com/China/Dynasty/dynasty-Mongol.html.
129. http://www.paulnoll.com/China/Dynasty/dynasty-Ming.html.
130. http://www.paulnoll.com/China/Dynasty/dynasty-Qing.html.
131. http://www.paulnoll.com/China/Dynasty/dynasty-ROC.html.
132. https://www.uschina.org/statistics/tradetable.html.
133. http://news.xinhuanet.com/english2010/china/2011-11/03/c_131228263.htm.
134. http://news.xinhuanet.com/english/business/2013-06/05/c_124811764.htm
135. http://news.xinhuanet.com/english/indepth/2013-07/20/c_125039658.htm
136. http://news.xinhuanet.com/english/business/2013-06/04/c_132430788.htm
137. http://news.xinhuanet.com/english/indepth/2013-07/28/c_132580396.htm
138. http://news.xinhuanet.com/english/indepth/2013-07/28/c_132580690.htm
139. http://online.wsj.com/article/SB10001424127887324081704578232650955659718.html.

140. http://online.wsj.com/article/SB100008723963904436966045776471022032905 14.html

141. http://www.huachun.com.cn/hc/en/news_view.asp?newsid=463.

142. http://www.google.co.in/imgres?hl=en&sa=X&rlz=1C1CHMO_enIN521IN521&bi w=1366&bih=600&tbm=isch&tbnid=sRHdiy6W-ay6oM:&imgrefurl=http://www. eia.gov/countries/cab.cfm%3Ffips%3DCH&docid=BV3I30ryiIEO8M&imgurl=h ttp://www.eia.gov/countries/analysisbriefs/China/images/crude_oil_imports_ source.png&w=554&h=467&ei=AeAlUbjOE8qIrAfWu4HACA&zoom=1&ved=1t:3 588,i:118&iact=rc&dur=747&sig=113499893185618779384&page=1&tbnh=180 &tbnw=221&start=0&ndsp=15&tx=67&ty=100.

143. http://articles.marketwatch.com/2012-01-19/economy/30788275_1_income-gap-china-reform-foundation-gini-coefficient.

144. http://www.chinadaily.com.cn/china/2010-05/12/content_9837073.htm.

145. http://community.travelchinaguide.com/forum2.asp?i=43913.

146. http://strategicstudyindia.blogspot.in/2013/01/myanmar-china-relations-post-myitsone.html.

147. http://www.tibettelegraph.com/2012/05/chinas-foreign-policy-debate.html.

148. http://news.rediff.com/column/2010/may/31/us-accused-of-strategically-encir-cling-china.htm.

149. http://groups.yahoo.com/group/Hinduism/message/5577.

150. http://www2.lse.ac.uk/IDEAS/publications/reports/pdf/SR012/breslin.pdf.

151. http://eprints.lse.ac.uk/44205/1/__Libfile_repository_Content_LSE%20IDEAS_ Special%20Reports_SR012%20China%27s%20Geoeconomic%20Strategy_ China%27s%20Geoeconomic%20Strategy%20_Firms%20with%20Chinese%20 Characteristics%20%28LSE%20RO%29.pdf.

152. http://www.thefreelibrary.com/Maritime+geostrategy+and+the+development +of+the+Chinese+navy+in+the...-a0156364589.

153. http://www.kdng.org/news/34-news/295-myanmar-china-relations-post-myit-sone-suspension--analysis.html.

154. http://www.canberratimes.com.au/world/burmas-suu-kyi-heckled-over-copper-mine-20130315-2g4kr.html.

155. http://www.watoday.com.au/world/burmas-suu-kyi-heckled-over-copper-mine-20130315-2g4kr.html.

156. http// eng.tibet.cn/2010/home/news/201204/t2012 dated 15 April 2012.

157. http://www.economist.com/node/16843717.

158. http://www.deccanherald.com/content/321148/china-pak-seal-secret-nuclear. html.

159. http://www.businessweek.com/articles/2012-03-21/indias-misguided-china-anxiety.

160. http://www.iol.co.za/business/international/china-s-role-in-africa-under-scruti-ny-1.1529528#.UgcWrJLI3Ys

161. http://business.time.com/2012/06/05/chinas-antiquated-financial-system-the-creaking-grows-louder/

162. http://www.news.com.au/business/worklife/china-labour-costs-like-us-within-

years/story-e6frfm9r-1226438065496#ixzz22K62hsDt

163. http://in.images.search.yahoo.com/images/view;_
     ylt=A2oKiZevLjtR9VcALGy9HAx.;_ylu=X3oDMTBIMTQ4cGxyBHNIY
     wNzcgRzbGsDaW1n?back=http%3A%2F%2Fin.images.search.ya-
     hoo.com%2Fsearch%2Fimages%3F_adv_prop%3Dimage%26va%
     3Dshale%2Bgas%2Bdeposits%2Bchina%26fr%3Dchr-greentree_gc
     %26tab%3Dorganic%26ri%3D1&w=500&h=379&imgurl=blogs.
     worldwatch.org%2Frevolt%2Fwp-content%2Fuploads%2F2012%2
     F08%2Faeb6708d6720111024-china-shale-gas-deposits-500x379.
     jpg&rurl=http%3A%2F%2Fblogs.worldwatch.org%2Frevolt%2Fchina-
     has-high-hopes-for-shale-gas-the-thorny-road-of-honor%2F&size=77
     .4+KB&name=aeb6708d6720111024-%3Cb%3Echina%3C%2Fb%3E-
     %3Cb%3Eshale%3C%2Fb%3E-%3Cb%3Egas%3C%2Fb%3E-
     %3Cb%3Edeposits%3C%2Fb%3E-500x379&p=shale+gas+deposits+chi
     na&oid=c5c79951fdc64826a1dcf6591c929552&fr2=&fr=chr-greentree_
     gc&tt=aeb6708d6720111024-%253Cb%253Echina%253C%252Fb%253E-
     %253Cb%253Eshale%253C%252Fb%253E-
     %253Cb%253Egas%253C%252Fb%253E-%253Cb%253Edeposits%253-
     C%252Fb%253E-500x379&b=0&ni=112&no=1&ts=&tab=organic&sigr=12vq27if
     v&sigb=140l2crc6&sigi=13erhl817&.crumb=5ZjJlJtunKD.

164. http://www.financialsensearchive.com/stormwatch/geo/pastanaly-
     sis/2007/0309.html.

165. http://in.images.search.yahoo.com/images/view;_
     ylt=A2oKiZevLjtR9VcALGy9HAx.;_ylu=X3oDMTBIMTQ4cGxyBHNIY
     wNzcgRzbGsDaW1n?back=http%3A%2F%2Fin.images.search.ya-
     hoo.com%2Fsearch%2Fimages%3F_adv_prop%3Dimage%26va%
     3Dshale%2Bgas%2Bdeposits%2Bchina%26fr%3Dchr-greentree_gc
     %26tab%3Dorganic%26ri%3D1&w=500&h=379&imgurl=blogs.
     worldwatch.org%2Frevolt%2Fwp-content%2Fuploads%2F2012%2
     F08%2Faeb6708d6720111024-china-shale-gas-deposits-500x379.
     jpg&rurl=http%3A%2F%2Fblogs.worldwatch.org%2Frevolt%2Fchina-
     has-high-hopes-for-shale-gas-the-thorny-road-of-honor%2F&size=77
     .4+KB&name=aeb6708d6720111024-%3Cb%3Echina%3C%2Fb%3E-
     %3Cb%3Eshale%3C%2Fb%3E-%3Cb%3Egas%3C%2Fb%3E-
     %3Cb%3Edeposits%3C%2Fb%3E-500x379&p=shale+gas+deposits+chi
     na&oid=c5c79951fdc64826a1dcf6591c929552&fr2=&fr=chr-greentree_
     gc&tt=aeb6708d6720111024-%253Cb%253Echina%253C%252Fb%253E-
     %253Cb%253Eshale%253C%252Fb%253E-
     %253Cb%253Egas%253C%252Fb%253E-%253Cb%253Edeposits%253-
     C%252Fb%253E-500x379&b=0&ni=112&no=1&ts=&tab=organic&sigr=12vq27if
     v&sigb=140l2crc6&sigi=13erhl817&.crumb=5ZjJlJtunKD.

166. http://www.globaltimes.cn/content/781566.shtml#.UZLcCLXI3Lk

167. http://www.globaltimes.cn/content/781627.shtml#.UZLb57XI3Lk

168. http://www.globaltimes.cn/content/785093.shtml#.UaWES9LIvYo

169. http://www.globaltimes.cn/content/785391.shtml#.UabOeNLIvYo

170. http://www.globaltimes.cn/content/785711.shtml#.UagkMdLIvYo
171. http://www.globaltimes.cn/content/787104.shtml#.UbAGAtLIvYo
172. http://www.globaltimes.cn/content/790733.shtml#.UcUyhfnI3Lk
173. http://www.globaltimes.cn/content/796936.shtml#.Uedj3dlwffl
174. http://www.globaltimes.cn/content/797375.shtml#.UejPYdlwffl
175. http://www.globaltimes.cn/content/797396.shtml#.UejPRdlwffl
176. http://www.globaltimes.cn/content/797634.shtml#.Uet6YY3I3Lk
177. http://www.globaltimes.cn/content/798547.shtml#.Ue9R-NIwffl
178. http://www.globaltimes.cn/content/798567.shtml#.Ue9Rztlwffl
179. http://www.globaltimes.cn/content/799516.shtml#.UfS1S43I3Ys
180. http://www.globaltimes.cn/content/800201.shtml#.UfiY8Y3I3Ys
181. http://www.globaltimes.cn/content/801460.shtml#.Uf8iltlwffl
182. http://www.globaltimes.cn/content/801948.shtml#.UgHFpNIwffl.
183. http://english.peopledaily.com.cn/90778/8282812.html
184. http://english.peopledaily.com.cn/90778/8297840.html
185. http://english.peopledaily.com.cn/90778/8334764.html
186. http://english.peopledaily.com.cn/90882/8353272.html
187. http://www.universalnewswires.com/centralasia/security/viewstory.aspx?id=13991
188. http://knowledge.wharton.upenn.edu/article.cfm?articleid=2962
189. http://knowledge.wharton.upenn.edu/article.cfm?articleid=3313
190. http://knowledgetoday.wharton.upenn.edu/2013/06/health-care-in-china-is-there-a-doctor-in-the-house/
191. http://knowledgetoday.wharton.upenn.edu/2013/07/as-china-changes-so-do-global-supply-chains/
192. http://thediplomat.com/china-power/china-and-latin-america-big-business-and-big-competition/
193. http://www.diamonds.net/News/NewsItem.aspx?ArticleID=40453&ArticleTitle=Global+Witness+Ties+Diamond+Business+with+Funding+Mugabe's+Military+
194. http://africajournalismtheworld.com/tag/mugabe-diamond-funds-for-election/
195. http://www.mining.com/chinese-diamond-mogul-funding-zimbabwes-mugabes-military-report/
196. http://www.chinadaily.com.cn/china/2010-05/12/content_9837073.htm
197. http://community.travelchinaguide.com/forum2.asp?i=43913
198. http://cinemarasik.com/2013/05/04/chinahandle-with-care.aspx

Index

9789382652663